Survey
Interviewing

Survey Interviewing

THEORY AND TECHNIQUES

EDITED BY
TERENCE W. BEED
AND
ROBERT J. STIMSON

George Allen & Unwin
Sydney London Boston

© Terence W. Beed and Robert J. Stimson 1985
This book is copyright under the Berne Convention. No
reproduction without permission. All rights reserved.

First published in 1985 by
George Allen & Unwin Australia Pty Ltd
8 Napier Street, North Sydney, NSW 2060 Australia

George Allen & Unwin (Publishers) Ltd
Park Lane, Hemel Hempstead, Herts HP2 4TE England

Allen & Unwin Inc.
Fifty Cross Street, Winchester, Mass 01890 USA

National Library of Australia
Cataloguing-in-Publication entry:

Survey interviewing.

  Bibliography.
  Includes index.
  ISBN 0 86861 436 X.
  ISBN 0 86861 444 0 (pbk.).

  1. Interviewing in sociology 2. Interviewing in
  market research. 3. Social surveys. I. Beed,
  Terence W. II. Stimson, R.J. (Robert John).

300'.723

Library of Congress Catalog Card Number: 84-72277

Typeset by Graphicraft Typesetters Ltd, Hong Kong
Printed in Hong Kong.

Contents

Appendixes

Tables

Figures

Abbreviations

ABS	Australian Bureau of Statistics
AID	Automatic Interaction Detector
ANU	Australian National University
ATC	Australian Telecommunications Commission
AT&T	American Telephone and Telegraph
BTE	Bureau of Transport Economics
CASSR	Centre for Applied Social and Survey Research, Flinders University
CATI	Computer-Assisted Telephone Interviewing
CCD	Census Collector's District
CSIRO	Commonwealth Scientific and Industrial Research Organisation
FCC	Federal Communications Commission (USA)
HES	Household Expenditure Survey
ICPSR	Inter-University Consortium for Political and Social Research
ISR	Institute for Social Research, University of Michigan
IYDP	International Year of the Disabled Person
LGA	Local Government Area
MRS	Market Research Society
NCHS	National Center for Health Statistics (USA)
PHS	Public Health Service
SSC	Sample Survey Centre, University of Sydney
STC	Standard Telephones and Cables Pty Ltd
VDU	visual display unit
WATS	Wide Area Telephone Service

Contributors

Terry Beed, Director, Sample Survey Centre, The University of Sydney

Iain Bell, Director, Spectrum Research (NSW) Pty Ltd, a market research agency in Sydney

Ken Brewer, Principal Research Officer, Survey Design and Development Section, Bureau of Agricultural Economics, Canberra

Charles Cannell, Research Scientist and Program Director in the Survey Research Center, Institute for Social Research, University of Michigan, Ann Arbor

Tony Cleland, Senior Lecturer in Psychology, Flinders University of South Australia, Bedford Park

Terry Cutler, Manager, Planning Research, Commercial Division, Telecom Australia Headquarters, Melbourne

Bill Faulkner, Director, Research and Statistics, Department of Sport, Recreation and Tourism, Canberra

Roger Jones, Head, Social Science Data Archives, Research School of Social Sciences, Australian National University, Canberra

Paul Korbell, Director, Spectrum Research (NSW) Pty Ltd, Sydney

Kevin Sharp, Director, Smith and Sharp Marketing and Research Consultants Pty Ltd, Melbourne

Bob Stimson, Director, Australian Institute of Urban Studies, Canberra

Foreword

Fundamental research into survey methods is very much undeveloped in Australia. In the last decade, however, there has been an increasing interest at the academic level in research design, data collection and analysis. This has been largely in response to the need to collect very accurate data, and to develop and evaluate policies and programs in the areas of health, welfare, education, employment, and community development. Increasing use of survey methods is also evident in government sectors at the federal, state and local levels, and in the business sector. All sectors have a mutual interest in the betterment of survey methods.

This book brings together survey practitioners from academia, various government instrumentalities, and the private sector. Survey research is an obvious area which can be used to promote interaction between universities and the wider community.

There is no doubt that Australia is about to experience a revolution in data-collection methods, such as the implementation of computer-assisted telephone sampling and interviewing. It is imperative that rigorous testing and evaluation of such methods be conducted so that we can find out the effects of sampling bias and assess the reliability of data. We also need to evaluate the cost-effectiveness of these innovations. Unfortunately, there has been precious little basic research in Australia so far on these fundamental issues.

This book is an edited version of papers given at two workshops on the theory and techniques of interviewing. They were held in Sydney on 21–23 October 1981 and in Melbourne on 18–20 November 1981. They were the first of their kind to be organised within the academic community in Australia and they are one outcome of collaboration in recent years between the Sample Survey Centre (SSC) at the University of Sydney and the Centre for Applied Social and Survey Research (CASSR) at the Flinders University of South Australia.

The program for the workshops was proposed by the Directors of the SSC and CASSR in 1979, and culminated in 1981 in bringing Professor Charles Cannell to Australia. Professor Cannell is a research scientist at the Survey Research Center, University of Michigan, and is a

recognised authority in the areas of assessment of interviewer performance, reliability and bias in survey data collection, and computer-
assisted telephone interviewing techniques.

The present book covers a range of both standard and innovative
approaches to collecting social data. Cannell focuses on interviewing
techniques and discusses the need for experimental research to evaluate
data reliability and validity. He also talks about the Survey Research
Center's experiments at Michigan on computer-assisted telephone
interviewing methods. His three chapters were prepared from edited
transcripts of tape-recordings made at the Workshop sessions. Brewer
looks at randomised response techniques and their use in the Canberra
drug survey. Faulkner's chapter outlines the use of simulation-gaming
methods for collecting information on intended travel behaviour in
response to environmental change. Cleland describes the use of
community panel discussions as an integral part of issues specification
and questionnaire design in community social surveys. The implications of using telephone interviewing in Australian surveys are taken up
in the Cutler and Sharp chapters on Telecom Australia's role in the
development of telephone interviewing systems. Jones discusses variations in household telephone accessibility and use in Australia, and Bell
and Korbel examine the demand for telephone surveys in the business
sector in Australia.

ACKNOWLEDGEMENTS

Publication of this volume has been assisted by a grant of funds from
the Centre for Applied Social and Survey Research, Flinders University, to which the editors extend their gratitude. The transcripts of
Professor Cannell's lectures and discussions were worked up by Pat
Keane, Bev Flynn and Muriel Turner. Pat Keane prepared the final
manuscript and John Roberts drew the diagrams. Special thanks are
due also to Mike Hutchinson for his comments and suggestions on
Faulkner's chapter, and Anona McKnight for her assistance in developing the simulation game in the Canberra experiment. The AID
analyses of the Household Expenditure Survey data used in Jones'
chapter was carried out by the Development and Research Section of
the ABS, Canberra. Ian McRae and Ray Chambers contributed
valuable comments. The papers by Brewer and Jones were published
in the *Australian Journal of Statistics* after the workshop presentations. We
are indebted to the editor of that journal for permission to rework them
for inclusion here as chapters 4 and 7. The views expressed by the

authors of each chapter do not necessarily reflect those of their employing organisations.

Terence W. Beed
Robert J. Stimson

C.F. CANNELL

Overview: response bias and interviewer variability in surveys

This book focuses on practical issues of survey research rather than on theory, specifically on interviewing procedures, and, incidentally, on problems of question design.

In an article I read again recently, Alan Barton (1958) wrote about an issue that is still a major one: how does one 'handle' questions that seek embarrassing information? What kinds of techniques does one use to get embarrassing information? Over the years the pollsters' greatest ingenuity has been devoted to finding ways of asking embarrassing questions in non-embarrassing ways.

Here are some suggestions from that article as applied to the question: Did you kill your wife?

The first thing one can do is to use a casual approach with the question:

'Do you happen to have murdered your wife?'

The second procedure is to give a numbered card:

'Would you please read off the number on this card which corresponds to what became of your wife?' (HAND CARD TO RESPONDENT)
1. Natural death
2. I killed her
3. Other (What?)
(GET CARD BACK FROM RESPONDENT BEFORE PROCEEDING!)

Three, the Everybody Approach:

'As you know, many people have been killing their wives these days. Do you happen to have killed yours?'

Four, the Other People Approach:

(a) 'Do you know any people who have murdered their wives?'
(b) 'How about yourself?'

The fifth is the Sealed Ballot Technique:

> 'In this version you explain that the survey respects people's right to anonymity in respect to their marital relations, and that they themselves are to fill out the answer to the question, seal it in an envelope, and drop it in a box conspicuously labelled 'Sealed Ballot Box' carried by the interviewer.'

Six, the Projective Technique. Here there are four stick-figure pictures. The first shows a woman with someone standing over her head with an axe. In the second the stick figure has fallen down and someone has a smoking gun. In the third, there is a cliff and one of the people is falling off the cliff. The fourth is a picture of the American flag. The question is:

> 'What thoughts come to mind as you look at the following pictures?' (Note: the relevant responses will be envinced by Picture D—the American flag.)

Number seven is the Kinsey techique:

> 'Stare firmly into respondent's eyes and ask in simple, clearcut language such as that to which the respondent is accustomed, and with an air of assuming that everyone has done everything, 'Did you ever kill your wife?'

Eight is putting the question at the end of the interview.

The question of error and bias in surveys has long been of importance and the new concept of *total survey error* is a particularly interesting one. In this case the attempt is made to find out how much error (or bias) is contributed by one of the stages in the survey process. To my knowledge, no one has actually carried this through to its logical conclusion and obtained measures of error at each of the stages of the operation. However, it does seem clear that a major (and perhaps the most important) source of error is found in the data collection stage. Detailed information on new research into data collection can be found in Cannell, Miller, and Oksenberg (1981) and Cannell (1982).

Formerly, error was more pronounced in sampling. Samplers now have a good grasp of the theory and techniques of probability samples, and the amount of error—error because of non-coverage of the population or because of the incorrect drawing of the sample—has been substantially reduced. There is of course the problem of non-response which detracts from the well-designed probability sample. In the United States, this is beginning to cause some real problems. The response rate for personal interviews has been declining over the past ten years. This is of some concern, and there have been attempts to increase the response rate—so far with a great lack of success.

As the telephone interview becomes more heavily used new sets of issues relating to response errors arise—in particular, problems of population coverage. In the household personal interview sample you can cover (at best estimate) 98 per cent of the population. For telephone surveys the issues are quite different because so many people do not have phones, and the people who do not have phones are characteristically different from people who do have phones. However, with these exceptions (and they are fairly large exceptions) the amount of sampling bias is usually pretty small for a well-designed personal interview study.

The main issues we will attend to here are twofold. One is the area of *interviewer variability*. If one assigns each interviewer a random sample of the population in which one is interested, it is characteristically found, in study after study, that there will be significant variation from interviewer to interviewer. This may be error or it may be bias. Interviewers may tend to force the answers in one direction, causing bias, or answers may simply be more spread out and thus become part of sampling error. It is a significant problem and one of the matters I will discuss in this chapter is techniques to reduce interviewer variability.

The second issue is *response bias*. Response bias comes about because the respondent reports either incompletely or inaccurately the information that is requested of him. This may be due to the wording of the question; it may also be due to the kind of information that is requested. Response bias and interviewer variability make the main contribution to total survey error. That is, more bias comes about at the stage of the process that we are now going to discuss than at any other part of the survey operation. I cannot support this with specific research, but there has been enough investigation into other aspects of bias to indicate that such an assumption is valid. One can no longer assume that if one asks a simple question, one will get a straightforward response. If this is surprising let me cite some data from a rather simple study to show what these biases look like and how rapidly they seem to come about.

RESPONSE BIAS

The problem of response bias has intrigued survey researchers since the beginning of survey research back in the thirties and early forties.

Sociologists and psychologists were using surveys, as were people in opinion polling, market research and product testing. In the early days there was very little attention paid to bias. The assumption was that given a simple question, the respondent would answer it accurately. Characteristically, most of the data collected were to do with opinions and attitudes: 'Do you believe this...or this?' or, 'Do you like this product or that product?' The validity of those responses was hard to verify.

What is the validity of an opinion? According to the market researcher, or the academic researcher for that matter, an opinion is valid if that is the opinion the individual states. It follows that beautiful classic definition of intelligence that psychologists used for years to reassure themselves: How do you define intelligence? It is what an intelligence test tests. By the same token, how do you define an opinion? The assumption was that it is what the person says when you ask a question. There was very little attempt in those days to test the issues of response bias or response validity. Then somebody made the 'mistake' of trying to predict how the federal election would come out. When this happened, not only the survey researchers but the public as a whole suddenly found that, on the one hand, here is what a poll says and on the other, here is how the vote went—and that they did not necessarily agree. Suddenly there was a considerable amount of interest in response bias in the fields of market research and polling.

Another example from these early days which is not in the polling field illustrates the types of studies that were done at that time. In 1929, Stuart Rice was doing a study in New York and he hired several interviewers to do a sampling of people who were destitute. This was during our Great Depression. The interviewers went around and asked people questions about their destitution. A few years later while re-reading some of the interviews, he noticed that there were a couple of themes which tended to go through the responses. He found that responses to one interviewer attributed most of the causes of destitution to economic factors (unemployment, inflation, all the rest of it). This was seen as the reason the person could not find a job and was destitute. Rice looked at the work of another interviewer and found that most of his respondents talked about the problems of alcohol; they had become alcoholics and this was seen as the reason for their destitution. He found those two interviewers and talked with them for a while. The first one was a socialist and the second was a prohibitionist. This suggested that the causes of bias are in some way located in the interviewer, and the whole concept of interviewer bias ran widely through the field. In fact it was proposed by Cantril (1947) that to avoid bias in presidential election polls one should hire an equal number of republicans and democrats as interviewers.

Similar research followed, but bias of this simple type does not really trouble us much anymore. We train people better, we do things differently, we ask better questions. We still get problems during election polling—and I gather people do in Australia too. But more recent tests indicate that extreme bias—where the interviewer guesses a response in line with his or her own attitudes or where the response is consistent with what the interviewer expects respondents to say—are not so prevalent these days. A recent study of interviewers' attitudes and expectations by Sudman and Bradburn and their colleagues (1977) indicates that neither the attitudes of the interviewers, nor their expectations of the results, have much effect. They found there was still some interviewer variability, but it was not related to the interviewer's own expectations.

If it is not the interviewer who is giving rise to bias, then where does it come from? What is going on? One begins to look at respondents and say, maybe there are some respondents who are doing well as respondents and maybe others who are not doing well. If you knew the characteristics of the respondents, you could predict where bias would come from. Inevitably, this became the next major activity of researchers: to look at characteristics of the respondents and to see whether respondents were reporting well or poorly. Essentially, the findings are mixed. There is no large or noticeable set of respondents who do a bad job in responding to survey interviews. Provided the questions are appropriately asked, whether respondents are on lower or higher income or of lower or higher education, they all seem to do a pretty good job.

There is, however, some variability with the kinds of questions that are asked. For example, when one is doing a national survey of the general population, the question is often raised by us researchers: should one use black or white interviewers to interview black respondents? Almost mindlessly, everyone says, 'Oh yes, you ought to use black interviewers.' The question is, why should you? Howard Schuman (Schuman and Converse, 1971) did a carefully designed study in which he had black and white interviewers and black and white samples. He randomly assigned black interviewers to black and white respondents, and white interviewers to black and white respondents and then compared results. For almost all the questions there was no difference, but as soon as one came to issues of blackness, or to where racial issues were important, there were some real differences.

By and large, it appears very unlikely there is any such thing as classes of 'good' and 'bad' respondents. The characteristics of the respondent *may* become of some importance for particular issues of investigation: we are likely not to know very much about those characteristics except in such obvious cases as the black and white one.

If we wash out the effect of the characteristics of the interviewers, and we find that respondents as a group are not characteristically good or bad, that leaves us one other dimension: the kinds of information we are asking about.

If one looks at the kinds of data that we are asking respondents about in the interview, one suddenly finds huge differences and huge effects. It appears to relate to the amount of burden we place on the respondent. This could be the burden of trying to recall information, or to retrieve data, or a matter of asking things that are socially undesirable or threatening. It could also be a matter of asking things that are salient or important, or not salient and not important. Most of the major, consistent and lawful rules of response bias are focused on the nature of the event that is being investigated and the burden that this places on the respondent.

A 1965 (Cannell, Fisher and Bakker, 1965) study of the reporting of hospitalisation in health interview surveys provided some useful material for us to work with and shows the magnitude of these issues. This study was the first that we did to understand more about this form of response bias. Many of the illustrations that I will be using relate to health. It is not that I am especially focused on health as a variable, but the Public Health Service has been very supportive of the kind of methodological research in which we are interested. Although most of the data are health-related, the generalisations that we make can be widely applied.

This study began as most studies of methodology do, when somebody found that they had a problem. In this case, the National Center for Health Statistics of the US Public Health Service is responsible for collecting and processing most of the health records of the US—information on illnesses and various aspects of health. One of the methods they use is a survey which is conducted every week of the year. Approximately one thousand interviews are taken every week except Christmas week, to represent the national population. The interviewing is done by the US Bureau of the Census. Like most of the government statistics agencies this is a highly reputable organisation using excellent techniques, and it collects all the data for the Public Health Service.

At the time of our study there was conflicting information about the number of people who had been hospitalised. The PHS survey results gave one figure, and data which came out at the same time from the American Hospitals Association (who got the data by counting hospital beds and how many people were in them) gave another figure. The figures from the American Hospitals Association were higher than the figures in the survey. As you can imagine, this was enough to create some interest. The Public Health Service asked us whether we could do a study to find out (1) whether there was a problem of reporting and (2) how accurately hospitalisation was recorded. A sample of approximately 2500 discharge records from hospitals was drawn. From a probability sample of hospitals, a stratified probability sample was drawn from within each hospital of the discharge records for the year preceding the time of the study. Thus, we knew these 2500 people had been in the hospital; we knew when they were there, how long they were there, and what their diagnoses were.

The census interviewers who did this work were simply informed that this was a special study. The reason for the study was very carefully screened from them by putting in a lot of extra interviews with respondents drawn from the telephone book or somewhere else, so interviewers would not be aware of the preponderance of hospitalised patients. The regular national health survey interview was used and in that interview the key question was: 'Were you, or was any member of your family in a hospital overnight or longer for any time during the last year, that is since . . .', and a date was stated. The answer was simply 'Yes' or 'No'. If it was a 'Yes', the interviewer asked how many times, what was the reason on each occasion, how long were they there, and things of that kind.

The data in Table 1.1 relate to the time that had elapsed between when the person was in hospital and when the same person was interviewed. I should make the point that this is not total bias. One cannot say that after the first ten weeks the PHS is underreporting hospitalisations by 3 per cent: they are probably overreporting. All we know is that in the 2000 cases that we finally interviewed, 3 per cent of the hospitalisations that occurred in those households were not reported. This is not an overall bias. It is essentially a failure to report events that we know occurred. But notice how those figures begin to

Table 1.1 Rate of underreporting by the number of weeks between hospital discharge and the interview (includes proxy respondents)

Number of weeks between hospitalisation and interview	Number of hospitalisations (from hospital records)	Percentage not reported in hospital interview
1–10	114	3
11–20	426	6
21–30	459	9
31–40	339	11
41–50	364	16
51–53	131	42

Source: Cannell, Fisher and Bakker, 1965

increase. For those episodes occurring 41–50 weeks before the interview, 16 per cent of the cases were not reported and for the last two weeks (51–53 weeks lapse) it goes up to about 42 per cent.

There is an increase in underreporting as time elapses, and that characteristic has been found in all kinds of data—in surveys of health, consumer purchases, and many other areas. As far as I know, where there are supporting data, this time-lapse effect shows up. As another example, we did a study asking for recall of visits to doctors during a two-week period. The question was: 'Last week or the week before, did you go to visit a doctor for any reason?' The underreporting can be seen in Table 1.2. In this study, 15 per cent of the visits accounted for in the clinical records were not reported if the visit occurred within one week of the interview; 30 per cent went unreported if it occurred within two weeks of the interview. Although we acknowledge problems with recall, this seemed very high.

Table 1.2 Underreporting of visits to doctors by weeks between visit and interview (includes proxy respondents)

Weeks between visit and interview	Number of physicians' visits (from clinic records)	Percentage not reported in household interview
1 week	196	15
2 weeks	202	30

Source: Cannell and Fowler, 1963

The nature and extent of proxy response is included in Table 1.1. About 60 per cent of these were self-reports and about 40 per cent were proxy. The proxy report is somewhat lower and as the relationship gets more distant the underreporting becomes greater. But even within self-reports it is approximately 3 per cent lower. The same curve of forgetting seems to occur; everything is the same.

Table 1.3. shows data on chronic conditions. It shows a tremendous lack of reporting on chronic conditions, some 59 per cent. This study was done by Madow (1967) of the Stanford Research Institute and was very dramatic. In that case they did know something about overreporting. The average underreport was about 40 per cent and the average overreport was about 20 per cent. If one considers figures of the range of 40 per cent and 20 per cent it gives some idea of the frailty of the data. It is fairly well established that this kind of variable is important.

We can examine yet another variable in Table 1.4. This is one of the variables that we consider to be a measure of either the importance of the event for the individual, or its *salience*. One notices that the longer

Table 1.3 Per cent of chronic conditions not reported in interview by number of days since last visit to clinic (SRI)

Number of days since last clinic visit	Number of conditions in records	Percentage not reported in household interview
1–7	116	9
8–14	218	28
15–28	440	24
29–56	683	42
57–84	574	37
85–112	513	42
113–140	476	45
141–168	355	46
169–224	372	57
225–280	1232	52
281–364	1078	58
365+	71	59

Source: Madow, 1967

Table 1.4 Underreporting of hospitalisations by duration of hospitalisation (includes proxy respondents)

Duration of hospitalisation (days)	Number of hospital records	Percentage not reported in household interview
1	150	26
2–4	646	14
5–7	456	10
8–14	352	10
15–21	111	6
22–30	58	2
31 and over	46	8

Source: Cannell, Fisher and Bakker, 1965

the hospitalisation (which usually means it was more serious) the better the recording. This is also found in Table 1.5: if the person had been to the clinic six times or more, the reporting is far better than if they had been only once. Again this is characteristic of these kinds of data.

In Table 1.6 we see the combination of duration of events and time lapse. The table clearly indicates that there are two main effects going on here (interaction is not so important in this case): one is time lapse and the other is importance or salience. When one is dealing with a hospitalisation of one day that occurred 41 weeks or more beyond the

Table 1.5   Per cent underreporting of chronic conditions by number of visits to clinic (SRI)

Number of visits to clinic	Number of conditions	Percentage not reported
1	3081	56
2	1281	47
3	643	35
4–5	639	26
6 or more	496	14

Source: Madow, 1967

Table 1.6   Per cent of underreporting of hospitalisations by number of weeks the hospital discharge preceded the interview and length of the hospitalisation (including proxy respondents)

Number of weeks hospitalisation preceded interview	Duration of hospitalisation (days)		
	5 & over	2–4	1
1–20	5	5	21
21–40	7	11	27
41–52	22	34	32
(N)	(1018)	(645)	(150)

Source: Cannell, Fisher and Bakker, 1965

recording, the underreporting is about a third, whereas if it is a recent one of four days or more, underreporting is 5 per cent.

To generalise, when events are less important or less salient to the individual they are recorded less well. Psychologists will say, 'Why sure, you are telling me the standard, classic definition of memory.' Memory depends on the frequency with which an event occurs and the importance of the event. That is a classic finding in most memory experiments. One wonders, however, if one has a person who has been in a hospital within the past year or has gone to the doctor within the past two weeks, is it really that he forgot those events? The question occurred to the public-health people immediately. They decided 'Yes, he forgot.'

In our studies we went back to all those people who failed to report their hospitalisation in Time 1 and to an equal number of people who had reported it faithfully. The interview was taken by the interviewing supervisor, and we asked the question on hospitalisation again. Approximately 60 per cent of the episodes that were not reported at Time 1 were reported at Time 2. Thus, they apparently did not forget this, but for some reason they did not produce the data when they were first asked.

Let me consider one more variable. Most social scientists are very much aware of the problems of acquiescence and social desirability. It is a very clear issue in this case. If the diagnosis is either embarrassing or threatening to the person in some way, it tends not to be reported (Table 1.7). Further, if it was a gynaecological episode, a urinary tract infection or a psychological problem, the failure to report that particular diagnosis went as high as 60 per cent. At least 25 per cent of those potentially embarrassing things were in fact not reported accurately.

To research these effects further, we devised a study where we asked a couple of samples from student classes: 'If you had this condition, how would you feel about your friends knowing about it?' We listed the conditions in the order of whether they would not want people to know about it. Then we compared that with the way people reported it. It was almost a perfect rank–order correlation. If the students said they would not want people to know about it, then (we assumed) the respondents did not either. These tendencies are just very clear, and are reproducible time and again in experiments.

Table 1.7   Underreporting of hospitalisation by diagnostic threat rating
(including proxy respondents)

Diagnostic rating	Number of hospital records	Percentage underreported
Very threatening	235	21
Somewhat threatening	421	14
Not threatening	1164	10

Source: Cannel, Fisher and Bakker, 1965.

Here, then, are some of the main characteristics of the interview process. What is going on with the failure of people to report? Why is time so important? Why is recording so bad with the low-salience events? What can we do about them? What can we do about the reporting of embarrassing conditions?

Our interpretation is that these requests for reporting amount to a heavier *respondent burden* than the respondent is willing to accept for that interviewer. How and why is this the case? If you think of an event that occurred at some time in the past, it takes some effort to retrieve that event, and obviously people are not willing to make it. If it is recent and if it is non-threatening, it is a very simple task and everyone reports it almost without difficulty at all. However, if it occurs in the past and it is not particularly important, the work that the respondent has to do to salvage this data, to retrieve it from memory, is more than he or she is willing to undertake. It says that the interview really has very little meaning for the respondent. He or she has very little incentive to respond in a diligent way; he or she is not motivated to work hard to produce what appears to be very simple data. So even this simple kind of request is not very well pondered by the respondent.

A MODEL OF THE QUESTION-ANSWERING PROCESS

Question comprehension

Figure 1.1 is a simple model of the question-answering procedure. It tries to set up a sort of a job description of what a respondent must go through if he or she is doing a diligent task. It starts with, 1: comprehension of the question. Let me suggest that simple questions are not really simple and let me use as an illustration the question we referred to earlier about visits to doctors in the last two weeks: 'Did you go to visit a doctor or a doctor's office at any time in the last two weeks?' Now what does the respondent have to do if he or she is going to do a good job on it? The first thing is to think, 'How do I answer the question? What is a doctor to you? Do you include a chiropractor in this? Do you include the doctor's nurse? When you say 'visit him', do you mean that talking to him on the telephone should be included, or what do you mean?' What, indeed, are the dimensions of that question? The understanding of the question is frequently a difficult task for what is a deceptively simple question.

The doctor question is a very good illustration of the problem. If (as a respondent) one is doing a good job trying to understand the question, a series of questions has to be asked of oneself. For example: 'Who do I include as a doctor? When did the two weeks begin and finish? What was the date of the two weeks that I am supposed to report? What about a telephone call?' In other words, one has to think hard about these things. Then, in doing the job properly you go through some sort of an episodic retrieval. You have to say: 'How do I go about this? I have got to think of what was happening two weeks ago, and I have to go through this day by day if I am doing a conscientious retrieval job. Or I may try to think of all the illnesses I have had in the last two weeks.' The search that is required for a lot of these data is much more difficult than we would imagine and it is at this very point that the respondent tends to get sloppy. The respondent does not always go through all this, particularly if he or she does not understand it properly. If you ask the doctor-visit question and you ask

Figure 1.1   A model of the question-answering process

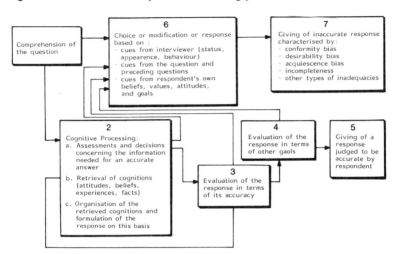

Source: Cannell, Miller and Oskenberg, 1981

a further question, 'Well, did you have to go for x-rays or a check-up, or something of that sort?', the respondent might say suddenly, 'Oh yes, well I did...I did not think about that.' 'Did you go for (this) purpose?' 'Oh yes.' So in addition to the question where the respondent should have recorded all these, you can pick up a lot more with these probes, indicating again that the respondent was not doing the task initially set.

In the original Public Health Service study they did not ask these probe questions, having assumed it was a simple issue. In the follow-up study that we did at the Survey Research Center, we included about seven or eight different probes and picked up a very significant number of doctors' visits previously unreported. So comprehension of the question in itself is difficult.

Cognitive processing

We should also consider cognitive processing of information versus the assessment of the decision about what information is needed to give an accurate response. We are also interested in attempts to retrieve the information and to organise the information in a way that is responsive to the way the question is worded. In terms of attitude questions, respondents have to understand what a 5-point scale is, in addition to understanding and pulling together what our own opinions or attitudes are, and then *we* have to understand the response made. If it is a 5-point scale, how to do I make my response into a 5-point scale; how well am I going to do this? Or if it is an open question, how well do I frame my opinions to report? Thus, it is not only the question itself and the information that the respondent has to work through; he also has to understand and work through the response categories.

I think we pay less attention to response category problems than we should, especially in relation to the telephone interview. This really raises the issue of how many points you should use for a scale and what the distributions look like. We have not done much work on this in the personal interview mode either. We go blithely ahead assuming people can handle a 5-point scale or a 7-point scale, and I am not sure that they can. That is the cognitive processing element of the exchange between interviewers and respondents, and again it is somewhat of a burden on the respondent.

Evaluation in terms of accuracy

The third point is evaluation of the response in terms of its accuracy. Once I have got the information and I am doing my job correctly I 'interview' myself again and say: 'Is this response accurate? Did I really visit the doctor only once, or could it have been twice? Is this the *correct* information?' By evaluating it properly I would be saying: 'Well no, I had better go back and try to retrieve another visit', or something of that sort. Thus there is a certain amount of evaluative processing in the retrieval of information and a reviewing of its accuracy.

Evaluation in terms of other goals

People sometimes evaluate their response in terms of other goals. For example: 'Sure, I remember I was in the hospital because I had a mental illness, but do I want to talk about it?' This is a *censoring* tendency, where the process I think is: 'What does this do to my self-image? What does this do to the image I am projecting to the interviewer? What should I do about it?' As a censoring process, it is an evaluation from various points of view: 'I know the information but I do not want to report it', or 'I know the information and it is quite alright to report it.' After going through all those processes, and if I am a conscientious respondent, I give a response which I judge to be as accurate as I can.

Modified and inaccurate response

Boxes 6 and 7 at the top of Figure 1.1 are where the problems of response bias show up most markedly. In every stage of the processing of questions and attendant information, the direct line which goes from box 1 to box 5 may be short-circuited. The response may reflect some other procedure or mode or some other activity than the one that we require. The respondent may say: 'It is too hard to me. I do not understand this question. I cannot comprehend all that. What shall I do? I will use some other cue to give the response.' And this may be particularly true in terms of attitudinal questions. If I were a respondent I may say: 'Well, what would that interviewer like me to say. What do I think this study is all about?' I may give the answers on that basis, or on whatever I think this interviewer really wants me to say. Or I may say: 'This is something the interviewer really wants me to say. Or I may say: 'This is somewhat embarrassing to me', or, 'I have not really thought about this very much.' We may therefore get a response on the basis of an acquiescence bias, conformity, incompleteness, or something of this sort.

The important thing is that at each stage, the responding process may break down and one may then get a response due to some cue or some characteristic which does not come from the proper processing of information. It may very well occur because the respondent says: 'I just do not want to work hard enough to go through all these steps and do it properly.' Or he or she may say: 'Well I think I am doing a good job; in fact I am doing a faulty job because I am not working hard enough.'

Summary—two important principles

There are two basic principles about the nature of the response task in the survey interview:

1 The task-demand level, or the difficulty, is the sum of the cognitive demands imposed by the requirement for information retrieval and processing, and the affective demands imposed by the threat of the information requested. This is a statement of difficulty or threat.

2 The quality of respondent performance is a function of the level of difficulty of the task and the level of the effort achieved by the respondent.

Thus it is a combination of the difficulty of the task and level of effort which the respondent applies to the solution of the task which seems to determine very largely how well the response process will work.

INTERVIEWER VARIABILITY

Respondent workloads

In our work we needed an insight into why people do not respond well and so we began to do some experimentation to improve reporting. As can be imagined, having been in the survey business for a number of years and finding the kinds of response problems we did, we were pretty shaken by the results, and we had to ask questions like: 'What are we doing anyway?' 'What is the use of all this?'

I have presented a somewhat biased picture; I picked those variables which show some vivid problems of recording, but they are not completely atypical. As I said, the generalisations about how people do a poor job of reporting seem to be pretty well established. Our next priority for research was to understand the factors that underlie reporting behaviour.

The study that was most revealing involved conducting a second interview with the respondents the day after they had gone through a regular health interview. The Census Bureau interviewer went to their home, conducted the regular health survey interview and the next day, one of our Survey Research Center interviewers arrived on the doorstep to ask the person about their experiences the previous day. Whereas the original interview took about a half-hour, we spent about an hour and a quarter asking them about that half-hour. Some very revealing information came out of it. We interviewed something over 400 respondents in this way.

The first finding was that virtually every respondent recalled the experience pleasurably. About 96 per cent of respondents said they really enjoyed it—it was interesting; the person was a very nice interviewer; everything went just fine, and it was a pleasant experience. They were very rewarding of the interviewer's behaviour and of the interviewers as people (this incidentally, is again characteristic of the way all respondents in all the studies I know of have reacted to interviewers—they like them and they get a pleasurable experience from the interaction).

Then we asked them *who* was doing this study. The answers then began to get very vague. Most respondents (over 50 per cent) said: 'Gee, I do not know, I really had not thought about that.' Only 45 per cent knew the study had been done by a government agency; only 11 per cent knew it was the Census Bureau. Then we asked them why the study was being done. Again about 50 per cent said: 'Gee, I do not know' or, 'Well, they wanted to collect some statistics', or, 'They wanted to get some information.' Our interviewers asked, why did they want the information?' 'Gee, I do not know, they are going to publish it somewhere.' Other people said: 'Oh sure, well, this was a study that was done by somebody who was doing a Masters thesis' or, 'This was done by the welfare department to find out how sick people are.'

In fact, before that interview the respondents had received a letter from the Census Bureau, an elaborate brochure from the US Public Health Service telling them why the study was done and how the data would be used. The interviewer had given a similar introduction and had shown indentification cards from the Bureau of Census, so the survey had been well introduced, as is the usual procedure. Yet respondents had almost no notion of how or why it was done. In other words, there was no concept of importance, no concept of why it would be important to do a good reporting job. We followed up with questions asking: 'Did the interviewer want you to report *all* your health conditions, or only the important things?' Respondents often said: 'Oh well, they only wanted the important things; they could not care about all those little details.'

So here one has the norm of people who did not understand the purpose and objectives of the survey. If one were a student of motivation one would say that there is very little in this experience that would get a person to make much effort to produce good data. One could think, as we did, that health ought to be a very interesting issue for people, that they ought to recognise its importance. The truth is, they do not. The thoughts in the respondent's mind are very likely: 'There was no tie between my contribution to this interview and any personal goal that I had. It does not contribute to my health even if I understand what it is doing. I do not perceive my participation to serve any useful goal.' The basic theories of motivation indicate that there needs to be some path to a goal to get good performance. That was clearly absent. We thought at this point that the brochures explaining the survey were not very good. We put several artists to work and they made elaborate brochures which were sent to a sample of people and then we interviewed them. Fifty per cent of the people said they thought they had seen something like that in the mail and others said they thought they had looked at it, or something. We asked what was in it and they did not know. It also made no difference at all to the quality of their reporting.

We have followed this up in some other surveys and got very much the same information. It seems very much that the respondent just does not share with the researcher the importance of the undertaking. The respondent does not see why this experience has anything to do with any goals they themselves have. They are glad to cooperate; it is a pleasant experience; they enjoy it and they do what is easy. If it is easy to report something and non-threatening, they report it. If it takes effort or poses a threat, they do not report it and there is no reason why they should.

Interviewer—respondent interactions and feedback

In the interviewing field, it has been considered for a long time that what carries an interview is probably the interaction between the interviewer and the respondent. This whole area of rapport and how one interacts with people is the fundamental linkage. It does not make all that much difference, perhaps, that the person does not know exactly what are the objectives. If the interviewer—respondent interaction is appropriate there may well be an intrinsic motivation that will drive or stimulate the interview.

About three studies were carried out in which we recorded several

Table 1.8 Per cent of kinds of interviewer behaviour over all interviews

Interviewer behaviour	Per cent of total interviewer behaviour	
Correct question	29.9	
Modified question	9.1	
Incorrect question	5.1	
Incomplete question	0.8	
Q. alternatives incomplete	2.2	
Not appropriate question	0.7	
Total question codes		47.8
Ask Q. out of order	0.1	0.1
Non-directive probe	6.2	
Anything else probe	1.3	
Directive probe	4.2	
Repeats question	1.5	
Total probe codes		13.2
Feedback	20.2	
Ongoing feedback	3.8	
Total feedback codes		24.0
Repeats answer	8.1	8.1
Gives clarification or information	0.3	
Polite behaviour	0.5	
Interruption	0.8	
Laughs	1.9	
Irrelevant conversation	2.1	
Extraneous interaction	0.4	
Uncodable (other)	0.8	
Total other codes		6.8
Total interviewer behaviour		100.0

Source: Lansing, Withey and Wolfe, 1971

Table 1.9   Per cent of kinds of respondent behaviour over all interviews

Respondent behaviour	Per cent of total respondent behaviour	
Adequate response	36.5	
Appropriate response	3.1	
Total adequate answers		39.6
Inadequate response	3.7	
'Don't know' response	1.6	
Refusal to respond	0.1	
Total inadequate answers		5.4
Other response	7.2	
Unusable response	5.8	
Repeats answer	2.8	
Closure	0.7	
Total other answers		16.5
Elaborates	19.1	19.1
Asks clarification	3.2	3.2
Feedback	1.3	
Ongoing feedback	1.5	
Total feedback		2.8
Suggests behaviour	0.2	
Polite behaviour	0.2	
Interruption	2.4	
Laughs	4.2	
Irrelevant conversation	4.2	
Uncodable (other)	2.2	
Total other		13.4
Total respondent behaviour		100.0

Source: Lansing, Withey and Wolfe, 1971

hundred interviews and coded the behaviour. We asked: What is the interviewer doing when asking this question? Is the interviewer asking it correctly, completely, incorrectly or incompletely? What does the respondent do as a result of this? If he gives an answer, is it a complete answer? Is it a partial answer or does he ask for information? Does he say: 'I won't answer it', or what does he do? Then what does the interviewer do next? We have a chain of behaviours that can be coded to record the behaviour of the interviewer and the respondent. From this you can evaluate the circumstances surrounding the respondent's reactions and the circumstances of the interviewer's behaviour. It was a powerful analysis, and there were a lot of data we had not seen before. In Tables 1.8 and 1.9 we see the results of one of these studies. This is just a straight tabulation of the frequency of responses and is fairly typical of the result of three or four such analyses. In the question codes, the interviewer is doing pretty well, having asked the questions really well. About half the behaviour takes the form of question-asking. The

19

next category of behaviour relates to probing, including non-directive probes; asking for 'anything else'; directive probing (which if course we frown on) or probes formed by repeating the questions.

The one fact that surprised us about this distribution and those of other similar studies, was that 24 per cent of interviewer behaviours constituted some sort of feedback. Feedback is defined, in this case, as being a comment or some reaction by the interviewer to what the respondent says. It is obviously one of the major components of communication of all kinds. It is frequently some sort of an attitude that is communicated: approval/disapproval or like/dislike. The thing that surprised us was that we had never thought of how much feedback was going on or what kind of feedback it was. We had not been training interviewers in feedback. We had been training them very thoroughly how to ask questions, how to probe, when to probe, how to be non-directive, how to clarify, and all these things. But we did not really tell the interviewers much about what kind of feedback they should use. Yet they were obviously using all kinds of feedback.

One danger was that they were frequently using feedbacks which could be interpreted as approval of the information which was reported. For example, one asks the respondent: 'Do you go to the dentist every six months to get your teeth cleaned?' and the respondent says, 'Yes.' The interviewer may say: 'That is good'; or 'Okay, fine'; or just simply nod and smile. How does the respondent interpret this? The probability is that he interprets it as approval of behaviour. Perhaps it is sometimes like this: 'I went to the dentist every six months like all good citizens do, and the interviewer is telling me that I am rather a nice person because of this.' When we asked people informally about some of these feedbacks, they would report that the interviewer tended to approve of what they were doing. Yet the probing is fairly good. There are some directive probes, but by and large the probing was well done and it was approved.

The important issue to us is, under what circumstances is the feedback being given? Feedback in this case was nearly always positive feedback; there was virtually no negative feedback. They were all 'Well, you are doing well'. Table 1.10 gives the probability of when the feedback was given. If the respondent gave an adequate answer he was almost as likely to get positive feedback. If he said 'Don't know' he got this kind of feedback.

If the respondent refused to answer the question he had the highest probability of interviewer feedback. Now the interesting thing about these statistics is that they are non-discriminating between good performance and bad performance. No matter what the respondent does, whether it is good, bad or indifferent, they are getting good, strong, positive support. Now think about issues of reinforcement. The whole notion of verbal reinforcement has intrigued psychologists for many years. It is now a form of therapy which is being used to modify or change behaviour by giving either positive or negative feedback or reinforcement. There are whole sets of classic studies which demonstrate that you can change all kinds of behaviour simply by the kind of feedback (reinforcement) you use. In this case, behaviour was changed because every time an appropriate behaviour is given by the respondent (or by the subject in this case) there is a positive feedback. Then if the subject does not do what one wants him to do, one gives him no feedback at all.

Table 1.10 Probability of interviewer feedback following respondent behaviour by kind of respondent behaviour

Kind of respondent behaviour	Probability that interviewer feedback follows
Adequate answer	.28
Inadequate answer	.24
'Don't know' answer	.18
Refusal to answer	.55
Other answer (code J)	.34
Elaboration	.30
Repeats answer	.32
Gives suggestion	.33
Other behaviour (not classified elsewhere)	.21

Source: Lansing, Withey and Wolfe, 1971

One can do such strange things as increase the number of self-references that a subject makes in the course of conversation. Every time the respondent says 'I' or 'me' or something like that, he gets feedback, and when he does not, he gets none. If one plots this over the course of a half-hour discussion one will discover that the personal references increase very significantly. If feedback is taken as a way of changing people's behaviour and then this particular application is considered, one may conclude that there is something the respondent can learn from this. But if you have a respondent who is just not interested, not involved and not working and you have an interaction that doesn't really focus on discriminating good and bad behaviour, feedback will be irrelevant. A lot of learning theory is based on notions of feedback. Yet there are often many situations when there is no reason why a respondent ought to report to an interviewer; there is no reason that we can understand why he ought to try to delve into his memory to come up with the information we want, or why he should take any risks of reporting anything that may reflect poorly on him. He does not know what it is all about, he does not see any value in it, and he does not learn much from the interviewer. This is still characteristic of much survey research.

Rapport

By rapport I mean the interpersonal exchange where there is some sort of affective relationship: I like you, you are good, you are interesting, you are a comforter, I am having a good time interviewing you. Rapport as such is not used much these days, and I have become a cynic in this area. The only reason people worry about rapport is for some of the reasons we have talked about: if I don't make that person like me, he isn't going to go through these 'stupid' questions I'm going to ask. I use rapport to develop a personal relationship with someone because I know he is not going to be interested or work hard otherwise. I think that there is the reason we talk about rapport so much and I do not think it is very useful.

The interviews we are going to be discussing in chapter 2 are what we would call task-oriented. Certain clearly defined tasks will be the focus of the interchange between the interviewer and respondent. And it is much more of a cognitive interchange than it is an affective interchange. One could assume that good rapport may in fact introduce bias. It may introduce bias because if I like that interviewer in some interpersonal sense and if I have to report something that is embarrassing, I am less likely to do it because I don't want to insult my new friend. So the affective exchange is not the kind of interaction which will stimulate self-revelation. This is much more likely to be accomplished where there is less personal and more task-oriented behaviour.

The best illustration of this is of course the medical interview. What happens in the medical interview when one visits a doctor? One goes in and sits down and there are obviously a few minutes of interchange, but the interview I am talking about is not a cold interview at all. It is a very personal interview. One might say to the doctor, 'It's raining this morning' or 'We've had good weather'. There may be a couple of minutes of that, then he changes. He sits up and fixes one with a beady eye. He says, 'Well, why are you here? What's going on?' And from that point on there is no rapport, it is oriented to the topic of this interchange—what is wrong with you, what kind of symptoms, what kind of conditions. It would be inappropriate in most interviews of this kind to change back to an interpersonal kind of exchange. It is almost always focused directly on the task in hand. I think that where an interview is of this kind, it is perceived as a task (and it needs to be perceived as a task which both people share in). That is the kind of interview that we are going to be talking about.

Summary—some important goals

I have been trying to emphasise the problems of the exchange between respondent and interviewer in a survey and to give some indications of why these problems occur. In later chapters we shall look at what we are going to do about them. But before doing so it is worth outlining some goals which will lead to a higher standard of respondent–interviewer exchange:

1 We need to teach the respondent what is expected of him or her in general to perform the task properly.
2 We need to inform the respondent and to provide cues on how to be most efficient in answering the particular question.
3 We need to stimulate and encourage the respondent to work diligently to recall and organise information and to report even potentially embarrassing material.
4 We need to develop procedures to standardise the techniques for greater comparability between and among interviews.

2

C.F. CANNELL

Experiments in the improvement of response accuracy

In chapter 1, I touched on some of the experimental techniques that we have been testing, introduced some concepts and terms and gave a few illustrations of data from various studies where we have been testing the methods. Here I would like to give some more extensive illustrations of what these techniques look like. In particular, I would like to discuss some of the methods and interviewing techniques we use with our interviewers and to outline some of the monitoring and supervisory techniques which are used. Finally, I would like to deal with response rates.

I will refer to a number of sets of example questions to illustrate the techniques as they are actually used in surveys. These are from a questionnaire used in a recent telephone survey but the questions are the same whether they are used in telephone or personal interviews.

PROBES AND FEEDBACK

Set 1

This is an extract from an interview, with a lot of questions and the introductory material omitted. The interview begins with a general introduction to the survey, a listing of all the household members and a random selection of the individual eligible to be interviewed. Then it goes to the material shown in Set 1. A commitment form was used. This was a telephone survey so there was no signing in it, but the form is very much the same. The first statement to the respondent (Q1a) was, 'This research is authorized by the Public Health Service Act...' and goes on to ask if he or she is willing to think carefully about each

OMB No. 68-578024
Expires: March 31, 1980

P. 468161

HOUSEHOLD ID NO. ☐☐☐☐

FAMILY AND PERSON ID NO. ☐☐

SURVEY RESEARCH CENTER
INSTITUTE FOR SOCIAL RESEARCH
THE UNIVERSITY OF MICHIGAN
ANN ARBOR, MICHIGAN 48106

INTERVIEWER: _____

DATE OF INTERVIEW: _____

EXACT TIME NOW: _____

HEALTH IN AMERICA

HIS/SRC **EP** QUESTIONNAIRE

1. INTERVIEWER CHECKPOINT

☐ 1. FIRST PERSON SECTION TO BE COMPLETED FOR THIS FAMILY, OR NEW R, THIS FAMILY

☐ 5. FIRST PERSON SECTION FOR THIS FAMILY ALREADY COMPLETED ──▶ GO TO EO QUESTIONNAIRE

1a. This research is authorized by the Public Health Service Act. It's important for the Public Health Service to get exact details on every question, even on those which may seem unimportant to you. This may take extra effort. Are you willing to think carefully about each question in order to give accurate information?

| 1. YES | 5. NO |

We appreciate your willingness to make the extra effort.

Since getting accurate information is important, it's necessary to get your agreement to think carefully if we are to continue the interview. ──▶ TERMINATE

For our part, we will keep all information you give confidential. Of course, the interview is voluntary. Should we come to any question you do not want to answer, just let me know and we'll move on to the next one.

1b. Many people feel it helps them to look at a calendar to recall dates of visits to doctors, illnesses, and other things asked for in these questions. Do you have a calendar handy? I'll be happy to wait while you get one.

| 1. YES | 5. NO |

The next few questions refer to the period beginning Monday _____ and ending this past Sunday evening, _____. This does not include any of the days since Sunday.

3. For this question, we'd like to get the number as exact as you can report it.
    During the two-week period, that is from _____ to _____, how many
    days did illness or injury keep you from <u>work</u>?.
    (FOR FEMALE): Not counting work around the house?

    _____ DAYS | 00. NONE |

                                            TURN TO P. 4, Q4.

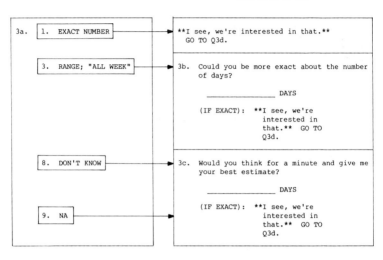

3a. | 1. EXACT NUMBER |————————▶ **I see, we're interested in that.**
                                   GO TO Q3d.

     | 3. RANGE; "ALL WEEK" |————▶ 3b. Could you be more exact about the number
                                          of days?

                                          _____ DAYS

                                          (IF EXACT): **I see, we're
                                                         interested in
                                                         that.** GO TO
                                                         Q3d.

     | 8. DON'T KNOW |———————————▶ 3c. Would you think for a minute and give me
                                          your best estimate?

                                          _____ DAYS

                                          (IF EXACT): **I see, we're
     | 9. NA |——————————————————▶   interested in
                                                         that.** GO TO
                                                         Q3d.

3d. On how many of these days lost from work did you stay in bed <u>all</u> or <u>most</u> of the
     day?

     _____ DAYS (IF EXACT) **F**

26

4.   What condition caused you to (stay in bed/miss work) during those two weeks? We'd
      like to get the name of the condition as well as you can report it?

_____

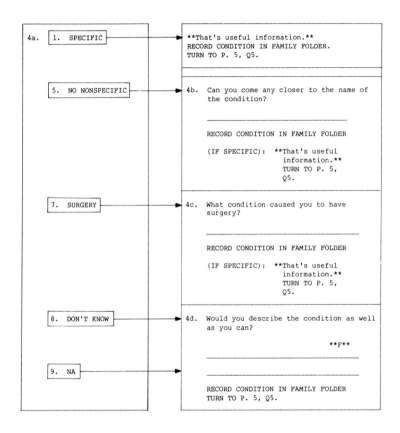

4a. ┌─────────────────┐   **That's useful information.**
     │ 1. SPECIFIC   ├────► RECORD CONDITION IN FAMILY FOLDER.
     └─────────────────┘   TURN TO P. 5, Q5.

     ┌─────────────────┐   4b. Can you come any closer to the name of
     │ 5. NO NONSPECIFIC├──►   the condition?
     └─────────────────┘
                              _____

                              RECORD CONDITION IN FAMILY FOLDER

                              (IF SPECIFIC): **That's useful
                                                information.**
                                              TURN TO P. 5,
                                              Q5.

     ┌─────────────────┐   4c. What condition caused you to have
     │ 7. SURGERY   ├────►   surgery?
     └─────────────────┘
                              _____

                              RECORD CONDITION IN FAMILY FOLDER

                              (IF SPECIFIC): **That's useful
                                                information.**
                                              TURN TO P. 5,
                                              Q5.

     ┌─────────────────┐   4d. Would you describe the condition as well
     │ 8. DON'T KNOW ├────►   as you can?
     └─────────────────┘
                                                          F
                              _____
     ┌─────────────────┐
     │ 9. NA   ├────►   _____
     └─────────────────┘
                              RECORD CONDITION IN FAMILY FOLDER
                              TURN TO P. 5, Q5.

11. (Not counting the days in bed and/or lost from work)

Were there any (other) days during that two-week period that you cut down on the things you usually do because of any illness or injury? This is sometimes hard to remember, so please take your time.

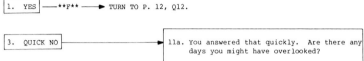

1. YES ——**F** ——▶ TURN TO P. 12, Q12.

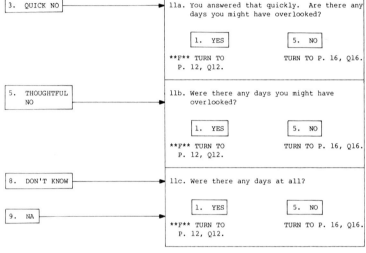

3. QUICK NO ──────────▶ 11a. You answered that quickly. Are there any days you might have overlooked?

        1. YES   5. NO

     F TURN TO   TURN TO P. 16, Q16.
     P. 12, Q12.

5. THOUGHTFUL NO ──────────▶ 11b. Were there any days you might have overlooked?

        1. YES   5. NO

     F TURN TO   TURN TO P. 16, Q16.
     P. 12, Q12.

8. DON'T KNOW ──────────▶ 11c. Were there any days at all?

9. NA ──────────▶

        1. YES   5. NO

     F TURN TO   TURN TO P. 16, Q16.
     P. 12, Q12.

22. In the next question, we're interested in medical advice obtained over the telephone (either through calls you made yourself, or through calls someone else made about you).

During that period, did you get any medical advice from a doctor over the telephone?

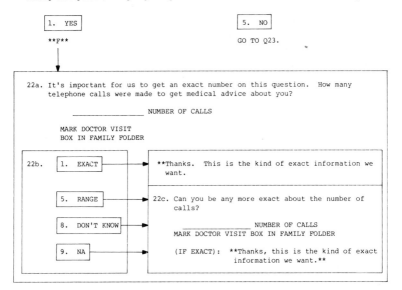

1. YES

F

5. NO

GO TO Q23.

22a. It's important for us to get an exact number on this question. How many telephone calls were made to get medical advice about you?

_____ NUMBER OF CALLS

MARK DOCTOR VISIT
BOX IN FAMILY FOLDER

22b.   1. EXACT   **Thanks. This is the kind of exact information we want.

        5. RANGE   22c. Can you be any more exact about the number of calls?

        8. DON'T KNOW   _____ NUMBER OF CALLS
                          MARK DOCTOR VISIT BOX IN FAMILY FOLDER

        9. NA   (IF EXACT): **Thanks, this is the kind of exact information we want.**

23. INTERVIEWER CHECKPOINT

☐   1. IF 1 OR MORE DOCTOR'S VISITS FROM Q20 - 22c. ──►TURN TO P. 20, Q24.

☐   2. IF 0 DOCTOR'S VISITS FROM Q20 - 22c. ──►TURN TO P. 24, Q30.

question before answering. If the response is 'Yes' there is a comment at the side, 'We appreciate your willingness to make the extra effort.' This is a kind of feedback or reinforcing statement. If the answer is 'No', the interview is terminated at that point. This being a telephone survey, there was maybe one person out of the 2500 who did not want to agree to it. The interviewer comments that, 'we will keep all the information you give confidential.' Question 1b is a kind of general instruction to look for a calendar to make answering easy.

In Q3 there is the instruction, 'For this question, we'd like to get the number as exact as you can report it.' Then the question itself: 'During the two-week period...how many days did illness or injury keep you from work?' If the respondent gives an exact number, the following statement is a feedback statement. The feedback statements are identified by two asterisks preceding and following: 'I see, we're interested in that.' If they give a range, then there is the probe: 'Could you be more exact about the number of days?' If they are more exact they get a positive feedback, and if not, they do not get it. 'Don't know' also has the probe there, and if they are then exact, they get a feedback.

This is the general format of a questionnaire which is set up to use these experimental techniques. It contains the probes, the feedback, and almost everything the interviewer is supposed to ask. The interviewer is allowed, if there is some problem with understanding the question, to repeat the question. If he gets information which seems to be either incomplete or not quite clear enough for the interviewer to understand, he is allowed to say, 'Can you tell me more about this?' or 'Can you give me more information on it.' These are about the only things they can do. They can sometimes define terms if it is allowed in the instructions, but in most cases it is not. In cases where the respondent says, 'What do you mean?' the interviewer can repeat the question or he can say, 'Whatever it means to you' or 'However you interpret it'. But with those exceptions the interviewer sticks exactly to the wording given.

The feedback '**F**' without any content is what we call a short feedback, such as 'I see', or 'I understand', or any of the single- or double-word feedbacks. The interviewer has a list of about five or six from which he can choose and a long list he cannot choose from. For example, interviewers tend, as we all do in conversation, to use perhaps most frequently the feedback 'OK' or 'Good', or something like that. These are bad feedbacks because they indicate too much approval. The interviewer can say, 'I see', 'Thanks', or 'I understand', but that is all. So the '**F**' simply means, pick one of those.

In Q4 notice again the instructions, this time following the question, 'What condition caused you to (stay in bed/miss work) during those two weeks? We'd like to get the *name* of the *condition* as well as you can report it'. If they give specific information, the feedback 'That's useful information', is used, if they give non-specific information, a probe, 'Can you come any closer to the name of the condition?' If they then give a specific condition the same feedback is used. If it was surgery the interviewer asks, 'What condition caused you to have surgery?' and there is the feedback. 'Don't know' answers are dealt with by asking, 'Would you describe the conditions as well as you can.' Note the instruction and the specified feedback. The most important characteristic of the feedback is that it reacts to the *process* of communication rather than to content, and is contingent on 'Name the condition as well as you can report it'. That is, a contingency is set up for the feedback to be used. The assumption is that in time the respondent will understand the instruction and the feedback, that this will improve the reporting, and that it will teach the respondent generally what is wanted in terms of reporting. The reinforcement will be rewarding.

In some of the questions there are words underlined. When we listened to a lot of interview recordings, it became clear that the interviewers were using varying inflections in the questions, and the inflections they were using sometimes changed the meaning of the questions or the context of the question. So we have been underlining the words we want the interviewer to emphasise in an attempt to standardise the stimulus. We never can completely standardise it, but this is at least one small step in that direction.

Q11 starts with a different kind of instruction: 'This is sometimes hard to remember, so please take your time.' If the person answers 'Yes', then we go on to the next. But if the answer is a quick 'No', (which is defined as anything within three seconds) the interview says, 'You answered that quickly. Are there any days you might have overlooked?' That is a probe, or a negative feedback, whichever you might like to call it. If they then give you a 'Yes', a short feedback is usual such as, 'I see' or 'Thanks'. If it is a thoughtful 'No', (that is, something over three seconds) then the interviewer asks, 'Were there and days you might have overlooked?', or if the respondent does not know, he is asked, 'Were there any days at all?'

In Q22 we are trying to define a little bit better what we mean to include by doctor's visits and phone calls, and so forth. The parenthesis in the introductory question indicates that if it is a single-family household that phrase is not used. The instruction is a definition: 'During that period, did you get any medical advice from a doctor over the telephone?' Again, the instruction is, 'It's important for us to get an exact number on a question. How many phone calls were made to get this medical advice about you?' If he gives an exact number, the feedback is, 'Thanks. This is the kind of exact information we want.' If a range is given, the interviewer asks, 'Could you be more exact about the number of calls?' The same probe is used for 'Don't know'. In effect, the respondent gets penalised, mildly of course, for not doing what we want and rewarded for doing what we want.

It works out that the respondent gets sometimes penalised and sometimes rewarded for not doing the right thing. If people learn that they are going to be rewarded for giving a specific number there are in fact no checks on whether they are giving the right information. The working hypothesis here is based on the assumption that if they report more information it is more likely to be correct—and by correct I do not mean exact. If they report four things, it is more likely to be correct than if they report only two. In some cases, however, the working assumption is the other way—for health, it is almost always that way. If you look at another study we did on use of medications, the desirable response is fewer or less. Thus, most cases have directional components, and we have to make some assumptions about them at the outset. The evidence is that people tend to report more when more seems to be better, and less when less seems to be better, and we do not know at all if what they are giving us is correct. I suspect one never knows that in survey research.

UNFOLDING TECHNIQUES, OPEN-ENDED QUESTIONS AND SCALES, COMMITMENT PROCEDURES

Set 2

This is concerned with the collection of demographic data. In this case, where we do not know what is good or bad, all the feedbacks are simply short feedbacks. No matter what the respondent says, he gets 'I see', or something equally innocuous. This is a technique which we have been trying in telephone surveys. Instead of using the usual tick boxes or something of that sort, we have tried a set of unfolding techniques to see whether we get more information or better information.

Collecting data on income always causes the surveyor in our culture the most problems. I remember a survey we did several years ago about family planning and we asked the women all the details of pregnancy and children; we asked them about frequency of use of contraceptives, methods of contraception, and success of contraception. When we asked the income they said, 'Wait a minute, that is personal.' If one found out what kinds of questions people object to reporting one could learn a lot about their culture. I can tell you that in the United States, the one thing that troubles people is reporting their income.

The unfolding techniques used on these data are just simple

OMB No. 68-578024
Expires: March 31, 1980
Project 468161

HOUSEHOLD ID NO.

FAMILY AND PERSON ID NO.

SURVEY RESEARCH CENTER
INSTITUTE FOR SOCIAL RESEARCH
THE UNIVERSITY OF MICHIGAN
ANN ARBOR, MICHIGAN 48106

INTERVIEWER: _____

DATE OF INTERVIEW: _____

HEALTH IN AMERICA

EP - EO

DEMOGRAPHIC SECTION

D1. Now, thinking about your (family's) total income from all sources, did (you/your family) receive more than or less than $15,000 in 1978?

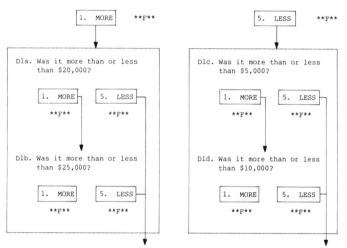

| 1. MORE **F** | 5. LESS **F** |

D1a. Was it more than or less than $20,000?

| 1. MORE **F** | 5. LESS **F** |

D1b. Was it more than or less than $25,000?

| 1. MORE **F** | 5. LESS **F** |

D1c. Was it more than or less than $5,000?

| 1. MORE **F** | 5. LESS **F** |

D1d. Was it more than or less than $10,000?

| 1. MORE **F** | 5. LESS **F** |

D2. I am supposed to ask these questions for our records. Other than the telephone number we're now using, could I reach you at home by dialing any other number?

| 1. YES **F** | 5. NO ──► TURN TO P. 2, D6 **F** |

D3. In total, how many telephone numbers do you have in your home?

_____ NUMBER

D4. Are any of these numbers for business only?

| 1. YES | | 5. NO | ──────▶ GO TO D6 |

F   **F**

D5. How many are used only for business?

_____ **F**
        NUMBER

D6. INTERVIEWER CHECKPOINT

☐ 1. ODD NUMBERED HOUSEHOLD ──────────▶ GO TO Q.D7

☐ 2. EVEN NUMBERED HOUSEHOLD ──────────▶ GO TO Q.D13

D7. These last questions ask for your personal feelings about your health and your life
     in general. In answering them, please think carefully about your experience in the
     past and what you expect in the near future. Of course, if you don't have any
     feelings on a question or if your've never thought about it, just tell me.

     Some people think about their health a great deal, while others take it for granted
     and don't think much about it. Would you say you think about your health
     very often, often, now and then, rarely, or never?

| 1. VERY OFTEN | 2. OFTEN | 3. NOW AND THEN | 4. RARELY | 5. NEVER |

     Now, I'll ask you to give me a number between one and seven that describes how you
     feel about your health -- "One" stands for "completely dissatisfied" and "Seven" for
     "completely satisfied". If you are right in the middle, answer "four". So, the low
     numbers indicate that you are dissatisfied, the high numbers that you are satisfied.

D8. We'd like to get your ideas very accurately on these questions so please take time
     and give me the number which best describes your feelings.

     First, what number comes closest to how satisfied or dissatisfied you are with your
     health and physical condition in general?

_____ **F** | 8. NEVER THOUGHT: NO FEELINGS |
        NUMBER

34

D9. And, what number best describes how you feel about your <u>physical ability to do the things you want to do</u>?

_____ **F**
NUMBER

8. NEVER THOUGHT: NO FEELINGS

D10. What number comes closest to your feelings about the <u>amount of energy or pep you have</u>?

_____ **F**
NUMBER

8. NEVER THOUGHT: NO FEELINGS

D11. And what number comes closest to how satisfied or dissatisfied you are with your <u>resistance to illness</u>?

_____ **F**
NUMBER

8. NEVER THOUGHT: NO FEELINGS

D12. We have talked about various aspects of your health. Now I want to ask you about your <u>life as a whole</u>, and I want to get your ideas very accurately. Thinking about <u>all</u> the parts of your life, which number comes closest to how satisfied or dissatisfied you are?

_____ **F**
TURN TO P. 9, D19

8. NEVER THOUGHT: NO FEELINGS

D13. These last questions ask for your personal feelings about your health and your life in general. In answering them, please think carefully about your experience in the past and what you expect in the near future. Of course, if you don't have any feelings on a question or if you've never thought about it, just tell me.

Some people think about their health a great deal, while others take it for granted and don't think much about it. Would you say you think about your health <u>very often</u>, <u>often</u>, <u>now and then</u>, <u>rarely</u>, or <u>never</u>?

1. VERY OFTEN	2. OFTEN	3. NOW AND THEN	4. RARELY	5. NEVER

D14. Now, thinking about your health and physical condition in general, would you say you are <u>satisfied</u>, <u>dissatisfied</u> or <u>somewhere in the middle</u>?

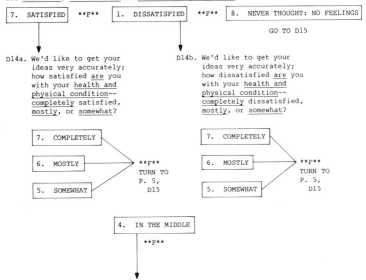

| 7. SATISFIED | **F** | 1. DISSATISFIED | **F** | 8. NEVER THOUGHT: NO FEELINGS |

GO TO D15

D14a. We'd like to get your ideas very accurately; how satisfied <u>are</u> you with your <u>health and physical condition</u>-- <u>completely</u> satisfied, <u>mostly</u>, or <u>somewhat</u>?

| 7. COMPLETELY |
| 6. MOSTLY |
| 5. SOMEWHAT |

F
TURN TO
P. 5,
D15

D14b. We'd like to get your ideas very accurately; how dissatisfied <u>are</u> you with your <u>health and physical condition</u>-- <u>completely</u> dissatisfied, <u>mostly</u>, or <u>somewhat</u>?

| 7. COMPLETELY |
| 6. MOSTLY |
| 5. SOMEWHAT |

F
TURN TO
P. 5,
D15

| 4. IN THE MIDDLE |

F

D14c. We'd like to get your ideas very accurately. If you had to choose, would you say you are closer to being <u>satisfied</u> or <u>dissatisfied</u> with your <u>health and physical condition</u>, or are you <u>right in the middle</u>?

| 5. SATISFIED |
| 3. DISSATISFIED |
| 4. IN THE MIDDLE |

F

36

D18. We have talked about various aspects of your health. Finally, I want to ask you about your life as a whole. Thinking about all the parts of your life, would you say you are satisfied, dissatisfied, or somewhere in-between?

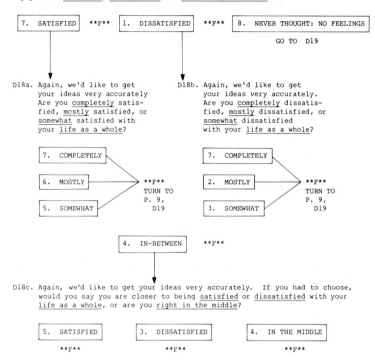

| 7. SATISFIED | **F** | 1. DISSATISFIED | **F** | 8. NEVER THOUGHT: NO FEELINGS |

GO TO D19

D18a. Again, we'd like to get your ideas very accurately Are you completely satisfied, mostly satisfied, or somewhat satisfied with your life as a whole?

| 7. COMPLETELY |
| 6. MOSTLY |
| 5. SOMEWHAT |

F
TURN TO
P. 9,
D19

D18b. Again, we'd like to get your ideas very accurately. Are you completely dissatisfied, mostly dissatisfied, or somewhat dissatisfied with your life as a whole?

| 7. COMPLETELY |
| 2. MOSTLY |
| 3. SOMEWHAT |

F
TURN TO
P. 9,
D19

| 4. IN-BETWEEN | **F** |

D18c. Again, we'd like to get your ideas very accurately. If you had to choose, would you say you are closer to being satisfied or dissatisfied with your life as a whole, or are you right in the middle?

| 5. SATISFIED | 3. DISSATISFIED | 4. IN THE MIDDLE |
| **F** | **F** | **F** |

37

feedbacks. Since this was a telephone survey, we tended to use more feedbacks than we do in face-to-face interviews, to try to compensate for the lack of visual cues. Almost every question is followed by some modicum of feedback to at least let the person know we are interested.

In QD2 and the following questions we have a different kind of experiment. We were trying to find out what happened when people used the telephone. In some cases we used open-ended questions and in other cases, 5-point scales and 3-point scales (see Miller, 1981; Schuman and Presser, 1981).

This is an interesting issue. When one switches from face-to-face interviews to telephone, how well do respondents understand questions? And how well do they grasp the notion of 5-point scales (or however many scale points one wants)? This is an issue which requires a considerable amount of investigation because there is some evidence that people tend to handle 5-point scales differently on the telephone than in a face-to-face interview. The evidence is not very good but enough to make one try to do some studies to tease out differences.

One of our hypotheses was that respondents select the end scale points and the other hypothesis is exactly opposite: that is, they tend to code themselves in the middle. Some researchers report one tendency; others, the other. We are trying to determine if there is a tendency toward a position of bias. It is important that the interviewer repeat the whole scale when necessary—not for every question, but whenever the respondent asks the scale to be repeated. Then, if it is clear that the respondent is not understanding the question, the interviewer has to repeat the whole scale. The most likely occurrence is that in a 5-point scale, the respondent will give a 2-point answer such as 'It's good or very good'. The interviewer now knows it is either one or the other and can say, 'If you had to pick one, would you say it was good or very good?' But if the answer given does not designate only two positions—such as 'Oh, it's fine'—then the interviewer should repeat the whole thing. In general, one should not have many 5-point scales all together because it becomes monotonous.

The length of the scales is a problem. For a lot of people it is difficult to grasp more than three points over the telephone and unfortunately, three points does not give one much discrimination, particularly if one wants to compare it with a 5-point scale later on. There have been all kinds of tricks devised to try to get respondents to understand scale positions, such as using the telephone dial and have them pick the numbers—that was fine until people started getting push-button telephones! There are various techniques of this kind, none of which have been very satisfactory, and I do not know what the answer is. It may very well be that a 10-point scale is more meaningful than a 5-point scale, simply because people do not think in terms of five but they do think in terms of ten. One might be able to say to the person, 'Now if you were to score this from one to ten for example, where would you score it?' Or perhaps one could use one to 100. The argument has been that in school people tend to get graded on a 100-point scale and if they think in terms of 100 points, it may be easier for them than one to ten. None of these have really been checked exhaustively (see Miller, 1981).

A problem here is that the bigger the scale the less normal is the distribution. A 10-point scale does not produce a normal distribution even in face-to-face interviews. Probably we have not used a 10-point scale long enough to know just what those bumps and dips look like. So one gets them piling up at twos and fives. This is a fundamental issue of problems of measurement and problems of scaling. One of the things that always troubles me is to try to get the respondent to translate his response from one set of categories to another. That is why I was always worried about the thermometer or the ladder or a lot of those other things that are used to translate 'I am feeling like this'—I have problems with this and I think respondents do. One small study which we did was to use several of these scales for some of the complex issues, and then we asked the respondent afterwards, 'How did you happen to pick that point?' The respondent said, 'I had to pick something: what the hell, that was there—so I picked that.' We had the feeling that they had a kind of general notion of directionality of scale, but the distinction between threes, fours and fives was pretty vague for them.

We chose a 7-point scale in QD14 and QD18 purely as an experiment. We wanted to know how many points people could handle, and what happens and what kind of distributions we could get. We were also trying to standardise the scale so that the person would not have to repeat the seven points all the time. The statement 'Now, I'll ask you to give me a number...' etc. is used to say, 'We are going to ask you a lot of questions on these scales and here is what the scale is.' The other alternative may be for the respondent to write the scales down.

Set 3

This is one of our early experimental studies, a face-to-face interview. There are some attitude questions, satisfaction scales and unfolding techniques where one starts with the two points and ends up with five points, and so on. The feedback here is non-contingent, that is, no matter what the respondent says, if he answers the question he gets some sort of a short feedback. Q6 refers to an agreement or commit-

1. This is a question about your health in general. Choosing one of these four categories, would you say that your health these days is excellent, good, fair or poor?

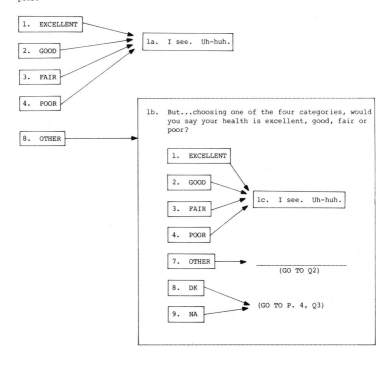

2. You said that your health is_____. Will you give me two or three ways in which your health is_____?

_____

_____

_____

2a. (CHECK ONE BOX)

┌─────────────────┐   2b. OK. Thanks. You've mentioned a
│ 1. TWO OR MORE │ ────────►   (couple/number) of things. Is there
│   MENTIONS   │   anything else?
└─────────────────┘
                                  _____

                                  _____

                                  _____

                              2c. (ANY MENTION) ☐ Uh-huh...I
                                                      see.

┌─────────────────┐   2d. Is there anything else?
│ 2. ONE MENTION │ ────────►
└─────────────────┘   _____

                                  _____

                              2e. (ANY MENTION) ☐ OK. Thanks.

                             Perhaps if I ask the question again you might
                             think of something.
┌─────────────────┐   2f. Will you give me two or three ways in
│ 3. NO MENTIONS │ ────────►   which your health is
│   OR DON'T   │
│   KNOW   │   _____?
└─────────────────┘
                                  _____

                                  _____

                                  _____

                              2g. (ANY MENTION) ☐ OK. Thanks.

41

3. Ok. Before we continue, I'd like to tell you more about this interview. As I said earlier, I will ask you questions about your _health_. The answers you give will provide _important information_. In order for your answers to be most helpful to us, it is important that you try to be as _accurate_ as you can.

Since we need _complete_ and _accurate_ information from this research, we'll be asking you if you will be willing to think hard to provide the information we need.

To give you an idea what the interview is like, we'll ask you a few more questions. Then I will ask you to decide whether you are willing to put in the _thought_ and _effort_ needed for this interview.

3. We'd like to know how many times you've been to the dentist since January 1st. We're interested in getting as exact an idea as possible so you will need to think carefully. Since January 1st, how many times have you gone to the dentist for yourself?

☐ R checks records, calendar, etc.   _____ NUMBER OF VISITS

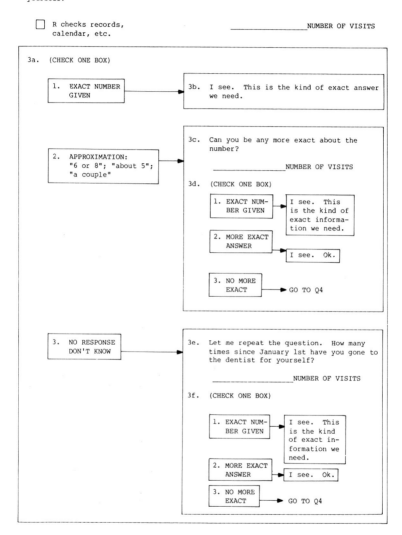

3a. (CHECK ONE BOX)

1. EXACT NUMBER GIVEN → 3b. I see. This is the kind of exact answer we need.

2. APPROXIMATION: "6 or 8"; "about 5"; "a couple" →
3c. Can you be any more exact about the number?

_____ NUMBER OF VISITS

3d. (CHECK ONE BOX)

1. EXACT NUMBER GIVEN → I see. This is the kind of exact information we need.

2. MORE EXACT ANSWER → I see. Ok.

3. NO MORE EXACT → GO TO Q4

3. NO RESPONSE DON'T KNOW →
3e. Let me repeat the question. How many times since January 1st have you gone to the dentist for yourself?

_____ NUMBER OF VISITS

3f. (CHECK ONE BOX)

1. EXACT NUMBER GIVEN → I see. This is the kind of exact information we need.

2. MORE EXACT ANSWER → I see. Ok.

3. NO MORE EXACT → GO TO Q4

43

5. Here is a question about people in general. What are the things that people can do to take care of themselves when they have a cold?

_____

_____

_____

_____

5a. (CHECK ONE BOX)

1. TWO OR MORE
   MENTIONS

5b. That's useful. Can you think of anything else?

_____

_____

_____

5c. (ANY ADDITIONAL MENTION) ☐ Ok. I see.

2. ONE MENTION

5d. Can you think of anything else?

_____

_____

_____

5e. (ANY MENTION) ☐ Ok. I see.

3. NO MENTIONS

5f. Maybe if I ask the question again you will be able to think of something. What are the things that people can do to take care of themselves when they have a cold?

_____

_____

_____

_____

5g. (ANY MENTION) ☐ Ok. I see.

6.   That's the last of this set of questions. The rest of the questions are about
     health, your daily life, and how you have been feeling lately. We are asking the
     people we interview to give us extra cooperation and try hard to answer accurately
     so that we can get accurate information about health. You are one of the people we
     hope is willing to make the extra effort.

     Here is an Agreement which explains what we are asking you to do. (HAND AGREEMENT).
     As you can see, it says, "I understand that the information from this interview must
     be very accurate in order to be useful. This means I must do my best to give
     accurate and complete answers. I agree to do this."

     We are asking people to sign this Agreement so that we can be sure they understand
     what we are asking them to do. The Agreement is for you to keep for yourself. It
     is up to you to decide. If you are willing to agree to do this, we'd like you to
     sign your name here (POINT OUT LINE). Down below there is a statement about
     confidentiality, and I will sign my name here (POINT OUT LINE). (PAUSE)

     (IF R HAS NOT ALREADY SIGNED):   [ ]   Are you willing to make the extra effort to
                                               continue the interview?

45

7. I want you to think about your <u>health</u> in the past two weeks. (HAND CARD WITH
PICTURE OF BODY). Here is a drawing of a (man's/woman's) body. You can see that we
have divided it into several areas, each with a different color. I will ask you
about what you have felt or noticed in the last two weeks within each of these areas
of your body. It can be something you noticed for the first time or something you
also noticed before.

Let's take the yellow part first. It includes the chest and abdomen. Please tell
me <u>all</u> the things you have felt or noticed here in the last two weeks.

_____

_____

_____

7a. (CHECK ONE BOX)

| 1. ANY MENTION | → | 7b. I see...We're interested in getting details like that...Was there anything else, even something small, which you felt or noticed here in the last two weeks? |

_____

_____

_____

7c. (ANY ADDITIONAL MENTION) ☐ Uh-huh, Thanks.

| 2. NO MENTION | → | 7d. But...in this question we want to be sure to get little things as well as the more important things. Was there anything at all, even something small, which you felt or noticed here in the last two weeks? |

_____

_____

_____

_____

7e. (ANY MENTION) ☐ I see...We're

interested in getting details like
that

46

SURVEY RESEARCH CENTER/INSTITUTE FOR SOCIAL RESEARCH/THE UNIVERSITY OF MICHIGAN

AGREEMENT

I understand that the information from this interview must be very accurate in order to be useful. This means that I must do my best to give accurate and complete answers. I agree to do this.

_____

Signature of Respondent

All information which would permit identification of the people being interviewed as a part of this project will be held in strict confidence. No information that would allow identification will be disclosed or released to others for any purpose.

_____

Signature of Interviewer

47

ment statement. This is the way we introduce the commitment for the face-to-face interview in this particular case, and it is noticeably lengthy. The agreement form is signed by the respondent. An example of such a form is included at the end of Set 3. The statement should be read at approximately two words per second, with pauses between the phrases.

LENGTH OF INTERVIEW AND EFFECT ON RESPONDENT

These surveys take about an hour to administer to each respondent. The respondent is told how long the interview will take only if he asks. The practice is that if the interviewer senses that the respondent is under any pressure of time he tells him that this will take some time and asks whether this is a convenient time to come. But if the respondent simply says, 'Come in and sit down', there is no statement of time. If he asks, the time is given quite honestly.

In telephone interviews particularly, we look for evidence of loss of concentration, but we have not found any. We started with the assumption that the telephone interview should probably last about ten minutes, or fifteen minutes at the outside, because people would stop listening, or get tired. But, as always happens in the survey business, when one needs more data one runs the interviews longer. We are now up to an average of about 30 minutes, and some of them go on 40 minutes. There was a recent study done by the Bureau of Social Science Research (Sharp and Frankel, 1981) which ran an experimental interview in one form lasting about twenty minutes and in the other form lasting around an hour. These were face-to-face interviews and they had the same main questions in various parts of the questionnaire. The issue was, what happens to the quality of data and what happens to response rates? As far as they could see, there was no difference. That was a very dull survey, however, on the details of housing and things of that kind. It was done for the Federal Housing Administration at the insistence of the Office of Statistical Standards of the Bureau of the Budget who had said that more than half an hour is too great a burden for the respondent. It turned out in this case that it was *not*, and I think generally this is the case. What happens is that the length of an interview tends to be guided by the interest of the respondent, and this is particularly true in an attitude study. If the respondent is really interested in the topic and does a lot of talking, the interview is longer. In our health studies the range of interviews is rather great, because if you have a lot of illnesses and a lot of conditions it runs longer. Quite often people love to talk about health. So there is a kind of compensation mechanism: if there is interest and involvement, interviews run longer and respondents usually enjoy it.

PROBING OF RECALL

It is important to understand that the questions we have been referring to above still contain experimental procedures. There are undoubtedly many better ways to achieve feedback. We need to try different techniques and different methods and to refine some of them. If one accepts the notion that the main problem of response bias is a motivational one, then the question is, what other techniques could one use to motivate the respondents?

There has been a lot of talk about the use of monetary rewards or other kinds of rewards to achieve respondent cooperation. We do not know what real effect they have and what is good and what is bad about them. Again, we have a folklore but we have no data. These techniques indicate that we can improve the responses and apparently improve their validity, but we cannot, it seems, improve them far enough to achieve valid data. I think this means that it is possible to change responses and that we can get respondents to work harder. We must, however, develop different techniques to improve the accuracy of reporting.

There is the anomaly that while respondents may not be familiar enough with medical terms to identify diseases accurately, interviewers are not allowed to help them to define their conditions. They are allowed only such probes as 'Can you tell me a little more about that' if the respondent is vague. The Public Health Service has been doing these surveys for 25 years and has a listing of conditions which are the kinds of things people actually say, though the physicians would probably not recognise them as clinically accurate categories.

It is well known that a major problem in surveys involves recall and accuracy of reporting on the part of the respondent. We know the theory of this problem, but we do not know how people behave in practice. We need to think of information as having been stored with different frames of reference. So, in the context of health surveys, if I think of my condition in terms of what happened to me ten years ago on a particular occasion, and if someone mentions that occasion, then the events are linked. But the same information is stored by various respondents in various mental compartments, depending on the way that information was coded in the first place. The simplest way to make it easy for the respondent is not to ask the respondent to go through these compartments himself, because that is hard work. We need to have a series of unfolding questions.

The procedures we have developed at ISR for use in health surveys have improved reporting quite considerably. For example, after the respondent said either 'Yes' or 'No' to the question had they been in a hospital in the past year, the interviewer said, 'Well people quite frequently forget, but it is more difficult to remember the events of hospitalisation where you were only in overnight...Did you have anything of that kind?' Sure enough, the respondent says, 'Oh, yes, I remember.' As there may have been some hospitalisations that occurred way back close to the beginning of the year, the interviewer asks 'Was there any chance you had something like this?' Then the respondent says, 'As a matter of fact there was.'

So one can use probes of this kind which attempt to say: here are what people tend to forget. If one can frame questions to get at those issues, one is more likely to get a good response. It is a memory cue. Usually what we do in surveys is to try to say to the respondent, 'Well, think again.' If he thinks twice, he is more likely to turn up things. That is useful but not quite as useful as this compartmentalised approach. In this way we both simplify things for the respondent and motivate him. We start with a simple-minded notion that here is a level of willingness of effort that this respondent is willing to give. If he is asked something which is contained within that level, he will retrieve it for you. The simpler it is, the more likely it is that it comes within the level of effort that he is willing to extend, but if the question asks him to expend greater effort than he is willing to do, one is likely to get a non-response. Thus, we word the question so that it comes within the level of willingness to which he is motivated.

I mentioned in chapter 1 that we found reporting of visits to doctors not reported by 15 per cent for the first week preceding the interview and 30 per cent for the second, which suggests that if we asked respondents to report doctors' visits over a one-month period, the curve ought to go down to a very small number of visits. Once a colleague came up to me and said, 'You know, the interesting thing is we have been asking about doctors' visits over a year's period and when we look at our figures, they were quite comparable to the national health survey figures for two weeks—if you extrapolate from your curve, we should be getting a far lower report of visits to doctors than we did.' It seemed to me after I had thought about it that what happens (and it happens to us in surveys all the time) is that the frame of reference (the recall) shifts from an episodic event to some sort of an estimation. It is as if I ask, 'What did you do yesterday?' then a respondent may say, 'Yesterday, oh, let's see. From 8 am on...' or whatever. He would need to review episodically what occurred to him during the day. Similarly, if I ask 'Did you go to a doctor last week?' he could say, 'Well, let's see. Monday, Tuesday, Wednesday', etc., and recall episode by episode. It is an episodic search of memory to retrieve information. But at some point the respondent says 'This is silly. Nobody expects me to try to review a year episodically and report doctors' visits.' So he uses an estimation procedure: 'How many times do I usually go to a doctor in the course of a year? Well, this would be about four times, maybe, and this was a good year, so maybe three.' So he will say, 'Three'. The question looks identical for the two modes of response—the respondent gives the same kind of response but the processes by which these data are reported is a very different one.

Then there is the final approach, which is a sheer guess. If I asked someone, 'How many times did you go to see the doctor in the last ten years?', he may say, 'Oh, hell, 100 times.' The difficulty is that again the diligent respondent is likely to attempt more episodic recall than the casual respondent would. That is, the harder he works, the more he is trying to recall specific episodic events. The respondent who is not working hard gives what sounds like a perfectly acceptable answer, except that he has used a different method to arrive at it. He has used some sort of an estimation, or guessing method, mainly to get me off his back. If one is attempting population estimates, estimation procedure may be quite adequate. Maybe the mean (the group mean) for estimations would be better than the attempt at retrieval. Thus, if I asked for doctors' visits for a month I would recognise that the respondent is not going to use an episodic recall and that there will be a lot of error in individual report. Determining the mean may be better than trying to get an episode recall. If all I wanted to do was to get a population estimate of the mean, I might use that technique. It raises problems if I want to do correlation analysis, because for any one individual the amount of error is unknown and likely to be great. We know this occurs. We know that people shift from one mode to another. We know that the researcher expects the respondent to shift from one mode to another because the question is identical. The researcher should realise that he cannot expect the respondent to learn this. This is an area that we just do not know much about at all. All we can do is hypothesise. We need fundamental experimental work to be done.

It might be possible to ask the respondent after the interview, 'How accurate did you think that response was?' Maybe we might use only those data that he thought were accurately reported. An example of how that worked is in some of our political studies where the study directors were interested in the response to some specific issues of an election campaign. They wanted to know how these issues were weighted to the potential vote of the individual and party identification. The survey took major issues of the campaign—maybe fifteen issues.

The respondent was asked, 'How do you feel about this on a 5-point scale and who do you think is more likely to produce this, the Republicans or the Democrats; and how strongly do you feel about that?' In the survey analysis the correlation between how people saw these issues and their stated party identification was very low. They then revised the procedures to say to the respondent, 'In any campaign there are lots of issues. Some interest some people and some interest other people, and people aren't interested in all of them, so let us go through the issues and see whether you are interested in them. Here is issue No. 1. Is this one that interests you or not? No. OK. (Issue 2)...is that something that interests you?' The respondent answers, 'Oh, yes. I am interested.' The interviewer then says, 'OK, now what is your position and how do you feel?', and so on. When we do that, the correlations line up just as they should. That is, the people who look like Democrats in terms of issues tend to say they are going to vote Democrat. We must give the respondent the opportunity to say 'Well, that is too difficult', or 'I don't know'. If respondents would only tell us that they do not understand the question, or that they do not know the answer, or that they do not care about something we would be better off, but they assume that if we ask them a question they are supposed to know it.

TECHNIQUES TO IMPROVE INTERVIEWER PERFORMANCE

Set 4

This is a summary form of a series of manuals and instructions that we prepared at ISR for interviewers and study directors. It is a very practical application of techniques.

In Section A there is a listing of things to be included in the questionnaires, such as questions underlined for standard phrasing; major probes or sub-questions, with examples of them; instructions; what is to be expected, with examples; and the commitment procedure. These are all included as part of the questionnaire. There is no feedback here because we are still debating how to handle it.

Under Section B we are developing manuals for specifying such things as how to ask the questions, clarifying them, probes, pauses, repeating all or part of the question, and feedback techniques. At the end of Set 4 there is a listing of the kind of feedback statements we think are acceptable for interviewers to use. They are a summary of things to work on, things that interviewers should be trained in, and things that should be incorporated in the design of questionnaires.

OUTLINE OF TECHNIQUES

A. **Included in Questionnaire**

1. **Questions** (underlined words for standard phrasing)

    Examples:
    --What do you think will happen to <u>interest rates</u> for borrowing money during
    the next 12 months--will they go <u>up</u>, stay the same, or go <u>down</u>?
    --Did you talk with the doctor about any <u>other</u> conditions?

2. **Major probes or sub-questions**

    a. Incomplete response (contingent on answer)

        (lack of precision, lack of specificity or details)

    b. Additional information (non contingent)

        (anything else, any other reasons, frame of reference, reasons why)

    Examples:
    --Can you be any closer about the |date?
    --Are there any <u>other</u> reasons why you feel that way?
    --You've mentioned ____ reasons why you think TV is not good for children.
      Can you think of any other reasons?
    --Is there anything else?
    --Can you be more exact?

3. **Instructions to Respondents**

    a. Role expectations (what is expected of R)

    b. Cues to R as to how to produce accurate answers:

        --How to retrieve information from memory,
        --How to organize information,
        --How to respond: selecting response categories, free responses, etc.

    Examples of Instructions:
    "In this interview we want to get as much information as we can."
    "This includes things which may seem small and unimportant as well as
    important things."
    "We said earlier that for some of these questions you would need to search
    your memory thoroughly. How difficult has it been to remember the things
    we have asked you so far...has it been very difficult, somewhat difficult,
    or not at all difficult?"
    "For this question you will need to think back and remember whether you
    have <u>ever</u> had any of them (health conditions) even if it might be a long
    time ago."
    "In answering the next few questions it may help you to be accurate if you
    check a program listing or TV guide."

"We're interested in all television watching, even short times. We find that if people think hard, they can sometimes remember other times when they saw or heard the television, even though they weren't paying much attention."

Exact Q.: "For this question, we'd like to get the number as exact as you can report it. During the two-week period, that is from ___ to ___, how many days did illness or injury keep you from work?

Exact Q.: "(Not counting the days in bed and/or lost from work) Were there any (other) days during that two-week period that you cut down on the things you usually do because of any illness or injury? This is sometimes hard to remember, so please take your time."

4. Commitment

"This is a study about women's health and their daily lives. I will ask you about your past health, your daily life, and how you have been feeling lately."

"In order for your answers to be most helpful to us, it is important that you try to be as accurate as you can. Since we need complete and accurate information from this research, we'll be asking you if you are willing to think hard to provide the information we need. To give you an idea what this is like, we'll ask you the first few questions. After these questions, I will ask you to decide whether you are willing to put in the thought and effort needed for this interview."

"You remember we said at the beginning, when you agreed to do your best to give accurate and complete answers, that you would need to search your memory carefully. How hard has it been for you to remember the things we have discussed with you so far?"

"I understand that the information from this interview must be very accurate in order to be useful. This means that I must do my best to give accurate and complete answers. I agree to do this."

"All information which would permit identification of the people being interviewed as a part of this project will be held in strict confidence. No information that would allow identification will be disclosed or released to others for any purpose."

Exact Q: "This research is authorized by the Public Health Service Act. It's important for the PHS to get exact details on every question, even on those which may seem unimportant to you. This may take extra effort. Are you willing to think carefully about each question in order to give accurate information?"

B. Interviewing Techniques

   1. Asking questions

      a. Exact wording
      b. Training in natural phrasing
      c. Proper inflection
      d. Slow pace

   2. Clarifying question

      a. Repetition of entire question or relevant part
      b. Define only if R asks and instructions permit
      c. R to define for self if not specified ("Whatever it means to you.")
      d. No clarification for opinion questions.

   3. Probes to focus responses on objectives and to motivate full responses
      (supplement to probes in questionnaire, used only when R fails to perform task properly or adequately)

      a. R uses incorrect frame of reference
      b. Irrelevant or non-responsive answer
      c. Partial response (after questionnaire probe)
      d. Response unclear to interviewer

Examples:

   Interviewers are allowed to use seven (7) different probes:

   1) A pause [Pause]
   2) Repetition of the Q or part of the Q
   3) "Would you tell me more about your thinking on that?"
   4) "Are there any other reasons why you feel that way?"
   5) "What do you think?"
              or
      "What do you expect?"
   6) "What do you mean?"
              or
      "How do you mean?"
   7) "Which is closer to the way you feel?"

```
┌─────────────┐
│ 1.  Pause   │
└─────────────┘
```

Exact Q: "Now I have some questions on how you feel about life in this country as a
            whole. Do you think there are some ways in which life in the United
            States is getting worse?"

R: "That's hard to say."

Interviewer: [Pause]

R: "That's a hard one."

Interviewer: "Let me repeat the question. Do you think there are some ways in which
            life in the United States is getting worse?"

R: "Yes, I guess the rate of violent crime is going up and the environment is
            getting more and more polluted."

```
┌──────────────────────────────────────┐
│ 2.  Repeat all or part of Question    │
└──────────────────────────────────────┘
```

Repeating the Question (RQ) includes repetition of the entire Q, of the remaining
response options, or of the misunderstood portion of the frame of reference. A
correctly used RQ is graded (RQ).

Exact Q: "How about the next year or two--do you expect that your family income
            will go up more than prices will go up, about the same, or less than
            prices will go up?"

R: "I would say either more than prices or about the same."

Probe: "So would you say your family income will go up more than prices or about
            the same?"

Exact Q: "How satisfied are you with the amount of education you received? Are you
            very satisfied, somewhat satisfied, not very satisfied, or not at all
            satisfied?"

R: "I'm quite satisfied."

Interviewer: "Would that be very satisfied, somewhat satisfied, or not very satisfied?"

R: "I would say 'somewhat' satisfied."

3. Would you tell me more about your thinking on that? or
   Would you mind telling me what you have in mind?

This probe is used under two circumstances:

a) When the Interviewer can't understand the R's reply,
   or
b) When the R gives an incomplete answer.

Exact Q C3a: "What were the main reasons you stopped your education when you did?"

      R#1: "I just felt like it."

Interviewer #1: "Could you tell me more about that?"

      R#2: "My mother has always greatly influenced my decisions."

Interviewer #2: "Would you tell me what you have in mind?"

5. What do you mean?

This probe is used:

a) When the Interviewer can't understand the R's reply,
   or
b) When the R gives an incomplete answer.

6. What do you think? or What do you expect?

This is used in the following circumstances:

a) To probe an initial "Don't Know" response

b) To probe an "I Hope So" response

Exact Q#1: "Now looking ahead--do you think that a year from now you will be better off financially, or worse off, or just about the same as now?"

      R: "I don't know. It's hard to predict the future."

> 7. Which would be closer to the way you feel?

> This is used when the R has narrowed his choices to a particular range. Record this description on your job aid **now**. If the R has not eliminated any choices, you should pause and/or repeat the response options (RQ) , rather than use this.

> Exact Q#1: "As to the economic policy of the government--I mean steps taken to fight inflation or <u>une</u>mployment--would you say the government is doing a good job, only fair, or a poor job?"

> R: "Somewhere between good and fair."

> Interviewer: "Which would be closer to the way you feel?"

> Exact Q#2: "By about what percent do you think prices have gone up on the average, during the last 12 months?"

> R: "Anywhere from 20 to 60%."

> Interviewer: "Which would be closer."

Interviewing Techniques (continued)

4. Feedback (to teach and motivate R's performance)

    a. To inform R on interviewer's reaction to his role performance
    b. To inform R on reaction to specific task performance
    c. To demonstrate approval of good task performance (not approval of response context)
    d. To withhold approval of poor task performance

Examples:

"As I mentioned, sometimes it's hard for people to remember everything. Perhaps if you think about it a little more, you will remember something you missed. Was there anything at all?"

"Thanks. This is the sort of information we're looking for in this research."

"It's important to us to get this information."

"These details are helpful."

"It's useful to get your ideas on this."

"Thanks, it's important to get your opinion on that."

"I see, that's helpful to know."

"It's important to find out what people think about this."

"Thanks, that's useful information."

"Uh-huh, I see."

"Let me get that down."

"I see, (Repeat Answer)."

"I want to make sure I have that right."

"I see, we need to find this out."

"This is helpful information."

5. Interviewing pace

   a. Slow rate of reading questions

   b. Pauses before probing or asking next question.

MONITORING OF INTERVIEWING PERFORMANCE

Set 5

It is always difficult for the researcher to try to evaluate the correct procedures and decide how well the interviewer is performing. We are now rather consistently using a kind of monitoring coding of the interviews, whether they are face-to-face or telephone interviews. The form in Set 5 is one of the procedures we have developed. The exact specifications of each form are set up for particular surveys. This one was set up for the health survey in Set 3, and is experimental; it delivers long feedback correctly. The attempt here is to sample periods of the interview for each interviewer. If it is a telephone interview the monitoring researcher is on-line listening to the telephone comment, which he codes as the interview proceeds.

This looks like an impressive code, but the monitors learn it easily and no longer have to check it. They find that most of the behaviours are good if an interviewer is functioning properly. This means that when they give feedback to the respondent, most of the comments are positive. It used to be the case that monitors taking notes on interviewers would almost always note the bad things, which produced an imbalance. In this case, one can specify to the interviewer what the problems were. We do this question by question, so the monitor can say, 'On question so-and-so, here is what you did.' It is a fine procedure for monitoring. When they first start training, the interviewers are introduced to this code. We talk to them about what the theory of interviewing is and try to communicate the notion of standardisation.

When we are practising interviews or when we are doing role-playing, we include the person who does the monitoring. You can hear an interviewer say, 'Oh boy, that was a 25. I shouldn't have done that.' It again sensitises them to problems; when the monitor goes through their regular procedures and gives them feedback, it is a natural thing, and it is very non-threatening because 90 per cent of the interviewers' performance is good so they don't object to the monitoring. It gives a standardisation of interviewer performance. One can sum up these forms across an interviewer and you can find out what kinds of consistent errors that interviewer is making over a period of a week or so. One can also find out what errors the whole staff of interviewers is making and redesign the training procedure. Equally fascinating, one can look at individual questions. If a question has a lot of incorrect reading there must be something wrong with it or one can ask, 'I wonder why lots of probes are used in this question?' One must then look at that question and see what the problems are.

CODES FOR MONITORING INTERVIEWER BEHAVIOUR

QUESTION-ASKING	11	Reads question exactly as printed.
	12	Reads question incorrectly - minor changes
	16	Reads question incorrectly - major changes
	17	Fails to read a question
	18	Reads inappropriate question (due to prior miscode)
REPEATING QUESTIONS	21	Repeats question correctly
	25	Repeats question - unnecessarily
	26	Repeats question - incorrectly
	27	Fails to repeat question
DEFINING/CLARIFYING	31	Clarifies or defines correctly
	35	Defines or clarifies - unnecessarily
	36	Defines or clarifies - incorrectly
	37	Fails to define or clarify
SHORT FEEDBACK	41	Delivers short feedback - correctly
	45	Delivers short feedback - inappropriately
	46	Delivers short feedback - incorrectly
	47	Fails to deliver short feedback
LONG FEEDBACK	51	Delivers long feedback - correctly
	55	Delivers long feedback - inappropriately
	56	Delivers long feedback - incorrectly
	57	Fails to deliver long feedback
PACE/TIMING	65	Reads item too fast or too slow
	66	Timing between items - too fast
	67	Timing between items - too slow
OVERALL CLARITY	75	"Unnatural" manner of reading item (poor inflection, exaggerated or inadequate emphasis, "wooden" or monotone expression)
	76	Mispronunciation leading to (possible) misinterpretation
MACHINE-RELATED	96	Lag due to backing up in questionnaire
	97	Slow machine response time

INTERVIEWERS' RESPONSE RATES

In the face-to-face interviews we have the interviewers make tape-recordings of their interviews; they are sent back to us and we then code them at the office. While they miss the fast feedback, the recordings do serve an extremely important purpose: they provide an objective evaluation of performance. A major problem is that we tended to evaluate surveys on the basis of response rate. If the response rate is 85 per cent, we say that is a good survey; if it is 60 per cent, we say that is bad. Making such recordings is really the only objective criterion that there has been for evaluating surveys. During the very first hospitalisation survey that we did, the Census people needed to hire a new field supervisor and decided to hire him from among the people who were working on that study. The question was which one of the interviewers was doing the best job? We agreed that so-and-so is the best interviewer and so-and-so has been the best supervisor. After the study was over we knew how accurate the response was. It turned out that the person with the lowest valid responses of any of the interviewers was the person who was evaluated as the best interviewer. That really shook us and we thought, why? What criteria are we using to pick this person? She had a high response rate; her work has always on time—nice neat work, with all the x's in the right boxes; she was very pleasant and very cooperative. Because we had been using response rate as the criteria, as the only objective criteria, she was really just acting like Pavlov's dog—she was being reinforced for getting things done on time, she was putting the x's in, but there was no negative or positive reinforcement on interviewing techniques. The result was she was doing better on what she was reinforced for.

It is essential that for quality in surveys there should be some procedure of this kind that permits us to evaluate the performance of the interviewer. How well is the interviewer doing compared with what we trained her to do? That I think is essential, and we hope we will get to the point where we will have an objective rating: here is the response rate and here is the average performance of the interviewer. That would do a great deal to improve the quality of survey data.

3

C.F. CANNELL

Interviewing in telephone surveys

The use of the telephone for survey research has been increasing very rapidly in the USA in the last several years and if one had to make a rough estimate of the proportion of market research that is now done by telephone it would probably be somewhere between 50 and 75 per cent. This high percentage is largely because the cost of conducting face-to-face survey interviews has been increasing sharply, and the excessive number of hours an interviewer takes to produce an interview is a problem. At the same time, the cost of telephoning has been coming down in the US. One can now have a leased line, called a WATS line, through which phone calls can be made anywhere throughout the country at a low rate. The other advantage of telephone use is saving time. Once the last interview is taken, the results can be rapidly tabulated. This assumes a central location for the telephone interviews.

In recent years, the last three or four specifically, academic groups and the US government have become interested in telephone surveys. We always used to look down our noses at telephone surveys and told ourselves that telephone surveys were done simply to save money; people were not worrying about quality. Then, the more we began to look at it ourselves the more we saw that telephone interviews had a real potential in data collection. We have now poured a lot of resources into looking at them in great detail.

One of the main problems of the telephone is the proportion of the population covered by household telephones. What has made telephone interviewing feasible in the US is that the household penetration figure is now close to 95 per cent. This means that for almost any survey, there is only a 5 per cent probability that one would introduce some serious sort of bias in terms of coverage. The people who do not have phones are the kind of people that one might expect. That is, they are of lower income, they are mostly single-person families, they are the lower-educated, older people, and they tend to be rural dwellers. But the main criterion of no phone is income. If one achieves only 95 per cent coverage, it is probably not going to hurt one too much. But if one were to do surveys of consumer expenditures or to find out what incomes and savings patterns were, one is likely to run into some serious problems of bias even with that kind of coverage.

If the coverage is lower in Australia, as I understand it is, it raises real questions about whether one should ever attempt a national survey where one is trying to get a sound representation of the population. If the coverage of phones is 75 to 80 per cent, it raises serious questions of bias. In this case I assume that the reasons for not having telephones are the same in Australia as they are in the US—namely, their cost and availability. At 75 per cent coverage, the potential for bias due to lack of phones is really very large. It may very well be, however, that if one were doing surveys in particular locations, such as the major cities, the coverage rates would probably be much higher and therefore more acceptable.

Our more recent work and newer ideas on telephone surveys run quite counter to our original concept of what they might be like. First, the response rate in telephone surveys has tended to be slightly lower than in face-to-face interviews—usually somewhere between 3 and 5 per cent lower. The reason is that it is much simpler to hang up the phone rapidly on someone than it is to slam the door in the face of an attractive interviewer. Most of the non-responses are refusals which occur during the first ten seconds or so of the interview, where the phone is simply hung up without a word being spoken. That is one of the problems of telephone surveys and it needs a great deal of research. I will describe some of the research we have been doing in the area of initial contact; most of it has not been very effective.

The second characteristic that distinguishes telephone from personal interviews is a basic communication difference. The absence of visual cues sets up quite a different communication pattern from what one gets in face-to-face communication. The literature indicates the significant amount of information that is communicated through visual cues. Of course that is absent in the phone interview and it appears that one needs to boost feedback mechanisms to help compensate for the lack of visual cues.

We discovered that when our phone interviewers began two or three years ago, they were doing a lot more talking than in the face-to-face interviews, and this terrified us sometimes. I remember I was showing some visitors through our set-up and I heard an interviewer saying, 'Oh, gee, you had that, well my uncle had that and he was very sick,' and I thought my goodness, what in the world is going on? Another interviewer was saying, 'Oh well, I know somebody else who had that kind of thing and it was also very uncomfortable.' I said to the interviewers later on, 'What is going on?' and they said, 'Well, you have got to do a lot of talking to keep these people communicating on the phone.' It turns out this is incorrect, but this was their perception of a major difference between telephone and face-to-face interviewing. In telephone interviewing, one needs to build in more feedback and give the interviewers 'harmless' things to say. These are of the type, 'Yes, I heard you', 'I see', 'Uh, uh', 'I understand' and so forth, just to indicate that communication is in fact occurring. Another major difference in the phone interview is the role of the telephone in society. Here, in contrast to my usual bias, I do think that there may be marked cultural differences. It seems that there are cultural differences between the US and Britain for example, and I suspect there may also be differences between the US and Australia. I base this on a couple of things. People in the US, by and large, have been brought up with the telephone. I do not ever remember when we did not have a telephone and almost none of my colleagues would remember such a time. That means that the telephone is much more widely used, and for many more purposes. Graham Kalton was a survey researcher in Britain and recently came to the US to join our organisation. He said spontaneously one night: 'The thing that amazes me is how free Americans are to pick up the telephone, make calls to people and conduct business on the telephone. Its use in Britain is more to find out are you going to be there so I can come to visit you?' So I do think there may be cultural differences. Indeed there are all kinds of reasons why they may be different.

Let us now consider a bit more how people use the phone. In the US there are really two reasons for making phone calls: either you are communicating with friends or acquaintances or strangers or you are doing some sort of business. You may call them and they may call you, but when you answer the phone and you hear a familiar voice, you know that this is some acquaintance of yours with whom you want to communicate. However, if some stranger is on the phone or the call is not immediately codable, one is immediately slightly suspicious. It is that suspicion that gives many problems to the phone companies, the phone being used now for selling things, for advertising and to do all kinds of things.

Differences in communication patterns do exist for various reasons. Communication is perhaps somewhat more difficult on the phone, and one has to take this into account when one is talking about interviewing techniques and types of survey questions. There is some evidence that it is more difficult to understand questions on the phone, and for that reason we may need to make them simpler. The difficulties we discussed in the last chapter—the type of response structure, how many point scales one can use, and so on—all these are new to the surveyor because none of us has really systematically used a telephone before; they are new methodological issues which need to be addressed.

It is of course comparatively easy and inexpensive to get together a group of interviewers in a central place where you can closely monitor and supervise them. This is one of the great advantages of phone interviewing. You can see what they are doing and then look at the cost records and the response rates rapidly. It is a much tighter administrative organisation and it is obviously far less expensive than a widespread face-to-face interviewing staff that covers the whole country. Our staff of 50 telephone interviewers work two shifts and they work two-thirds of the time during the month: we have regular monthly surveys that use telephones so they are busy most of the time.

The main question about telephone interviews is how do the data compare with face-to-face interviews? The other basic issue is response rate and response coverage. How do the characteristics of response differ from those of personal interviews? Several studies done over the past seven or eight years indicate that the differences are not very large. Some studies find that the telephone seems to be getting slightly better information. The explanation appears to be the anonymity offered by the telephone: it appears easier to report threatening or embarrassing information over the phone. But conversely, some of the findings are that the face-to-face interview seems to be getting better data because of the whole notion of rapport, and that face-to-face contact seems to be better, even if most of these studies are not sufficiently well designed to make general conclusions. However, it was enough to make a lot of the methodologists think that this comparison really needs to be studied.

EXPERIMENTAL WORK

The National Health Survey, as I mentioned earlier, is conducted by the Census Bureau every week and has been going on for some 25 years. Like all federal agencies, its sponsors are getting increasingly worried about funds. They were having to cut their samples, and thought if there was some cost advantage to telephone interviews they had better find out about it. They contracted with us to do a parallel study with the Census Bureau and it is now nearing completion.

The Census Bureau collected data using their regular probability samples throughout the nation for one quarter of the year. They collected about 20 000 interviews. We designed the study shown in Set 3. It was as close as we could make it to the face-to-face interview questionnaire. The questions were identical except for one where there was a show card which we could not use, of course, over the phone, but aside from that the wording was the same. The interview was conducted with a household respondent who reports for herself and all respondents and you cannot quite have a direct parallel to that on the telephone. But we tried the best we could to get any responsible adult and asked if other people were there whom they might want to question as the interview went on. It did not work very well, but there also did not seem to be very much difference between the face-to-face and the telephone. Time was spent with the Census interviewers and we made recordings of their interviews. We catalogued their procedures for interviewing as thoroughly as we could and we trained our telephone interviewers in those procedures. The survey was done in exactly the same quarter of the year, though with only 8000 interviews. We did everything we could think of doing to make this comparison good. In Table 3.1 there are three columns of data. The first is the telephone surveys we conducted; the second is the household interviews conducted by the Census Bureau and reported for houses which had telephones, and for which we should expect an exact comparison. The

Table 3.1 **Per cent of NCHS–SRC sample with one or more events reported in the telephone and personal surveys**

| | Telephone survey SRC | Personal survey (NCHS) | |
		Households with telephones	All households
Health event or behaviour	N=2099	N=18 388	N=19 800
One or more events reported for the past two weeks:			
Days in bed	7.7	7.7	7.8
Days away from work	6.7	5.5	5.4
Days of reduced activity	8.8	7.1	7.0
Visits to physicians	17.9	14.1	13.9
Dental visits	6.9	5.3	5.2
One or more events reported for the past 12 months:			
Days in bed	52.4	45.1	46.3
Visits to physicians	72.4	73.5	73.2
Hospital episodes	13.9	13.3	12.5
Some limitation of activities:	20.1	18.7	18.9
Mean number of acute conditions:	.174	.116	.122
Mean number of chronic conditions:	.420	.415	.458
Rate health as good or excellent:	82.9	84.1	84.4

Source: National Center for Health Statistics and University of Michigan Survey Research Center, 1981

third column shows all households, including those which did not have telephones.

There is some interesting information there. This is really a preliminary table based on unweighted data. Weighted data are unlikely to give differences which are statistically significant. The first similarity is how comparable those figures are and it is only when you take all households that there is a slight difference. In some cases, such as visits to physicians, about a 4-percentage-point difference emerges, but that is the largest one. Aside from that the differences are really very small and a lot of them are at best only marginally significant. In fact the estimation for this survey is that there is no significant bias in the phone data.

The second thing that one notices about these data is that the telephone survey has tended in each case to get higher reporting than face-to-face interviews. This is something we had not anticipated. Again, on the assumption that more is better, the telephone in fact got a somewhat significantly better reporting of health conditions. What is the explanation? We are interpreting this as saying that the telephone survey is better. But what we do think happened is that because of the proximity of all the interviewers, it meant we could do our monitoring much easier, we could supervise the interviews more closely than you can in face-to-face interviews. The interviewers had the opportunity to interact with the researchers and with each other and morale was very high. Again I think what we are looking at here is simply a difference in the enthusiasm and the morale of the interviewing staff—it does not have any significance in terms of the general conclusions.

The interviewing staff knew that this was an experimental parallel study. We had every reason to think the interviewers were a little more conscientious than the Census interviewers who were doing the same thing face-to-face. I do not conclude that all telephone surveys are better as such. I do conclude from this and from other data that we have looked at that as far as we can determine, the telephone survey tends to get data which are quite comparable with the face-to-face surveys. After seeing this, we went back and looked at some of the other studies to see what differences there were. There were very few in the other studies, no matter what the content was, or what the substance was. It appeared that respondents were reporting quite as well over the telephone as in face-to-face interviews.

For part of the sample for the NCHS telephone survey we used the experimental techniques that we talked about before. In particular, we used the instructions, reinforcement and the commitment procedure. In the control group we attempted to replicate as closely as we could the Census procedure, and in the experimental group we used these three procedures. Table 3.2 shows that there is an increase in most of the episodes of health care due to the experimental procedures. The same interviewers were using both procedures and so it is not interviewer differences. They are technique differences and at least half of them are significant differences.

The general conclusion from this experiment is that the telephone seems to be a very feasible instrument for collecting data. There seem to be no major problems with any of the subgroups and their reporting by telephone; the subgroups line up in just about the same way as the total group does. There seem to be no education or income effects in the data; there are no interactions that one can find—it is a very comforting way to have experimental data come out if you are thinking of using the phone. There is one other piece of data that encouraged us further.

Most of the studies of interviewer variability have been done on face-to-face interviews, and in almost every one they show significant interviewer variation. In this case it was easy to randomise respondents to interviewers. We had a series of about 28 or 30 small random samples for which we could compute the variability. We have done that now in three telephone-based studies and, with the experimental procedures and the monitoring, it very substantially reduces the variability

Table 3.2 **Per cent of sample from the NCHS–SRC telephone survey by control and experimental interviewing techniques**

| | Per cent reporting one or more events | |
| | Control | Experimental |
Health event or behaviour	N=4217	N=3993
One or more events reported for the past two weeks:		
Days in bed	7.5	9.9
Days away from work	6.4	8.8
Days of reduced activity	8.3	11.4
Visits to physicians	15.3	16.6
Dental visits	6.9	7.5
One or more events reported for the past 12 months:		
Days in bed	51.0	55.5
Visits to physicians	72.8	74.5
Hospital episodes	13.4	12.4
Some limitation of activities:	20.9	27.9
Mean number of acute conditions:	.170	.196
Mean number of chronic conditions:	.421	.529
Rate health as:		
Very good or good	84.1	82.6
Poor or very poor	14.8	16.4

Source: National Center for Health Statistics and University of Michigan Survey Research Center, 1981

between interviewers. While we think our enthusiasm for the telephone was in the first place mainly financial, we are now coming to the conclusion that this may actually be an inherently better way of collecting data. The opportunity for close supervision, for easy training, and for doing such things as monitoring interviewer performance closely is what attracts us to the telephone. It appears to be no worse than any other method and it appears to have a lot of potential for development.

The federal government is now putting a lot of work into telephone interviews—they have a federal commission studying the use of telephones. The US Health Department and the Census Bureau have been leaders in the field and I think it will be a very short time before there is regular data collection by telephone in government surveys. The government has in the past used telephones to collect data on non-responses for their current population survey. They have never used it for a total design, but I think they are about to.

Two other issues need to be addressed here. The first is sampling. We use random digit dialling. In our case, we can get a booklet from American Telephone and Telegraph (AT&T) which lists area codes for the first three digits and the local office codes for the second three digits. Then one has a 4-digit number which is randomly generated. So we can stratify by area code for the first stage and we can stratify for a second stage if we want by local office code. Then we can randomly generate the last four numbers. So we come up with a good stratified probability sample of households. The one difficulty is that one makes a very large number of fruitless phone calls because of the number of businesses that are in the telephone directory.

There are a couple of schemes that are being used now to try to reduce the number of fruitless calls made. The one we use is called the Waksberg system. It amounts to the discovery that the phone company tends to put out banks of 100 or so numbers and they tend either to be held-back or unused numbers—the numbers have been assigned but they have not been assigned to individuals. So here are some numbers but they are not used; or here is a block of 100 or so that is used mainly for businesses. The University of Michigan, for example, has one central office code and no matter what you dial in that central office code you are going to get the University of Michigan, one place or another. The scheme is to draw the first two numbers at random of these 4-digit numbers and make three or four calls in each bank and if you find only businesses, or no numbers at all, you give those a much lower probability of selection. This means you can build up the probability that when you dial you will be successful in reaching a household instead of a business.

This does mean one can also dial numbers that are not allocated at all, though I do not know what the probability is, maybe 2 or 3 per cent of the numbers are not allocated. When a phone is given up, that number is put in the reserve pile and it is kept for about three or four months before being reassigned. We may get one of those, and there are great variations in telephone companies. Some of them have a ringing device and that number will ring merrily away even though there is nobody on the other end, not even a phone on the other end. Others will have an intercept saying the number is not working. We found some places where the same number could be reaching two office codes. There is one place where the state line goes right through a telephone directory. Those people living there were listed with two numbers—one for the exchange areas on each side of the river. These problems do not occur very often but they are enough to drive a sampler mad if he is trying to do the job properly.

One of the classic stories of random digit dialling emerged when one of our interviewers called a random number and somebody answered the phone and said, 'Yes, who is this calling?' The interviewer said, 'This is the University of Michigan, Survey Research Center.' 'What are you calling about?' 'Well we are doing a survey.' 'How did you get this number?' 'It is random digit dialling.' 'Who did you say was calling?' The interviewer got slightly annoyed and said 'It is the University of Michigan, but why are you asking me all these questions?' 'Madam, you have reached a number in the Pentagon that no one is supposed to know anything about.'

The other story is mainly for samplers. The interviewer explained that we list the people in the household and then randomly select one to be interviewed. Speaking to the housewife, she listed the people in the household and said 'It is your husband I need to talk with—is he at home?' She said 'Yes he is at home, just a minute I will get him.' She came back and said 'I'm sorry, we have two lines into our place and he can't come now. You see he is being interviewed by an interviewer from the University of Michigan!' The probability of that happening is of course very remote!

What are some of the other problems of the telephone? We have talked about response rate. This is a very great problem in all interviews—the response rates generally tend to be going down in surveys in the US and if the response rates go down much more, we will be in some sort of desperate straits. We mentioned that a lot of the non-response comes from central cities, from those heavily industrialised, urbanised areas where interviewers do not like to operate. We think that the possibility of a dual-mode data collection procedure, where some of the data are collected by telephone and some are collected by face-to-face interviews, may be part of the solution to a lower response rate. At least it may help to compensate for that varying potential bias if you get a 50–60 per cent response rate in central cities and 95 per cent in rural areas. That is being studied by the samplers at the present time and I expect within another few months we will test some of these multi-phase designs to see what will come of it. The rates for face-to-face interview have also been going down generally in the US over the past ten years. The reason for both rates dropping is probably that people are concerned about the invasion of privacy, or that the general fear of violence means they do not want to let someone into the house. I do not see these as very serious concerns, but they give people a good reason for refusing. The problem of saturation, or wearing a place out with surveys, is probably not an issue, but there does seem to be an issue in the conflicting use of the phone for different purposes, such as selling. There are salesmen who use the telephone and face-to-face interviews. They do bogus surveys in order to try to sell something and the Better Business Bureau in the US has been very actively concerned with disciplining this group. But there is still a lot of selling on the pretext of surveys and we are getting more and more of it on the telephone. The worst device was that owned by a newspaper. It had a continuous tape machine which automatically dialled numbers, and when it got somebody to answer, the tape read off, 'You can get the such-and-such news now for so much money.' It just kept going round and round and its owners were very proud of how many people it could talk to in the course of an hour. A few more things like this and the telephone interviewers are in trouble too.

As I have said, response rates generally in the US are a very serious problem. Face-to-face rates are going down, the telephone rates seem to be 3 to 5 percentage points lower, and the question is, what do we do about it? Some studies were tried with all different kinds of introductions. We tried about four different kinds of introductions: we started right off by asking a question instead of introducing ourselves; we tried saying we were from the Public Health Service first instead of the University of Michigan. We did all kinds of different things but the content of those introductions made very little difference—maybe one percentage point—in the response rate. We tabulated the data on refusals and the finding was that about 50 per cent of them occur within the first ten seconds and that most of the rest occur after the first introductory statement.

I have been asked if I find it just as easy to get to the designated person with a telephone as I do in face-to-face interviews. It is when one is doing the household listing that one tends to get the second major bulk of refusals. The first bulk occurs within ten seconds, then one introduces the survey and one does the listing of the people in the household; it is at that point one is likely to get the second big cluster of refusals. But it is also at that point that one tends to get most of the refusals in face-to-face interviews. I cannot say how much difference there is but it is enough that we tried modifications of the Kish system to get around the listing. The procedure was to designate a household as a male or a female household randomly at the very beginning before a number was called at all and if this was designated as a male household, when the phone answered, the introduction was 'How many males live here?' And if no males, how many females. Then you only had to list the one sex. Since most households contain only one male, one female over eighteen would be eligible, and in most cases you did not have to do any listing.

Leslie Kish is studying this approach in more detail now to see if there is any major bias, but at present we think there is no great bias in the procedure and it is of course much simpler to use. In this case, people do not even have to give the names because if there is, for example, a relationship such as father–son, one knows who is the oldest and one can use the random system to choose the person. The procedure is now used consistently in the interviews to choose people at random and it seems to be that it works pretty well, but it does mean that a lot more refusals are experienced at this point.

We also have the interviewers make call-backs on refusals. As a rule, they pick up about 25 per cent of the original refusals and convert them to interviews. We tell the interviewers not to push too hard and if they are really getting resistance to back off and say, 'You are probably busy now, I will call you back.' We work on two assumptions: one, that the second time somebody else may answer the phone; and the second, that refusals tend to be momentary. That is, the respondent might say, 'I have had a hell of a hard day . . . Now I come home and I am just about to do something for myself when the stupid phone rings and somebody wants to talk to me . . . and I don't want to talk to them. If you call the next day when I am more at ease I may be ready to be interviewed.' Another tentative hypothesis is that sometimes the person is turned off by a particular phone voice. We do not have much evidence for this, but I know the interviewers will suggest that someone else call back the next time because she may be able to get an interview, and it seems that she sometimes can.

Refusal is a very difficult research area to handle. Along with finding out when the refusals occur, we were able to compute the response rate for each of the interviewers, or the refusal rate for each of the interviewers over a long period of time. Since we do a study about every month, we had interviewers who worked for six months. We looked at their response rates over this period and found that there were some interviewers who were getting higher refusal rates while some were lower—in fact the variability was about 30 per cent—some of them were getting a 60 per cent response rate and some were getting 90 per cent response rate and doing this rather consistently from study to study. We knew they were getting random samples, so we could not expect any sampling bias. When this happened to us in personal interviews, the interviewers would say, 'Well, that is a very tough area and that is why refusals are occurring in this area.' We would say, 'Sure, we understand.' Now we cannot say that any more because when one is interviewing randomly sampled people on the phone over a number of interviews the responses ought to even out. They do not: there is still a big difference. We thought of course that it was probably what the interviewer said. We standardised content by allowing the interviewers with the best response rate to generate an introduction that they thought was the most effective. Interviewers with both the high and the low response rate used that introduction in a small study and the refusal rates were still the same. It does not take much deduction to figure that what is left is a void. It is clear however, that people sound different on the telephone and it is clear that some people respond well to some voices and not well to other voices.

This has got us into the whole paralinguistic literature which I did not know anything about, but I find it absolutely fascinating discovering the kinds of things that get communicated by voices in terms of the personal attributes of the speaker. Our procedure was to record four of the best interviewers and four of the worst interviewers. We recorded their introduction and we played them to a couple of seminars. We asked how would you rate these voices in terms of being trustworthy, honest, mature, pleasant, and nice. People made discriminations such as, 'This is the person I would like to talk to; she sounds pleasant, she sounds as if she has a lot of integrity and lots of assurance, but these people down here, I am not sure I can give an interview to them.' Then we said, 'Well, what is there about that voice that communicates these feelings?' At that point everything blew up; nobody knew what it was. But there was some agreement about who they would like to be interviewed by and who they would not. This tends to check with other studies in the field which show that the pitch, the rate, the amplitude and several other voice characteristics characterise particular speech and that these are correlated with personal attributes. There is not very much useful literature on this but this is where we are at the moment.

The really worrying thing is if we should find that one kind of voice is well received by one group but not by another. For instance, some people may react well and others badly to highly cultivated voices, or even just male voices. We hope we can make some sort of generalisation about this; if not, we are in trouble.

An interesting development in this area is the telephone surveys conducted by the Columbia Broadcasting System/*New York Times* Poll. They frequently use unemployed actors and actresses as interviewers.

Here is a group who ought to be able to figure out what voice qualities to use to establish positive relations with the respondent on the other end of the telephone. We are beginning a systematic analysis, funded by the National Science Foundation, to see whether we can come up with generalisations on voice qualities as they relate to refusal rates. We are using ratings both from population groups and acoustical analysis of interviewers' voices. This is in the very early stages, but we have hopes that we may be able to identify 'good' and 'poor' voices and either select or train people for more acceptable speech.

We have already talked about two general sorts of problems that confront both face-to-face and telephone interviewing: response rates and non-response problems. Face-to-face response rates have been decreasing over the last decade partly because of the growing concern in the community about violence and letting people into the house, and partly from other causes that we do not know about. I must say that our effort in trying to find out why people refuse has not been very successful. A second major issue of response rate for face-to-face interviews is not only the generally decreasing rate, but the imbalance of response rates between the central urban areas and the rural areas. So if one is thinking about the potential bias of non-response we would be looking at roughly a 60 per cent response rate in central cities and up to 90 per cent in smaller urban, suburban and rural areas, with the response rate going up rather consistently as you go away from central cities to rural areas. This gives one a big imbalance in the overall response rate. If one is analysing data in which urbanisation is relevant, or attitudes of city versus town and rural people and one then looks at means of population estimates, the estimates are likely to be considerably in error. It does mean some sort of weighting is necessary. I want to talk a little more about weighting later on, but briefly one can do some weighting for non-response and this type of weighting is a little tricky. We assume of course that one starts with a well-designed probability sample; it will deteriorate as one encounters non-response problems.

For the telephone, the response problems are somewhat different. First of all there is coverage; people without phones are clearly different from the people with phones. Most importantly, they are different in terms of income. They tend to be the poorer segments of the population. I have emphasised that in Australia the bias may be even greater because of the higher cost of telephones when compared with the US. This means it would exacerbate the problem of income imbalance if one were to draw a sample. The second problem is of course the lower penetration of the population by telephone. The non-response factor would tend to look like the non-coverage problem. Non-respondents would tend to be of somewhat lower income and older. Thus, we have both of these factors going in the same direction and the total effect of non-coverage and non-response can be rather devastating. The lower the coverage, the more devastating it is likely to be.

Weighting comes in here, and it is not a simple problem. Suppose one weights for income; suppose one does find some people of low income with telephones and you use that as a basis to weight the data up to get the population distribution correct for income. But income may not be the proper thing to weight the data on. The one thing we do know is that more often than not, the lower-income people who have telephones are different; some have telephones and some do not. In this regard we do not know what the telephone ownership pattern means. It may reflect a higher-educated, lower-income person; it may reflect a person who is more socially oriented; it may reflect a lot of things that we just do not know about. Simply using income as a weight variable is a rather dangerous exercise, particularly if we conclude that by weighting for income we have got back to representing the usual population parameters.

The main thing I am concerned about is that weighting to get the sample to look like the population in terms of some key characteristics may not reflect the real differences in the population. The differences may be due to factors that one cannot weight on or that one does not know about, for example, certain attitudes, the level of sociability, whether they have more friends and neighbours than others, or whether they are sick and need telephones. There are all kinds of reasons why some people have telephones and some people do not in the lower-income groups. Unless one can find out some of these things and weight for them, the weighting may not help very much. This does not mean that one should not use weighting at all. I am simply warning, or viewing with some alarm, the use of telephone surveys where one knows that the coverage is not good and the non-response is specific. The more people are doing these post-survey adjustments and weighting, the more they are discovering it is a very tricky procedure.

The problems in coverage and low response rate in phone interviews leads us to contemplate other solutions. One is to think of a mixed-mode approach because it does appear that non-response in the two modes of telephone and face-to-face interviewing is somewhat different. The characteristics of the people who do not respond and the reasons they do not respond are different. If proper samples can be designed to take the most advantage of the two modes, I think this may be part of the solution to the general non-response problem. The experimentation with introductions that we have tried in both face-to-face and telephone interviews have not been productive.

Every other year we have a methodological conference in the US that includes all the major survey methodologists. At each of these we have a session on non-response problems, and it is always the shortest session in the whole conference. Everyone views non-response with alarm and there is hardly a single idea about how to improve it. Clearly it is a very difficult problem—one that has not really had the systematic attention that for example, sample bias or sampling error has had, and it is getting worse. We need to think about the kinds of research that might help us all in the survey business to improve response rates. I am convinced it is going to become, if it is not already, a real threat to the use of survey research. One can have the best questionnaire and the best everything else, but if one is unable to interview a small but crucial proportion of the population, then generalisation from that sample to the population is a hazardous exercise. This is one of the major areas where not much research is going on at the present time, in fact no serious research that I know of, yet it really needs the most urgent attention.

Mixed-mode methods are going to require considerable design effort to merge the two kinds of samples. Already, there is work going on in that area. The mathematical statisticians at the US Census Bureau and other places are spending quite a bit of time thinking about that issue. It will probably help somewhat, but the solutions are a fair way off in the future. Thus, non-response problems and non-response bias are major problems facing the survey field in both face-to-face and telephone interviewing; they look a little different in each area of interviewing but they are very serious in both. The coverage problems in telephone surveys are considerably worse in Australia than our coverage problem in the US. There is also a substantial problem in response bias, no matter which survey mode one uses. It appears however, that the type of response bias and the magnitude of response bias are generally comparable between phone and face-to-face interviews.

There are two recent studies which attack these problems. One was done by Theresa Rogers (1976). She used both the phone and face-to-face mode and found that the rate of voting reported in the presidential election was about the same for the two modes, but both overstated the vote by about 25 per cent. Similarly, a study by Bill Locander (Locander, Sudman and Bradburn, 1976) found only minor reporting differences between face-to-face and phone interviews but did find widespread invalid reporting in both modes: 17 per cent overreporting of being registered to vote; 31 per cent overreporting of actual voting; 21 per cent overreporting for holding a card at the public library, and an underreport of 56 per cent of being charged for drunken driving. The message here seems to me that response bias is a most serious problem; it is a problem which affects both modes apparently about equally; and the characteristics of the bias appear to be about the same in both modes. The conclusion one comes to is that the goal of telephone interviews is not to make the telephone mode as good as the face-to-face mode but to try to improve both modes and to try to maximise the validity of both modes. For a long time, all of us who were dedicated to face-to-face interviews thought that the objective was to improve the telephone mode so that it would be as good as the face-to-face mode. Now I say that the goal is to improve both methods and to use the advantages of both methods to improve response overall.

The above comments state the agenda for the methodological research issues—non-response and response bias. The materials we have been working with suggest there are ways in which we can apparently improve reporting. But there are ways in which we can change the respondent behaviour through the interaction of the interview itself. However, what we have done so far is simply scratch the surface of the problem of response bias. As with the non-response issues, these are really critical areas of research for which solutions are needed if survey research is going to be useful for academic work, policy planning, or business decision-making: it is increasingly apparent that there needs to be much more development of good survey methodology. This is the agenda that survey researchers need to face. We should try at least to design some small methodological episodes into continuing studies. It seems to me that is the way we are going to progress. Among the many opportunities to design experimental modules into continuing surveys are small experiments of one sort or another: small things one can manoeuvre in the course of a survey. There might be different introductions, for example; different use of pre-interview information sent to respondents; different ways of starting the interviews. When all these are added up, none of them is suddenly going to make a great breakthrough. If there were to be a dramatic breakthrough, it probably would have been made by now. But there is a lot to be said for a whole series of small studies that gradually add to the literature and give other people ideas about what kind of research they might want to do. If there was a way in which such incidential research could be circulated it would be a very great boon to the survey business. Everyone needs, when designing their own surveys, to attend to some of these issues of either non-response or response bias. Our work at Michigan came along at a time when big response bias problems suddenly became obvious. Everybody panicked at that point and the result was that we had very generous support. The Public Health Service supported us on a seven-year program grant, at about $250 000 a year. One is not going to get that any more and it was glorious while it lasted. But for about six or seven years this is only as far as we got and there is clearly a tremendous way to go beyond this. I really get concerned about the future of surveys and think we all have a responsibility to help make methodological improvements.

THE UNIVERSITY OF MICHIGAN CATI SYSTEM

CATI is the acronym for Computer-Assisted Telephone Interviewing. Using this system, the interviewer is seated in front of a VDU screen. The questions appear on the screen and the interviewer enters the responses by means of a typewriter-keyboard console. The responses may be either numeric or may be open-ended, in which case responses are typed in.

Here is a simple example of a CATI questionnaire. Suppose we ask Q1 on the screen, 'Do you own a car?' 1. Yes, 2. No. The respondent says, 'No, I don't.' The interviewer then punches a 2. The next question that appears on the screen is, 'Do you plan to buy a car in the next 12 months?' And so it goes on. Here is another respondent: 'Do you own a car?' The answer is yes, but the interviewer makes a mistake and punches a 5 instead of a 1. The screen says invalid code, recode'. The interviewer cannot use a wild code and CATI prevents this. She may make a mistake, but at least she has to punch a 1 or 2 or the next screenful will not come. So she goes back and corrects that and punches in a 1 which says, 'I own a car.' The next question that comes up is, 'How many cars do you own?' The code may be 1, 2, 3 or more. Let us suppose the respondent says, 'I own one car.' The interviewer punches in a 1 and the next question is, 'What is the *make* of your car?' Now if she had punched a 2 or 3 for the number of cars the question would have come up, 'What is the make of your first car?' Thus, CATI takes advantage of what information has been coded. On the basis of that, there is usually a listing of cars with codes, so each car is preceded by a code. Suppose the respondent says, 'It is a Ford.' The interviewer looks down the list of codes on the VDU and sees that a Ford is number 24 so she punches in a 24. The next question that comes up is, 'What *model* is your Ford?' Then there will be screen lists of models of cars and the interviewer will punch in that information. At that point, if the respondent had reported two cars the next question that comes up is, 'What is the make of your second car?', and you repeat the sequence for model and so on. If there was only one car the screen says, 'Do you plan to buy a car next year?' It then goes back to where it recycled off in the first place.

What this means is that the interviewers can make very few errors. There are no wild codes permitted. Most of the wild-code checking that one usually does by hand is redundant and a lot of consistency checks can be built directly into it. It does not mean that all the coding is correct but at least it eliminates wild codes. It also means that if the interviewer punches the wrong code the probability is that she is going to ask questions that do not make sense. For example, if I say, 'Do you own a car?' and the answer is no, and I punch a yes by mistake, the next question that comes up is, 'What is the make of your car?' That is absurd, so you have to go back and correct it. So there are a lot of self-correcting mechanisms in the CATI system. It means also that you can make the questioning pattern much more complex. There are channels within channels within channels to take one through all kinds of conditional or filtered situations: the machine handles it without any trouble.

Some things which are much too difficult for an interviewer to follow can be readily programmed on the computer. One can do such things as change the order of questions randomly; one can randomly change sequence or change question words. Whatever that computer can do, one can redesign the questionnaire to fit its capabilities. One can take advantage of information that was collected in some parts of the interview for later on. For example, one could set up a question earlier at the stage where one listed the members of the family. At that point one probably asked what some of their ages were and now, later in the interview, one wants to ask some questions about each family member in order. After one asks the first one, the next person comes up on the screen and the question is, 'You said your son John is 19 years old...' Then you can go on and ask the question. It keeps those things straight and picks up other information that one used earlier if one wants. From this point of view it is extremely flexible in what one can do in designing questionnaires, and in keeping the interviewers straight. Consequently, the interviewers make far fewer errors in this than in the regular complicated pencil-and-paper questionnaire format.

The programming of the questionnaire on the VDU screen at the beginning is really very simple. The typist sits down at the keyboard terminal and types in the questionnaire. The computer asks the operator various questions: what are the acceptable codes and what are the unacceptable codes, so that she would reply in this case, 'A 1, 2 and 5 are acceptable and 6, 7, 8 and 9 are not admissable codes.' The instruction to the operator is, 'Where do we go in case the code is 1, what question comes up next, what variable is next?' Thus the operator can type in all the information that is needed to format the question-naire and lead the interviewer through the questionnaire. Another advantage is the flexibility it offers for testing. For example, on the basis of the first interview of a pretest one might discover that question 23 is not working at all. So one just types in another question 23 and goes on with the pretest. It is a very rapid change; if need be one can type in the question while the interviewing is going on.

We had problems with the development of this system. About four or five years ago we developed a system internally and used it on two studies. It had some good parts and some bad parts. The bad part was interviewer–machine response time. After each question the next screen was too slow in coming up. We had various consultants come in to look at it and they said, 'Well, you have got it on the wrong hardware.' We were using four-phase at the time and they said as long as we kept it that way it would not work any faster. We tried to jack it up by getting another four-phase to take only half the work. It would not work very well and we concluded that it was not properly designed. By this time we were intrigued enough with the idea of CATI to want to use it.

The issue was, should we start to redesign a whole system ourselves or buy something off the shelf? There were a number of systems in the US that were being used, and after reviewing these we found two of them that seemed to at least come close to what we wanted. The one we finally went with was being used by a market research firm in Detroit. We went with them because they were only 40 miles from Ann Arbor, they had a system that was good and they were quite willing to allow a lot of adaptation. I think it was the third system they had tried and it had been operating for a couple of years. It was functioning beautifully, but our demands on the system were estimated to be far greater than theirs. For a start our questionnaires were more complicated and we also wanted much more control. Our people put a lot of effort into developing different software to meet our needs. It has been in development now for over a year and it is still not complete. We are operating on the system but it does not have all the things on it that we wanted to have. From seeing our own systems and those of other people I concluded that one is likely to underestimate the time and the cost of getting a CATI-type system into full operation by something like 50 per cent.

This seems to be the history of every system I have ever heard of. They swallow up development costs and time at an incredible rate. The programmers say we can do things this way or that, and as soon as they do it that way, something crashes and they have to go back and rebuild it. I think the first true CATI system was probably the one developed by the Chilton Company, a market research firm in Philadelphia. They were doing work for the telephone company and they decided to go with telephone interviewing. They had a huge IBM 370 that they did not quite know what to do with, so they decided to launch into computer-based telephone interviewing. It was a very simplistic system when compared with current systems: it simply projected the questions on the VDU. It gave Chilton a lot of competitive advantage for a while—it seemed everyone was buying the system.

Since then CATI systems have become far more complex. The first academic system was at the University of California, Los Angeles, and that started from a different tradition. That was designed originally for psychological experiments and then it was adapted for use in telephone interviewing. That had some problems with it. It was then redesigned by the University of California, Berkeley, and in specification was close to the one we are now using in Michigan.

On the first study in which we were comparing telephone and face-to-face interviews, we divided the sample randomly into halves. Half of it was done using a hard-copy (pencil-and-paper) telephone questionnaire and half of it was done using computer-based screens. The results were identical. The same interviewers worked one week on one form and the other week on the other form and afterwards we gave them a big questionnaire to find out how they liked it. About half of them said they preferred to work on-line and about half said they preferred off-line. There was almost no serious complaint about either mode. A few people said they were probably getting some eye strain from the glare but other people did not seem to feel that. The main difficulty that we had was in the original training of the interviewers. There was a direct correlation with age as to how long it took people to learn how to handle the computer: the younger people were so acquainted with computers they all went right into it. The older people said, 'If I touch that button, is there something bad about to happen?' It took quite a while to get them over their concern about breaking the machine, so we told them first, 'Go in there and touch buttons. You do anything you want with it and you will see that the machine is tolerant of a lot of error of this kind.' The market research people faced this issue and what they did was to program a lot of games into this system—you can play tick tack toe, or golf— so the introduction to the system is to say to a new interviewer,'Well, I am going to be busy for half-an-hour, why don't you sit down and here is how you get on to these games. Why don't you just start playing games?' As soon as they get on to it and it becomes fascinating, they learn the system very rapidly.

The system is also a marvellous record keeper. In fact that saves us a great deal of money. When the interviewer tells the machine she is ready for another telephone number the machine has an algorithm built in to search all the unanswered phone numbers and to try new phone numbers which are stored in it. The algorithm has determined the best time to recontact that number, but of course this is not always effective as people might still be out or uncontactable. For example, if one called at 2.00 in the afternoon on a Monday and did not get anybody, one could try Wednesday at 7.00 at night. The machine will isolate these numbers. We have studies on the way now to try to find out when it is that people are home, so we can make the algorithm more effective. The interviewer really does not have to think. The number comes up on the screen—it has the area code and the office code and random digit—and that is the number that is called. If no answer comes up, the number and outcome of the call is coded and it goes into the record. It then keeps track of every completed interview, every refusal, the time taken and the length of the actual interview. It also keeps track of how many hours the interviewer has worked each week, or even each day. One can get a complete output of that interviewer's response rate, her costs, the total response rate overall, how the sample is going—everything is just automatically available. It is a great cost-control procedure. It also then reduces or eliminates the need for coding and for punching, not only with the time but the errors that may creep into that procedure. The only manual process that is needed at that point is the coding of the open questions.

Another main advantage to this system is again the control it gives over the interviewing process. One can now not only listen to that interview, but using a slave screen one can see what the interviewer is actually entering; if it is an open question one can compare what one is hearing the respondent say with what is being entered.

A question that was raised in our own minds was what do the respondents think of this method of being interviewed? It happens that when the console keys are punched there is a clicking sound audible over the telephone line. We found in the first experimental work that some of the respondents were saying, 'What is that noise?' With great fear and trembling the interviewer said, 'You see I am sitting at a computer console and putting this information directly into the computer.' Instead of saying 'Oh, my God', the respondent says, 'Is that right...now isn't that interesting?' We have got such positive responses now that we include after the first question of each interview words to the effect, 'You may hear a clicking noise in the background; you see, I am entering this material directly into the computer.' The overwhelming response to that is considerable interest. In fact there is much enthusiasm about it.

As an aside, the climax came when our old machine crashed. Our first idea was to give the interviewer a hard copy so she would just move to that in case of a breakdown but we decided not to on this occasion. So now the interviewer said to the respondent, 'I'm sorry but the machine just crashed and I can't go on with the interview right now, can I call you back?' The respondent said, 'Is that right? I never knew those things broke down, what happened to it?' The interviewer said, 'I don't know.' Obligingly, the respondent said, 'Sure; call me right back.' When the machine came back up, we called the respondent and she said, 'Well did they get it fixed?' Where we had thought there would be concern or anxiety over the use of computers, or the invasion of privacy in a computer-based society, the next query was, 'Does that computer show The Muppets?'

So the concern that we had over the respondent's reaction to the computer was unfounded. The main problem with the use of the system, however, is the cost. The PDP 1170 is dedicated to the interviewing and to the coding and there are 60 parts potentially available—we are using about 40 at the moment. The 1170 cost somewhere between $175 000 and $200 000. It is maintained and used only for the interviewing and coding, so you have reduced a lot of the coding cost but you have added a lot of machine cost. We think the two probably balance out.

4

K.R.W. BREWER

Randomised response techniques: the Canberra drug survey

Randomised response techniques for dealing with sensitive questions were first introduced by Warner (1965) and have been used on a number of occasions since. The only uses of the technique in Australia appear to have been in a pilot test on drug use conducted by the Australian Bureau of Statistics for the South Australian Royal Commission into the Non-Medical Usage of Drugs (Goode and Heine, 1978), and in the present study. In both instances the sensitive questions were about marihuana usage, which is illegal throughout Australia.

The ABS finding was that the technique 'did not significantly increase the number of affirmative responses to the controversial question, and was rather time-consuming'. The results obtained in the present study, conducted in Canberra, indicate a substantially and significantly lower level of marihuana use when the question is randomised than when it is asked directly. Despite the very different nature of these findings, they are both explicable in terms of a reluctance on the part of non-users to give an affirmative response to the randomised question.

SAMPLE AND EXPERIMENTAL DESIGN

Questions on the use of marihuana and a number of other (legal) drugs were commissioned by the Commonwealth Department of Health in the September 1978 round of the then ANU Survey Research Centre's Canberra Population Survey. This was a survey of private households in the defined Divisions (suburbs) of Canberra. The sample was based on responses obtained at 528 out of an eligible 604 private addresses.

At these addresses, members of the households normally resident in Canberra were listed in 'Person Number' order, beginning with the head of the household (as commonly understood), the spouse of the head (if any), followed by the remaining household members in descending order of age. Each address was allocated an Address Number. At odd Address Numbers, household members aged fifteen and over with odd Person Numbers were selected for a sample of individuals and the same was done with even numbers. The marihuana questions were asked of people aged 15–39 only: 379 of these were selected and 365 responded.

The manner in which the answers to the drug questions was elicited is best described in the preamble used by the interviewer. This ran as follows:

> The Department of Health has commissioned us to ask some questions on the use of alcohol, tobacco, medicines and drugs. Each item is covered by three questions, set out on one of these cards. If you would just look at the top card, you'll see that the first question asks whether you have ever used Pain Killers and there is a list of the things we mean by that. The second one asks on how many days, if at all, you have used them in the last week, and the third asks about use in the last four weeks. What we want you to do is just read through the questions on each card, giving the answers as you go. So for this card first, would you give me your answer to Q1? Just Yes or No.

The card in question contained a list of commonly used pain killers and three questions:

Q1   Have you EVER used headache pills or powders or pain killers of any type?

Q2   On how many days IN THE LAST WEEK (meaning the last seven complete days ending last night) have you used any pain killers?

Q3   On how many days IN THE LAST FOUR WEEKS have you used any pain killers?

This first set of three questions was followed by seven similar sets. The second was on a non-sensitive topic (stomach settlers for half the sample, vitamin and iron supplements for the other half), the third on sedatives, the fourth on tranquillisers, the fifth on tobacco, and the sixth on alcohol. The seventh was for half the sample on marihuana directly, and for the remaining half on marihuana randomised with the non-sensitive topic not previously used (vitamin and iron tablets if the stomach-settler questions had already been asked, and vice versa). The manner in which randomisation was performed was as follows:

The last question is about the use of the drug marihuana, and because some people may be unwilling to give answers about this, we use a method which protects you from anyone, even me, knowing whether you are talking about the use of marihuana or the use of something else. You have two cards left, one with the questions about marihuana, and one with the same questions but about vitamin supplement. I'll turn away, and I want you to toss this coin. If it comes down heads, then will you answer the questions on marihuana truthfully? If it comes down tails, then you answer the questions on vitamin supplements. Either way no-one will know which questions you are answering. Is that OK?

The cards for marihuana, vitamin and iron tablets and stomach settlers followed the same pattern as for pain killers.

The experimental design is summarised in Table 4.1 below. It will be seen that for odd Address Numbers the design is exactly that of the 'two alternative questions randomised response model' of Folsom, Greenberg, Horvitz and Abernathy (1973), while the even Address Numbers were used both to increase the sample sizes for the two alternative questions and to provide a comparison with the marihuana questions asked directly.

As will be seen, there was a design flaw of critical importance in the interaction between the experimental design of Table 4.1 and the manner in which the sample of individuals was selected (described above). As it stood, the technique of Folsom and associates would have been applied only to those sample individuals with odd Person Numbers (predominantly heads of households and predominantly male) while the direct questions on marihuana usage would have been asked only of sample individuals with even Person Numbers (predomi-

Table 4.1 Experimental design

Questionnaire type (Address Number)	Technique	Interviewer Number	
		Odd	Even
Odd	Randomising device	Sample 1 ⎰ Marihuana ⎱ Stomach settlers	Sample 2 Vitamin supplements
	Direct question	Vitamin supplements	Stomach settlers
Even	Direct question	Sample 3 Marihuana	Sample 4 Marihuana
	Direct question	Vitamin supplements	Stomach settlers

nantly wives of household heads). Fortunately this flaw was detected during the course of interviewing and the remedial action taken appears to have been sufficiently effective for the results to be capable of meaningful analysis.

The remedy was to instruct interviewers, at a time when approximately half the interviewing had been completed, to switch questionnaires, so that from that point on the individuals with *even* Person Numbers were subjected to the Folsom technique while those with *odd* Person Numbers were asked the marihuana questions directly. These instructions were understood and executed by all but one of the interviewers.(The remaining one switched selections as well as questionnaires, so that there was no net effect.) As a result the Folsom technique was applied to some 58 per cent of individuals with odd Person Numbers and 42.50 per cent of those with even Person Numbers. For both of these sub-populations, therefore, a comparison with the direct questioning is practicable.

It may, of course, be objected that within each of these two sub-populations there are differences between those who are easy and those who are hard to contact, and that the comparisons must be invalid. Against this it can be argued that the most obvious difference in accessibility is precisely that between household heads and their wives, which would not affect the *validity* of the comparison but would tend to reduce the overall proportion of those to which the Folsom technique was applicable. Thus, in the extreme, interviewers might have interviewed all the wives before the switch and all the household heads after it, leaving no one to face a randomised question at all. In fact, of the 365 respondents, 187 (51 per cent) faced randomised questions.

Table 4.2 shows the sex composition of the four samples for odd and even Person Numbers separately. It will be seen that, after controlling for Person Number, there is no significant difference (at the 5 per cent level) between the samples in this characteristic, which, given the nature of the 'mid-survey switchover' device used to remedy the design flaw might be expected to be the first to be affected. In fact, combining the χ^2 values over odd and even Person Numbers yields a value slightly smaller than the chance expectation.

If the two 'randomised question' samples and the two 'direct question' samples are combined, the resulting values of χ_1^2 are 0.22 for odd Person Numbers and 0.53 for even Person Numbers, indicating that there was rather less than the average chance deviation from exact proportionality.

The age composition (under and over 30) of the four samples is shown in Table 4.3. Once again there is no significant difference detectable, and combining the χ^2 values over odd and even Person

Table 4.2 Sex distribution by sample and Person Number

Sex	Sample 1 (Randomised) M	F	Sample 2 (Randomised) M	F	Sample 3 (Direct) M	F	Sample 4 (Direct) M	F	χ_3^2
Person Number									
Odd	47	17	47	9	32	5	33	16	6.47
Even	2	30	5	31	7	40	6	39	1.47

Table 4.3 Age distribution by sample and Person Number

Age	Sample 1 (Randomised) < 30	30+	Sample 2 (Randomised) < 30	30+	Sample 3 (Direct) < 30	30+	Sample 4 (Direct) < 30	30+	χ_3^2
Person Number									
Odd	31	33	31	24	20	17	33	16	4.10
Even	21	11	21	15	28	19	28	17	0.47

Numbers yields a value slightly smaller than the chance expectation. Combining the two 'randomised question' samples and the two 'direct question' samples, the values of χ_1^2 are 1.84 for odd Person Numbers and 0.01 for even Person Numbers. Yet again, if the two groups are considered together there is less than the average chance deviation from exact proportionality. The absence of any significant effect in this area (after controlling for Person Number) provides a considerable reassurance about the meaningfulness of the subsequent analysis. In any event, the magnitudes of the effects observed are so large that no conceivable difference between easy-to-contact and hard-to-contact subgroups could suffice to explain them.

STATISTICAL ANALYSIS AND RESULTS

The analysis used follows closely that of Folsom and associates (1973), the main difference being that with four samples instead of two there was the opportunity to estimate the incidence of affirmative replies to the non-sensitive questions more accurately. The exact nature of this analysis, together with the entire relevant set of numerical data, is available in a longer version of this chapter, obtainable from the author on request.

Two points, however, should be noted in particular. Both binary and quantitative variables were obtained in the survey, but when the

Table 4.4 Estimates of marihuana use for five categories of individuals and three characteristics

	Person Number	n	Randomisation estimate	Direct estimate	Difference	Weighted difference[a]	Est SE	t
Persons 15–39								
Ever used?	Odd	206	.167	.442	−.275	−.267	.082	−3.24
	Even	160	−.093	.163	−.256			
Last week?	Odd	206	−.037	.070	−.107	−.120	.046	−2.61
	Even	160	−.115	.022	−.137			
Last 4 weeks?	Odd	206	−.096	.070	−.166	−.195	.049	−4.02
	Even	160	−.200	.033	−.233			
Males 15–39								
Ever used?	Odd	159	.169	.400	−.231	−.193	.120	−1.61
	Even	20	.494	.385	−.109			
Last week?	Odd	159	−.077	.062	−.139	−.093	.061	−1.53
	Even	20	.344	.077	.267			
Last 4 weeks?	Odd	159	−.155	.062	−.217	−.157	.061	−2.56
	Even	20	.388	.077	.311			
Females 15–39								
Ever used?	Odd	47	.189	.571	−.382	−.316	.114	−2.78
	Even	140	−.167	.127	−.294			
Last week?	Odd	47	.141	.095	−.046	−.139	.067	−2.08
	Even	140	−.188	.013	−.201			
Last 4 weeks?	Odd	47	.134	.095	−.039	−.230	.069	−3.35
	Even	140	−.295	.025	−.320			
Persons 15–29								
Ever used?	Odd	115	.259	.585	−.326	−.250	.111	−2.25
	Even	98	.071	.232	−.161			
Last week?	Odd	115	.063	.113	−.050	−.047	.076	−0.61
	Even	98	−.007	.036	−.043			
Last 4 weeks?	Odd	115	.018	.113	−.095	−.120	.078	−1.53
	Even	98	−.112	.036	−.148			
Persons 30–39								
Ever used?	Odd	90	.058	.212	−.154	−.261	.166	−2.26
	Even	62	−.361	.056	−.417			
Last week?	Odd	90	−.148	.000	−.148	−.201	.031	−6.58
	Even	62	−.279	.000	−.279			
Last 4 weeks?	Odd	90	−.228	.000	−.228	−.287	.035	−8.16
	Even	62	−.343	.028	−.371			

Notes: [a] Weight proportional to n

paradoxical nature of this response to the binary questions was noted, no attempt was made to analyse the quantitative variables. Furthermore, as a result of the 'mid-survey switchover' the selection probabilities for odd and even Person Numbers varied from sample to sample. Classical sampling theory therefore required that the odd and even Person Numbers be analysed separately. Without controlling for Person Number it will be seen that Samples 1 and 2 (which were subjected to randomised response questioning) were predominantly male, and Samples 3 and 4 (which were not so subjected) were predominantly female. The difference in the sex ratios is almost significant at the 5 per cent level ($\chi_1^2 = 3.59$, $\chi_1^2 (.05) = 3.84$).

A summary of the results is given in Table 4.4. It will be seen that the randomisation estimates fall consistently below the direct estimates, especially for females, and that the effect is particularly pronounced for current usage by people aged 30 and over.

DISCUSSION

With the difference between the randomisation and direct estimates so consistently negative, the traditional view of randomised response as being conducive to the admission of sensitive characteristics cannot be a useful one in this situation. Similar though less extreme results were obtained in a study of racial, prejudicial, political and moral opinions conducted by Wiseman, Moriarty and Schafer (1975). Their six possible explanations are considered below.

Interviewers

Although the interviewers used for the survey differ greatly among themselves in professional interviewing experience, they were generally of high calibre, had been carefully trained, and understood the technique well. The results cannot simply be attributed to the incompetence of the interviewer.

Sample demographic composition

The separate analyses for odd and even Person Numbers which was made necessary by the design flaw mentioned before appears to have been adequate to remove any deficiencies due to the different demographic compositions of the relevant samples (see discussion on Tables 4.2 and 4.3 above).

Time lapse

In this experiment the two sets of questions were being asked simultaneously, but the result of the 'mid-survey switchover' was that the odd Person Number respondents were being subjected to randomised questions early in the fieldwork and direct questions later, while the opposite was true for even Person Number respondents. Since however, the entire fieldwork was conducted within a period of about five weeks, the effect of time lapse should be inconsequential.

Sample size

The fact that two of the t-values are of the order of -7 or -8 indicates that the sample sizes are sufficiently large for the paradoxical results to be treated seriously.

Lack of confidence in the randomising device

An ordinary coin was chosen as the randomising device largely to ensure respondents' confidence. Wiseman and associates found that 20 per cent of their respondents lacked confidence in their poker-chip device. It is unlikely that as many as 20 per cent would lack confidence in such a familiar object as a current coin, and in any case this kind of distrust, if traditionally interpreted, would only serve to explain an approach of the randomised estimate to the direct one, and not the completely paradoxical results obtained here.

Misunderstanding of the game

This is the only one of the six possibilities considered by Wiseman and associates which comes even close to explaining the observed results. Even so, it appears that it was not a simple misunderstanding that was responsible. Discussions with the interviewers after the fieldwork had been substantially completed indicated that there were three reactions of respondents to the technique which could have served to invalidate the answers to the randomised questions. In order of importance (so far as the interviewers could judge the matter) these were as follows:

1   *Embarrassment.* The interviewers' consensus was that the introduction of a lottery was felt by the respondents to be unnecessary and embarrassing. It broke the flow of the interviewers' technique and

interfered with the level of communication. As a result, many respondents (in the interviewers' opinion) did not take the randomised questions seriously, though many others—as was shown by their care in answering questions on the frequency of usage— evidently did.

2 *Sinister associations.* Although marihuana use is illegal throughout Australia there was not, at that time of the survey, any expectation that there would be much enforcement of the laws against marihuana use in Canberra. In consequence, the direct question (where appropriate) was asked, in almost every case, without embarrassment, the chief exception being in the asking of young people when their parents were present. The randomising of the question however, introduced a sinister element into the proceedings and may have put people on their guard.

3 *Desire to help.* The intention of the randomised question clearly being to measure marihuana use, it was noticeable that a number of respondents were eager to help over and beyond the answering of the question. It is quite conceivable that other respondents randomised to non-sensitive questions considered it would be more helpful if they were to answer the marihuana questions instead.

Three other possible explanations were considered, but were believed by the interviewers to operate on a very small scale, if at all. These were as follows:

4 *Conformity to perceived peer-group expectation.* A few of the younger respondents, perceiving a peer-group expectation that they should have tried marihuana, may have answered 'Yes' to the direct question without having used it in fact. (This explanation is obviously inappropriate for the over thirties, where the paradox is sharpest.)

5 *Over-sensitivity of non-users.* Some non-users of marihuana may have been so reluctant to run the risk of association with marihuana that they answered 'No' when they were supposed to answer 'Yes' following randomisation to the non-sensitive questions on vitamin and iron supplements or stomach settlers. It is largely this consideration which led Greenberg, Kuebler, Abernathy and Horvitz (1977) to advocate the use of non-sensitive questions with proportions of positive responses approximately equal to the proportions for the sensitive question. The present results are, in fact, fully consistent with the arguments presented in that paper, the only counter-evidence being a strong feeling on the part of the interview-

ers that this was not the most common reason for the respondent's behaviour.

6   *Deliberate falsification by non-users.* Wiseman and associates suggested that one of their problems might have been the eagerness of respondents to have their opinions recorded. Corresponding to this, a person who was strongly opposed to marihuana might be unwilling to answer 'Yes' when randomised to a non-sensitive question if he felt that he was thereby contributing positively to the estimate of marihuana use.

It is interesting that the ABS pilot study (Goode and Heine, 1979), which also used a coin as the randomising device, did not obtain paradoxical results. There were however, many differences between the two studies. In the ABS study there was only one non-sensitive question, 'Were you born in the months of January, February or March?' with a known incidence of occurrence (0.25) much lower than that for use of vitamin supplements (ever used, 0.78) or stomach settlers (0.75). Further, the 444 respondents had already completed a self-administered form containing the same question on marihuana use asked directly, which may have had a considerable influence on the subsequent randomised response. The proportion of persons indicating on this questionnaire that they had used marihuana was 17.1 per cent ± 1.8 per cent, which was lower than the estimate of use from the randomised response technique (18.7 per cent ± 3.8 per cent) but not significantly so. It does not appear that the ABS study sheds any particular light on the present findings, but perhaps the single most important difference between the two surveys lies in the incidence rates for the non-sensitive characteristics. Not only do high incidence rates for these characteristics give greater respondent protection (though at the cost of reduced accuracy), but departures from the standard model of behaviour can be more easily detected when these incidences are very different from that of the sensitive characteristic.

5

H.W. FAULKNER

Simulation games as a technique for information collection: a case study of disabled person transport use in Canberra

Social researchers have generally relied upon structured interview–questionnaire formats to obtain information about the behaviour and attitudes of particular groups. Typically, the researcher devises a series of questions encompassing various facets of the problem being investigated according to his or her understanding and conceptualisation of that problem. Similarly, response categories are usually identified in advance, although there is often scope for recording responses which do not conform with these expectations. Interviews usually involve the researcher and respondent in a rather sterile, essentially non-interactive communicative situation, with the latter responding to a battery of questions from the former, who classifies and records the answers.

While they can produce useful quantitative information about certain aspects of the attitudes, motivations and circumstances of individuals, conventional surveys provide only a limited and often superficial perspective on factors influencing human behaviour. Surveys tend to be structured to receive a particular type of information; their scope is too often constrained by the preconceived notions of the researcher; and priority in their design seems to be given to the collection of large volumes of data in a form which facilitates analyses rather than effects communication. Some of these limitations can be rectified by allowing surveys to evolve through a comprehensive series of pilot studies before questions are defined. All too often, however, they are designed by ex cathedra inspiration incorporating untested biases and judgments. The emphasis placed on this single fallible approach highlights the necessity for developing alternative approaches which do not have the same limitations and which, in particular, are suitable for strengthening the 'front-end' exploratory phase of the survey process.

This chapter's purpose is not to present a critique of conventional survey techniques. Rather, it aims to describe a different and complementary technique—the game simulation approach—which avoids some of the limitations referred to above. We begin with a brief outline of a research project, A Study of Transport for the Disabled in Canberra, in which the technique has been applied. The Canberra study provides a context for describing and explaining the approach. The rationale for adopting a game approach in this instance is then considered and the game-interview procedure is described. Some of the findings of the Canberra study are described, but only to the extent that is necessary to indicate the nature of the information produced by the technique. Finally, attention is drawn to some of the major benefits of the game approach, its potential uses and its limitations.

THE CANBERRA STUDY OF TRANSPORT FOR THE DISABLED

The purpose of the Canberra survey

An individual's access to community facilities and opportunities for social interaction is largely determined by his or her personal mobility. In an affluent society where high levels of car ownership have become the norm, the degree of mobility required to enjoy all the benefits of modern urban life has become increasingly dependent upon one's ability to make use of whatever transport is available. One of the achievements of the International Year of the Disabled Person (IYDP) program has been to draw attention to that substantial minority of people who have disabilities which restrict the range of transport services they can use, and which consequently further limit their opportunity to live the sort of life most able-bodied people take for granted. This increased awareness has added impetus to innovations in urban transport aimed at accommodating disabled people. However, to appraise the effectiveness of these developments and to identify those deficiencies that undoubtedly remain, it is necessary to develop a clearer understanding of the travel behaviour of disabled people, the problems they experience and the modifications to urban transport systems required to overcome these problems.

The Bureau of Transport Economics' study (1982) of disabled

people in Canberra aimed at taking a step towards rectifying this gap in knowledge. More specifically, the purpose of this study was to explore the travel behaviour and preferences of disabled people of Canberra in order to identify:

1 how they presently cope with their travel demands;
2 what problems they encounter in relation to their transport arrangements; and
3 what deficiencies persist in existing and recently introduced transport services specifically designed for this group.

Selecting an appropriate survey approach

Clearly, the study required the collection of detailed information on the needs, constraints and interdependencies affecting the organisation of individual disabled persons' activities. Such information could only be collected by consulting disabled people themselves, and their families, within a survey framework. However, certain characteristics of the research problem made a conventional survey approach inappropriate.

Given the exploratory nature of the study, the limitations of the structured survey approach mentioned earlier became particularly pertinent. Such an approach is too restrictive in terms of the scope and depth of the discussion it generates, and also because it is insufficient as a framework for discussing the complexities of individual travel behaviour at an appropriate level of detail. A technique was required which combined the flexibility of open-ended discussion with a structured format to facilitate the systematic collection and organisation of data on actual and preferred travel arrangements.

Open-ended discussion was considered as an alternative approach because it enables the degree of flexibility required—see, for example, Michelson (1966) and Carter and Thorne (1972). However, this approach is limited where complex relationships between individual and household, actual and preferred travel behaviour are being considered. A more systematic, semi-structured format incorporating some of the features of the open-ended approach was therefore necessary to clarify discussion on these more complex issues. The same technique was adopted mainly because it hinges on a model which provides tangible cues and props for such a discussion.

Games have been used as a framework for interviews in a variety of research fields generally related to behaviour and preferences in residential settings. They have been used to explore preferences in the use of leisure time (Chapin, 1971; 1974; Chapin and Hightower, 1965); to measure residential environment preferences (Wilson, 1962; Berkeley, 1968; Hoinville, 1971; Rowley and Tipple, 1974; Rowley and Wilson, 1975); and in planning practice to gauge community preferences (Bourgeois, 1969). This technique has also been adopted in research situations more closely related to the subject of the Canberra study. It has been used to investigate travel preferences and related decision-making processes (Hoinville and Berthoud, 1969; Jones, 1979), and transport problems experienced in remote suburban communities (Faulkner, 1981; Faulkner and Rimmer, 1982).

In most of these cases, the game has a fairly simple structure. Respondents are invited to express their preferences by manipulating a model representation of particular aspects of their residential environment. No unpredictable contingencies such as the effects of actions taken by other participants are included, nor is there scope for the inclusion of rewards since there is no way of ranking responses in order to apportion pay-offs. In short, games have generally been used mainly to simplify questions and to simulate aspects of the environment which require a trade-off between certain options rather than to simulate the type of conflict situation in which game theorists are interested.

THE DISABLED PERSONS TRANSPORT GAME

The game-interview technique developed in the Canberra study involves three distinct components: preliminary questions; setting up the gaming board; and the game itself.

Preliminary questions

Background information on the nature of the individual's disability and the effect it has on their mobility was gathered by means of a conventional survey approach. Questions about family relationships, economic circumstances and residential history were considered later in the interview because such questions are likely to be perceived by the respondent as being personal and not entirely relevant if dealt with at the outset.

Setting up the gaming board

Attention was then focused on a map (the gaming board) upon which a record of the respondent's existing travel pattern was compiled by placing a flag at the destination of all trips undertaken regularly (i.e. at

Figure 5.1   The Canberra gaming-simulation Board (BTE photograph)

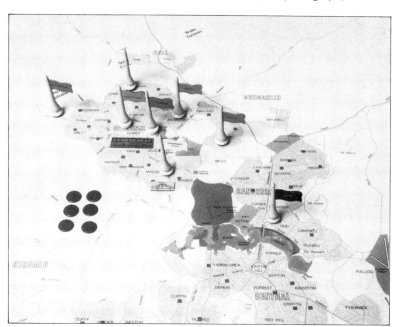

least once a month). The gaming board, with flag markers and other equipment used in the survey, is shown in Figure 5.1. As each destination was registered, information was sought on trip purpose, frequency, mode of travel, assistance required, difficulties encountered and other destinations incorporated in the same journey. With the benefit of hindsight, it is apparent that the quality of the information collected at this stage could have been improved by having the respondent compile a travel diary over a period of several weeks before the interview, and then using this information as a guide for setting up the gaming board. However, time and logistic constraints imposed upon the Canberra study did not allow such a step.

Apart from its obvious purpose in enabling certain information about travel behaviour to be collected, this step would have provided an opportunity for participants to become familiar with the gaming board. It also provided a framework for them to consider their existing travel arrangements in a systematic fashion which reduced the possibility of omissions, and encouraged respondents to consider difficulties experienced and possible alternative travel strategies. Once all trip destinations had been plotted on the board, the scene was set for the game itself. Before progressing to the game stage, however, one more critical question was put to respondents. They were asked to indicate the destination of any trip they would like to include in their itinerary, but couldn't for some reason. If such trips existed, the reasons why they presently cannot be undertaken were sought.

The game

The previous stage mainly served to draw attention to what respondents presently do. An opportunity was provided for the expression of preferences, but this was done without respondents being required to consider the consequences of enacting these preferences. Thus, the intention of the game itself was to create a situation which encouraged respondents to consider alternatives realistically in terms of economic and organisational constraints.

At the outset of the game alternative forms of transport were presented for respondents to consider. Their choice was constrained by the requirement that each trip be paid for by means of counters—the units of currency used in the game. The price structure of the transport options reflected their relative costs in the real world with some concessions being made for the sake of simplicity. The scope of the respondent's transport choice was manipulated by altering the amount of currency allocated. At first, their choice was restricted by being given fewer counters (30 per cent less) than was required for them to keep to their present travel pattern. This 'belt-tightening' procedure was designed to direct participants into a reassessment of their travel priorities and a consideration of alternative travel strategies. The options open to respondents were then expanded by the allocation of a 'mobility allowance' equivalent to an additional 30 counters (approximately \$12 per week) above their current expenditure level. In the final stage of the game, the financial constraint was eliminated (i.e. all trips were made free). This allowed the degree to which the individual's travel behaviour was restricted by economic factors to be revealed.

Two points about the rationale of the game should be noted at this stage. First, although financial constraint was the explicit variable introduced to seek respondents' reactions, it was through observation of the process (as much as the product) of travel adjustments that insights into the real behavioural factors under study were gained. Thus the financial constraint served as much as a catalyst for discussion as it did as a proxy for policy changes.

Second, some consideration needs to be given to what is implied by the expression of travel preferences in the context of the travel game. Transport handicap is a relative concept in the sense that the degree to which someone is disadvantaged depends upon comparison with 'normal' levels of travel behaviour. This suggests that a logical method for identifying mobility handicaps associated with disability would have been to compare the travel patterns of disabled people with those of a control group comprising individuals with similar characteristics but who do not have disabilities (Brog et al., 1981). However, since this approach requires a broader study of travel patterns among various socioeconomic groups, it was not feasible in the present study. Instead, a simpler and perhaps less rigorous approach was adopted whereby the disparity between actual and preferred travel behaviour was taken as the disadvantage experienced in each case. This approach assumes that what a disabled person would 'like' to do in respect to travel approximates the norm of their able-bodied counterparts, and that disabled people are prevented from acting according to their preference mainly because of their disability. There is a possibility that estimates of disadvantage based on this assumption will be exaggerated by unrealistic expression of preferences. However, there is some basis for believing that this danger was minimised by the way the interview technique was explicitly designed to encourage respondents to take relevant constraints into account when considering their preferences.

ADVANTAGES OF THE GAME-SIMULATION APPROACH

The approach described above was limited in the sense that it yielded mainly qualitative information about a fairly small number of people. However, it had features which counteracted several limitations and disadvantages of conventional survey techniques and made it especially suitable for an exploratory investigation. In summary, these features include flexibility, communicative advantages and the ability to simulate aspects of the real decision-making environment.

Flexibility

One of the main limitations of the conventional survey approach is that the interviewer's schedule of questions tends to become a restrictive recipe for interviews. Consequently, information which does not conform to the researcher's expectations about what constitutes the relevant dimensions of the problem is often screened out. The technique used in the Canberra study overcame this problem to the extent that it fostered a free-flowing open-ended discussion in which unexpected variations in responses could be explored in depth. As mentioned previously, this feature of the technique makes it especially applicable to the exploratory phases of research.

Communicative advantages

Perhaps the main advantage of the game technique is that it facilitates communication—not only between respondent and interviewer, but also between individual members of the household concerned (Brog and Erl, 1980). This feature of the game was significant in the context of the Canberra study not only because it contributed to a more thorough exploration of the issues, but also because disabled people often depend on help from others, and their transport problems often have an impact upon the mobility of other members of the household.

The physical model used in the game provided a tangible prop for discussion. Questions and answers were clarified by referring to the model; participants were able to visualise their travel patterns and remind themselves of omissions as they cumulatively reconstructed their record of travel behaviour; and alternative transport systems being presented for consideration were more easily described. Furthermore, the novelty of the game and the model representation of the respondents' behaviour and environment sustained their interest, and avoided the tedious repetition that occurs when conventional survey techniques are used to obtain data on travel behaviour.

Simulation of aspects of the decision environment

The final advantage of the game is concerned with the way it simulated certain aspects of the environment. By imposing a budgetary constraint on the individual's choice, the game simulated the restrictions of choice in the real world. Thus, respondents were forced to assess their priorities and trade off one alternative against another.

In his analysis of the advantages of the game technique, Jones (1979) emphasises how surveys frequently fail to predict responses to proposed changes. People often respond differently from what they say they will do before the event. This lack of correspondence between expressed intentions and eventual behaviour arises because people seldom fully understand the consequences of their choice. Preferences expressed in the survey interview situation are therefore suspect whenever respondents have no previous experience of a particular option and the adjustments which may be required to use them. In the Canberra study, the game technique aimed to overcome this problem by presenting transport options in a manner which enabled participants to explore some of the practical implications of enacting their preferences.

PATTERNS REVEALED BY THE CANBERRA STUDY

It is beyond the scope of this chapter to provide a detailed description of the Canberra study's findings (see BTE, 1982). However, a brief outline of variations in responses to the game at this stage provides some insights into the nature of the information it produced.

An analysis of trip-making patterns among survey respondents, levels of satisfaction with travel arrangements and constraints affecting such arrangements revealed that the sample could be divided into four different groups.

Forty per cent of the sample had either ready access to a private car or were able to use other forms of transport independently. Being relatively unrestricted in their use of transport, this group travelled frequently, and their satisfaction with existing travel arrangements was reflected in a lack of interest in expanding travel when the opportunity arose in the game. The remainder of the sample generally had limited access to a car and was unable to use any form of transport independently. Lower trip rates were consequently recorded by a majority of the sample (60 per cent), but, as their different responses to the game revealed, the precise reasons for this varied.

Some of these 'non-travellers' (16 per cent of the sample) indicated that they were satisfied with their low rates of travel and did not increase their travel when they were given extra resources to do so in the game. Most members of this group had adapted to their disability by replacing activities which would require travel with home-based activities and by relying on others.

Among the 'non-travellers' who were dissatisfied with their situation, the game distinguished between those whose travel was restricted mainly by characteristics of the transport system such as fare levels and physical obstacles and others who were inhibited by psychosocial barriers. The former group (27 per cent of the sample) could readily resolve their transport problems within the constraints of the game through the allocation of extra funds to travel. The latter group (17 per cent of the sample), on the other hand, could not find a remedy to their transport problems within the structure of the game because their problems were not simply economic. Members of this group were discouraged from travelling mainly by less tractable social and psychological adjustment problems such as: feelings of self-consciousness, inadequacy or inferiority; lack of companionship; and reactions to attitudes of drivers and fellow passengers when public transport is used.

CONCLUSION

A game-simulation approach like that used in the Canberra study has considerable potential as a tool for examining the transport needs of disadvantaged groups in general as well as disabled people in particular. While the physical equipment that is used facilitates the description of travel arrangements, problems and alternatives, the game framework enables preferences to be expressed with due regard for the constraints involved and the consequences of choosing particular options. In general, this technique has potential particularly in exploratory research where a complex trade-off among conflicting options is necessary (and needs to be understood rather than merely measured) before preferences can be expressed, and/or where respondents need to be encouraged to consider the consequences of making certain choices.

As with any single technique, however, this approach also has limitations which should be acknowledged. Indeed, many of its limitations are a product of the advantages. First, the game requires more pretesting and experimentation than is customary with conventional questionnaire surveys (notwithstanding the earlier reference to a tendency to inadequate pretesting of such surveys). Second, since tional surveys, sample size may be restricted unless a large number of interviewers can be used in the study. Third, the detail of information about each case and the fact that much of this information is qualitative makes the data produced somewhat more difficult to analyse and less amenable to statistical inference. These limitations reiterate the point made earlier about the undesirability of relying too much on any single method, and reinforce the argument for applying a combination of techniques which compensate for each other's limitations (Webb et al., 1966). In this respect, the game technique should not be construed so much as an outright alternative to the conventional approach, but rather as a supplementary device which may be applied either to facilitate the design of conventional surveys or to clarify their findings.

6

E.A. CLELAND

The use of panel discussions in questionnaire design

One of the basic tools in market research and in many planning situations is what has variously been known as group discussions, panel discussions, search conferences and even motivation research. This paper examines a variation on these techniques which has been adopted at the Centre for Applied Social and Survey Research as a preliminary step in questionnaire design. The technique has been found to be particularly valuable in situations where the researchers have little first-hand experience with the subject matter of the survey. The aims of these panels have been to discover the 'range' of problems, as opposed to the 'extent' of them, in some population, and the language used by the population to describe these problems. Armed with this information, the researcher may design a questionnaire that has relevance and meaning.

ALTERNATIVES TO PANELS IN QUESTIONNAIRE DESIGN

The type of panel discussion to be examined here refers to small group discussions. The group or panel typically consists of interested, reasonably articulate and, one hopes, informed people chosen from the target population of a proposed survey. The participants are not chosen because they are 'experts' on the subject—as in many search conferences—nor do the participants remain in the 'panel' over a period of time. Rather they form a panel of discussants for one meeting only. Some researchers have used each of the above alternative types of panels, and in fact, the 'in-depth interview' with individuals, in an attempt to satisfy similar aims. Sometimes these other approaches are used as *the* research method to replace a sample survey. It therefore seems that a digression is warranted to show why each of these alternatives was discarded in favour of the present approach.

If one were to adopt an approach in which 'experts' in the subject matter of a survey were invited to define the range of problems in a community and the type of language used, one would do so at considerable risk. The risk relates to the fact that 'experts' (like the researcher) typically are middle-aged and middle-class, with language and values to match. Regardless of their attributed expertise, they are often poorly informed about the problems facing the community at the non-expert level. This is not to say that 'search conferences' are not excellent vehicles for answering some classes of questions, but most people who have used this approach, in the health and welfare area particularly, are aware that expert panelists are often very much removed from ordinary people. They tend to delight in technical jargon and talk more in terms of pet solutions to unidentified problems rather than getting down to precise definitions of problems that will be recognised by the respondent at his or her kitchen table.

Market research organisations often employ a panel of people from which they select groups to discuss predetermined aspects of products they have been asked to test. While of value for the purpose for which it was designed, this approach is clearly not applicable to preliminary research in questionnaire construction. Unfortunately the approach is sometimes also used in survey research in which the same sample is repeatedly used to study changes in behaviour or opinions and attitudes over a period of time. Researchers who have adopted this approach have not recognised the effect that earlier interviews have on subsequent responses. The case of a recent 'panel' survey to investigate the length of time new mothers breastfeed babies will serve to illustrate this point. A panel of mothers was interviewed at regular intervals by the typical middle-aged, friendly female interviewer. As long as breastfeeding continued, regular visits continued, and continued and continued. Whether all the respondents actually were still breastfeeding is not known, but it was clear that many had learnt to respond in what appeared to them a socially desirable way. One can only wonder about the effect of such demand characteristics and learning effects in many similar panel surveys such as changes in unemployment. These effects would considerably reduce the usefulness of this type of panel for the present purposes.

Training in certain disciplines seems to predispose researchers to adopt an approach in which a small sample, selected in whatever way, is subjected to what is proudly called the 'in-depth interview'. A particular requirement of the in-depth interview is that no questionnaire is used. It is argued by its proponents that this approach obviates the need for panel and follow-up survey research, as it produces valid answers when conducted by a skilful interviewer (usually the researcher). The opportunity for error however remains, even if the technique is only used to replace panels.

THE PANEL

Regardless of how well one may have conducted library research on a subject, those conducting surveys often have little personal knowledge or recent experience with many of the topics under investigation, or of what people outside their immediate circle think about them. A sample of recent problems investigated by the author may serve to illustrate this point. In recent years CASSR has conducted surveys into problems faced by school leavers; needs for health and welfare services in remote areas; the effects of management changes in the crayfishing industry; and attitudes to environmental issues in different types of rural areas.

If one wishes to design a questionnaire that does more than answer a few, often trite, predetermined questions and gets down to issues relevant to respondents, some method must be adopted that overcomes middle-class academic jargon and bias. The type of panel discussion described here is offered as a solution. It is seen as providing an overall appreciation of the area under investigation and thus providing new points of departure for literature searches rather than replacing them. It can ensure that all the relevant questions are asked—and that all the questions are relevant and asked in appropriate language. It also promotes good public relations, response rates and validity of responses.

SELECTION OF PANELISTS

The personal requirements of panelists is that they be concerned about the issues, be able and willing to discuss them and be 'reasonably' representative of the target population. The use of the word 'reasonably' is not intended as a quibble about randomness. A truly representative sample is not required, as the aim of the panel is not to estimate population parameters. Thus articulateness and concern are seen as more important than representativeness.

A problem does exist about the heterogeneity of panelists. In an homogeneous group little can be gained by having people who all agree with one another discuss some issue. One can be confident that an issue is relevant when the discussion becomes heated. Thus a fair degree of heterogeneity is needed. However, one must be sensitive to the possibility that there may be a limit to the desirable degree of heterogeneity. It was found, for example, that in the study of the crayfishing industry mentioned above, when skippers and deckhands were mixed in groups, several issues, seen as vital to deckhands (for example, workers' compensation) in segregated panels, were not even mentioned. Schoolchildren in the country were prepared to discuss racial problems only when the group did not include Aboriginal children.

How does one encourage participants to attend these discussion groups? I can offer no real answer to this vexed question. CASSR panels typically have been well attended. It should be noted that most work has been done in rural areas, or, as the examples above show, in areas which are of considerable interest to many sections of the community. They have all been well advertised and personal invitations have been extended. The point that most surprised panel organisers was that very poor attendance was recorded on the only occasions that incentives were offered to participants. There may be a lesson to learn from this experience—but the sample is very small.

PANEL PROCEDURE

The aim of a panel discussion is to determine what issues the panel considers important in some research area. This information is to be obtained from panelists through their interaction with one another with as little direction from the researcher as possible. In as much as the researcher directs the discussion, he or she will only receive confirmation of preconceived notions, which is often the case with the in-depth interview. Thus the researcher introduces the topic and defines the role that the panelists are to play. This usually involves their discussing what they consider to be the important issues and how each affects their community. One explains how the information will be used and gets the permission of the participants to use any mechanical recording devices, having explained also how these are to be used. The researcher should then be able to sit back and take notes but should be prepared to join in when the discussion drifts away from the topic, or if one area has been exhausted and there is a need to move on, or in some instances, to avoid physical violence. (Farmers sometimes have differences of opinion on environmental issues.) Above all, one should avoid offering an opinion oneself (this is harder to avoid in the panel situation than in the personal interview because up to twenty people may be looking at the researcher expectantly). The techniques of interviewing discussed elsewhere in this book are relevant and the need for many prompts can be anticipated and should be rehearsed in advance. When all else fails it should be remembered that a pregnant pause will probably be more embarrassing to participants than to a thick-skinned researcher. It is best to let the panelists fill in the pauses where possible—after all that was the role that was defined for them.

RECORDING PANEL DISCUSSIONS

Almost invariably, people embarking on their first panels arm themselves with a variety of electronic recording devices. It is only when they, or some unfortunate stenographer, is faced with the task of transcribing several cassette tapes that it becomes obvious that the task of taking notes has simply been very expensively postponed. The technique adopted by CASSR has been for two people (usually the person running the panel and a colleague) to take notes during the discussion. Between them they write a report on the panel. The only time a cassette tape is played is when there is some disagreement or uncertainty between the research staff.

Video tape-recorders have recently been introduced successfully into panel discussions. Video recordings have not been used as an aid to note taking (although at least in this medium one may be able to keep track of which participant says what). The main use has been, with the permission of participants, to show sections to future panels to promote further discussion about such things as differences between towns, or specific groups of people, and to show to the agency which commissioned the study. The latter use has proved to have a remarkable impact on certain funding bodies. Strong support for this or that issue may be a rather surprising statistical result from a survey—and produce little more than a brief acknowledgement from a report reader. Show the same reader a videotape or *one* person supporting that issue and it immediately assumes importance. Perhaps it is a sad commentary on the way survey reports have always been written, or worse still on the way the research consumer absorbs information. Cameras were not introduced with panels without some trepidation as it was believed that their presence would inhibit discussion. Experience has shown however, that after some initial preening, the camera is ignored. Most participants however, are delighted to see the playback—which often provides some secondary elaboration or explanation. One possible exception—again the sample is small—is that some schoolchildren of about the age of fifteen (typically of one gender) pay more attention to the camera than to the discussion. It may however, relate more to the skill of the researcher as children at this age typically seem to seek more direction and have been less spontaneous in their discussions.

CAN PANELS REPLACE SAMPLE SURVEYS?

The alternative approaches to panel discussions talked about earlier are often used as the only method of generating data, and quite successfully in the case of appropriate uses of the group in market research and the search conference. However, the type of panel discussion outlined here was designed purely as a preliminary step in questionnaire design. It should be noted that the sample is not drawn at random from the target population, and that panelists interact. Thus what is achieved is a description of the *range* of problems or issues in a community rather than their *extent*. One example may serve to demonstrate this distinction. Three independent panels conducted in a country town in South Australia indicated some need for speech therapy. Such independent 'validation' tended to suggest a widespread need. However, the subsequent survey of a 10 per cent sample of the town unearthed very few with this need. It appears that the same few in need were well known to all panelists.

There may be special situations where the panel approach could be considered a stand-alone method. These would necessarily be situations in which one was more interested in *range* than *extent*. One such situation could be in evaluation of the effectiveness of community intervention. As an example the author has used the approach to examine the effectiveness of a job-creation program. It was not feasible to sample from all 'unemployed', so what was sought in this project was the range of negative and positive features as seen by panelists who were and were not in the program. These were subsequently studied by the client to determine if suitable modifications to the program could be made to improve its effectiveness. It must be recognised however, that while this approach is fairly cheap and can be effective, it is second best and here it is only advocated as a preliminary step in research.

CONCLUDING REMARKS: PANELS AND PUBLIC RELATIONS

The primary aim of the panel discussion was seen as having a community define the problems which will be investigated in a subsequent survey. Effectively, in inviting people to join a panel, the researcher says that some agency has recognised a need in the community and that panelists are required to define the nature of this need and to help design the research. People who attend such panels feel—and rightly so—that they are designing the questions which will be asked of their community. People who attend talk amongst themselves as well as at panel discussions. Again, the results are informal, and relate mainly to rural areas, but interviewers have regularly reported that respondents have heard about the panels and have been encouraged to participate in surveys because they have believed that their community had some input into the study. Thus it may be argued that panels as described here ensure that relevant questions are asked, that important issues are not overlooked, that public relations (and thus response rates) are enhanced and that perhaps even the validity of responses is improved.

7

R.G. JONES

Variations in household telephone access: implications for telephone surveys in Australia

The most common methods of data collection in the sample survey are the face-to-face interview, the self-completion mail questionnaire, and the telephone interview. For surveys of the general population, the response rate obtainable in a mail survey may be too low to give reliable estimates, while the cost of face-to-face personal interviews may be prohibitively high. The telephone survey shares many of the advantages of the face-to-face interview over the self-completion questionnaire, yet is far less expensive.

Although the use of telephone surveys has grown considerably over recent years among market researchers in Australia, the relatively low level of telephone access raises strong reservations about the validity of estimates made for the general population. In 1975, Telecom Australia (ATC 1975) estimated that approximately 60 per cent of dwellings had a telephone service, with country households as low as 49 per cent. A more recent report (Telecom Australia, 1980d) based on data obtained from the Roy Morgan Research Centre over the period 1964–78 shows that telephone service to private dwellings is increasing at about 3 per cent per year and should now be close to 80 per cent overall. The report shows considerable variation by 'occupation of breadwinner', income and geographical area.

In general, however, there is very little published information on levels of telephone access and characteristics of telephone users in Australia, and thus very little evidence on which to base a decision about the value which might be obtained from a telephone survey. This is not to say that relevant data is not available. Almost every interview survey carried out by the major market research agencies over recent years contains a question on household telephone access, and comparisons between respondents with telephones and those without telephones would indicate the types of characteristics for which reasonable estimates could be obtained.

There would be no problem in estimating population parameters from a telephone survey if the characteristics, behaviour, beliefs and attitudes of serviced households and non-serviced households were essentially the same—that is, if there were no relationship between telephone access and the characteristics being estimated. Available evidence indicates, however, that telephone access is relatively higher among high-income groups, groups with higher occupation status, in metropolitan areas, for example, and these effects presumably carry over to differences in behaviour and attitudes. If no adjustment is made to the results of a telephone survey to take account of these relationships, the estimates obtained may be heavily biased.

In most cases I believe the relationship between telephone access and behavioural and attitudinal variables is largely spurious, being the result of the differences in the basic demographic characteristics of serviced and unserviced households. Thus, by identifying the combinations of demographic characteristics which determine telephone access, subgroups of the population can be defined in which differences between telephone users and non-users will be minimal. The use of appropriate methods of sample selection and appropriate weighting techniques based on these subgroups would then provide suitable population estimates.

Using data obtained from the Household Expenditure Surveys undertaken by the Australian Bureau of Statistics during 1974–75 and 1975–76, combinations of the demographic characteristics of households have been found which identify subgroups of the population homogeneous with respect to telephone access using the Automatic Interaction Detector (AID) technique. The next section contains a description of the data used in the analysis, and the AID results are given after that. A final section discusses the use of these results in further research on telephone surveys.

THE HOUSEHOLD EXPENDITURE SURVEYS

The Household Expenditure Surveys were based on samples of private dwellings, which included houses, home units, flats, caravans, and any other structures being used as private places of residence. Hotels, boarding houses, institutions, etc., were outside the scope of the surveys. The information used in this analysis was collected through personal interviews by trained interviewers with the head of household, usually the male 'breadwinner', or wife, with the interviews in each survey being spread evenly over the twelve-month survey period from July to the following June.

The 1974–75 sample was restricted to the six state capital cities and Canberra, and complete responses were obtained at 9095 of approximately 12 600 households included in the sample which met the criteria for inclusion. The difference is accounted for by households which could not be contacted, were unable to participate fully over the diary period required to collect expenditure details, or were otherwise non-respondent. In order to improve the accuracy of the estimates the sample within each city was allocated in such a way as to increase the representation of pensioner, migrant, and low-income households while maintaining adequate representation of other groups. While this increased representation was adjusted for in the published estimates, the data used here is unweighted. A detailed description of the survey objectives, scope and coverage, concepts and definitions used, and sample design and methodology is given in ABS (1977).

The 1975–76 sample was smaller and more widely distributed than that of the previous year but was otherwise similar. From a sample of approximately 8017 eligible households, 5869 complete responses were obtained, with representation from capital cities, other than urban areas and rural areas in all the states and from the Northern Territory and the ACT. Details of the survey are given in ABS (1978).

A range of demographic information concerning households and household members was collected in both surveys, including household composition, the age, sex, marital status, occupation and employment status of people, the country of birth and period of residence in Australia of the head of the household, the dwelling type, size of dwelling and tenure of dwelling. Telephone ownership, or, more accurately, the availability of a telephone in the household, was determined by the question 'Do you have a telephone at this house/ flat?'

On the basis of the demographic information, approximately 40 household variables were available for use in the analysis to explain variations in levels of telephone ownership. Use of all of these variables was impractical and would anyway have made interpretation of the results extremely difficult. In selecting the subset of variables to be used, a primary concern was to include only those which would normally be collected in a household or personal interview survey. Also, sets of strongly associated variables were reduced to a single variable in order to simplify interpretation. For example, if both income of head of household and household income were included in the analysis, the two are likely to compete strongly with each other for inclusion. This is basically similar to the problem of multi-collinearity in regression analysis. Some preliminary analyses were then carried out and variables which had no effect on the final outcome were eliminated. Country of birth and marital status of head of household are excluded for this reason.

This reduction of variables resulted in the selection of dwelling type and tenure; the age, occupation, employment status and income of the head of household; and the location of the dwelling as the variables to be included in the final analysis. Table 7.1 gives the number of households in each sample with a particular characteristic and the percentage of these with a telephone. It should be noted that the overrepresentation of pensioner, migrant and low-income households in the sample almost certainly lowers the level of telephone ownership in sample households compared to the population.

Clearly income is an important variable in explaining variations in the level of telephone ownership. Telecom's analysis of the Morgan Research Centre data (Telecom Australia, 1980) found that an exponential relationship between the proportion of households with a telephone and the household 'breadwinner's income' explained over 80 per cent of the variation in telephone ownership levels. The analysis below shows, however, that there is considerable variation in levels of telephone ownership within income categories, particularly at lower income levels. For example, the very low income group contains significant proportions of both the under 25s and the over 65s, with the latter group having much higher levels of telephone ownership. The Telecom 2000 report (ATC, 1975) points out that 'this can probably be accounted for by the fact that pensioners are entitled to a subsidy of 33 per cent of the rental cost of the service. There are at present over 500 000 pensioner concessions in force, representing nearly 25 per cent of all household telephone services'.

Comparisons across surveys of the percentage with telephones in general show similar patterns of variation around the overall average except for the middle income groups. This is presumably because of a high concentration of 'other urban' households in these categories and the relatively low levels of telephone access among these households.

AID RESULTS

AID is a method for exploring the relationships between a dependent variable and a set of independent or predictor variables using a binary segmentation approach. Firstly the sample as a whole is split into two subgroups so that the 'distance' between the subgroups, measured in some appropriate way, is maximised. The 'distance'

Table 7.1 Distribution of sample households and percentage with telephone

	1974–75 survey		1975–76 survey	
Variables, category codes and labels	No. of households	% with telephone	No. of households	% with telephone
Dwelling Type				
1 House	7229	72	4875	67
2 Flat	1803	42	830	35
Tenure				
2 Renting unfurnished	793	26	481	25
3–4 Renting furnished (govt or private)	1903	42	1108	36
5 Rent free	265	70	278	63
6 Buying	3682	77	1909	74
7 Owned outright	2444	79	1929	76
Age of head of household (5-yr groups)				
1–2 15–24	773	28	499	28
3 25–29	1273	52	734	46
4–6 30–44	2817	67	1774	66
7–10 45–64	2964	74	1810	71
11 65 and over	1260	77	888	72
Occupation of head of household[a]				
0 Not employed	1837	68	1329	62
1 Professional and managerial	1949	82	1401	80
2 White-collar	1231	69	682	65
3 Skilled manual worker	1536	57	710	54
4 Semi-skilled manual worker	1454	55	810	52
5 Unskilled manual worker	1079	52	773	47

Employment status of head of household	1975–76		1974–75	
1 Self-employed	83	833	86	921
2–3 Employee (full-time & part-time)	58	3543	62	6325
4–8 Others—includes unemployed, students, retired, not in workforce	62	1329	68	1841[c]
Weekly income of head of household				
1 Less than $50	63	983	66	1403
2–5 $50–$149.99	58	1973	56	4141
6–7 $150–$199.99	53	1256	68	1973
8 $200–$249.99	69	700	82	847
9 $250–$349.99	79	549	91	516
10 $350 or more	88	244	96	207
Area				
0 State capital city	68	2223		
1 Other urban—including Canberra and Darwin	55	2680		
2 Rural areas	72	802		
City / State or Territory				
1 Sydney / NSW	62	1572	69	2251
2 Melbourne / Victoria	70	1313	71	2542
3 Brisbane / Queensland	55	820	57	1117
4 Adelaide / SA	66	547	63	983
5 Perth / WA	60	499	59	1089
6 Hobart / Tasmania	61	421	63	562
7 — / NT (Darwin)	43	228	—	—
8 Canberra / ACT (Canberra)	67	305	66	543
All households included	62	5705[b]	65	9087[a]

Notes: [a] Recoded from the Census Occupation Classification used by the ABS into the major groups of the ANU I Occupation Status Scale
[b] Includes four cases which were given occupation codes
[c] Excludes dwellings which are not houses, flats or units
[d] Includes 55 caravan dwellings

Figure 7.1 1974–75 Household Expenditure Survey AID analysis of households with telephones

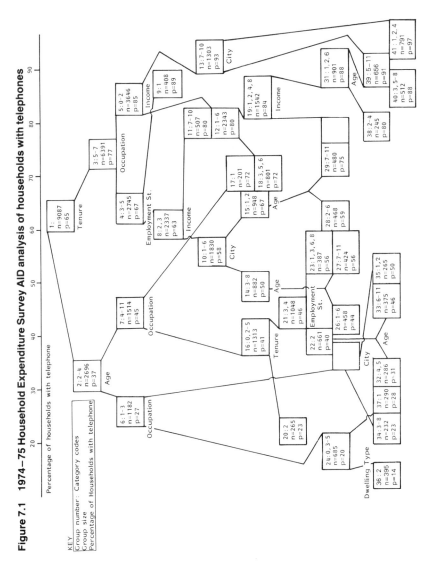

KEY
Group number : Category codes
Group size
Percentage of Households with telephone

118

Figure 7.2 1975–76 Household Expenditure Survey AID analysis of households with telephones

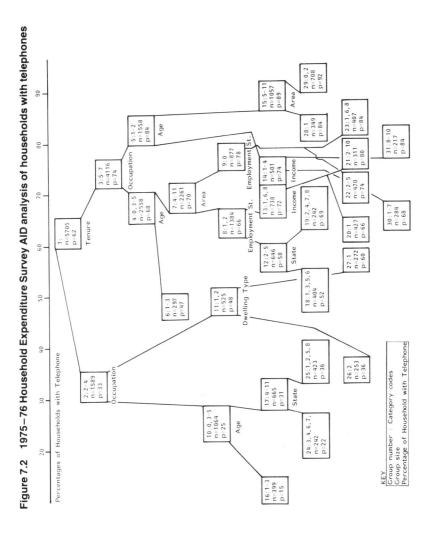

KEY
Group number : Category codes
Group size
Percentage of Household with Telephone

119

criterion used here was to maximise n^2, the ratio of the between group sum of squares to the total sum of squares or, equivalently, the proportion of the total variance in telephone access, defined as a dichotomous variable, explained by the binary split. The subgroups obtained are then internally as homogeneous as possible (in the sense that the within groups sums of squares are minimised) for a binary split on the predictor variables.

The analysis continues splitting subgroups sequentially until a subgroup is either too small to be split (a minimum size of 200 households was specified) or is such that the relationships between telephone access and the predictor variables are inconsequential. The result is a hierarchical tree of subgroups, as shown in Figure 7.1 and Figure 7.2 for the 1974–75 and 1975–76 data respectively. Each box in the figure contains the group number, indicating the order in which splits were made, the group size (n) and the percentage of households in the group with a telephone (p). In addition the division of the categories of the predictor inducing the binary split of the 'parent' subgroup are shown. Table 7.1 gives an explanation of these category codes. For the Income and Age (of head of households) variables, only splits which maintained the monotonic order of the category codes were allowed, whereas the combinations of categories of other predictors were free of any restrictions.

In both surveys the most significant division is that between renters and buyers (including rent-free and outright owners), with very few renters reaching the higher levels of telephone access achieved by buyers. Both trees show considerable asymmetry, suggesting some element of interaction between the predictors. A fairly high degree of association between predictors may also be responsible for many features of the tree. If one predictor is used, particularly at an early stage, then it may use up some of the predictive power of others with which it is associated. 'In such circumstances they may only turn up at very late stages in the tree with reduced predictive power and often may not appear at all' (Fielding, 1977:243). Thus the inclusion of occupation and age may suppress the income effect, while occupation and income suppress the age effect.

Nevertheless, our interest here lies in the final subgroups and the combination of predictor categories which identifies these subgroups. The fact that the two analyses give different results may only be different means of achieving the same end, although the different sample sizes and coverage of the surveys clearly have an effect.

In both surveys, age and occupation play the main role in subdividing renters. Group 11, Figure 7.2 could just as well be split into 'aged under 30' (n=268, p=36) and 'aged 30 and over' (n=257, p=61) as between houses and flats, and this is more compatible with the results of Figure 7.1. An initial division of renters into the four groups defined by the head of household characteristics: aged under 30—aged 30 and over; manual workers or not employed (professional, managerial or white-collar worker) therefore seems appropriate.

In the 1975–76 survey, three of these subgroups are too small to be split further, while Group 17 is split by State. Apart from New South Wales however (n=222), the number of respondents in each State is too small to provide reliable estimates of State differences at this level. Comparison of this distribution with that for all renters in Group 2 shows that the age and occupation controls have little effect, and there only Queensland (n=193, p=18) and Canberra (n=125, p=42) differ from the norm to any significant degree. The only other variable showing strong differences in Group 17 is area, with households in the State capital cities (n=257, p=40) having higher levels of telephone access than those in other urban areas (n=358, p=25). Area differences are also apparent in the other groups (Group 16: capital cities n=166, p=18; other urban n=210, p=11. Group 11: capital cities n=204, p=53; other urban n=283, p=42). The number of renting households in rural areas is small but they appear to have a level of telephone access more like that of capital city dwellers than those in other urban areas.

Unless there is a reasonably strong association between age and dwelling type, the differences between flat and house renters shown by the division of Group 11 will carry through to the aged under 30—aged 30 and over subgroups. Evidence from the 1974–75 Survey indicates such an association with two-thirds of flat renters as against 45 per cent of house renters being aged under 30. This reduces the difference in telephone access between flat and house renters aged under 30 in professional, managerial or white-collar employees to less than 10 per cent, while the larger difference among the aged 30 and over is explained by differences between professional or managerial workers and white-collar workers.

The larger sample size of the 1974–75 Survey (Figure 7.1) allows further splitting of the four age–occupation groups suggested by the 1975–76 data, much of which occurs within the aged 30 and over group (Group 7). Heads in professional and managerial occupations (Group 17) and the self-employed (Group 16: n=65, p=74) have a very high level of telephone access relative to others in this group. The separation from Group 16 of households renting furnished accommodation (Group 20) should be restricted to those in furnished flats only (n=194, p=14), while the white-collar employees included in Groups 20 and 22 (n=166, p=51) have similar access levels to the part-time employees (n=38, p=53) and the not employed (n=295, p=53) of Group 23. This suggests that improved homogeneity of telephone access within subgroups will be obtained by replacing Groups 20, 22, 23 and 17 respectively by those containing households where the head of household is aged 30 and over and is:

1 a manual employee or not employed, renting a furnished flat (n=194, p=14);
2 a manual employee, renting a house or unfurnished flat (n=583, p≈38);
3 not employed, renting a house or unfurnished flat (n=305, p=52) or a white collar employee (n=166, p=52);
4 a professional or managerial worker (n=201, p=72) or self employed (n=65, p=74).

Among households where the head is aged under 30, the self-employed again have relatively high levels of telephone access (Group 6: n=73, p=55). The differences between professional or managerial workers and white-collar workers (Group 25) and between manual employees and the not employed (Group 24) are much less than in the older group of renters, and the only subdivisions of these subgroups competing with those shown as the split of Group 25 into 'aged under 25' (n=249, p=24) and 'aged 25–29' (n=248, p=50) or the selection of the few cases where the head of household's income is over $200 (n=71, p=63).

Among home 'buyers', occupation determines the first split in both surveys, although the not employed are allocated differently. Examination of the distributions shows that three groups would be most appropriate at this level, namely manual employees, white-collar employees or not employed, and professional or managerial workers or self-employed.

In the 1974–75 survey, manual employees are split on income into those earning $175 a week and over (Group 11) and those earning less than $175 a week (Group 10), with the larger latter group being split further between Sydney or Melbourne (Group 15) and other cities (Group 14) and between those aged under 45 (Groups 26 and 28) and aged 45 or more (Groups 27 and 29). The nearest equivalent group in the 1975–76 survey is Group 22, and here again the best split would be on income, into those earning $200 a week and over (n=106, p=91) and those earning less than $200 a week (n=364, p=70). Manual employees living outside the capital cities in New South Wales, Queensland, Tasmania and Western Australia (Group 18) have relatively low levels of telephone access.

The 'not employed' are contained in Group 5 on Figure 7.1 (n=1339, p=79) and are then almost entirely transferred to Group 12 (income less than $175 per week: n=1316, p=79). The differences on city

(Groups 18 and 19) and on income (Groups 30 and 31) are maintained for these respondents, while the age split on Group 31 can be ignored since practically all the 'not employed' in this group are aged 35 and over (n=270, p=90). Group 30 is almost entirely the 'not employed' (n=617) and the same income split on Group 18 gives similar results (income less than $50 per week: n=296, p=67; assuming all are not employed, the remaining 133 cases give p=80). In Figure 7.2, the not-employed buyers fall almost entirely in Group 7 (n=999, p=73) and are divided between Group 13 (n=615, p=69) and Group 23 (n=336, p=83) on the basis of area. The importance of the split on income at $50 per week is seen to carry over to other urban and rural areas (Groups 20 and 21).

Self-employed manual workers are immediately split off in Figure 7.1 (Group 9), while in Figure 7.2 they are divided between Group 6 (n=28), Group 29 (n=15), Group 21 (n=108, p=82) and Group 23 (n=71, p=87). Over all these groups, their level of telephone access is sufficiently similar for them to be treated as a single group (n=222, p=83).

For professional, managerial and white-collar workers, income and age are the main determinants of telephone access, with the combination of being aged under 35 and earning less than $175–$200 per week indicating a relatively low level of telephone access (Figure 7.1, Group 38; Figure 7.2, Group 30). Figure 7.1 shows differences between Sydney, Melbourne or Adelaide residents and those in other cities (Groups 18 and 19, Groups 40 and 41), while Figure 7.2 indicates lower levels of telephone access for residents of 'other urban' centres.

In summary, the AID analysis provides a breakdown of the sample into subgroups which are internally relatively homogeneous over the categories of the predictors used on levels of household telephone access. Those subgroups with similar average levels can then be recombined without disturbing this homogeneity, and these groups provide a basis on which adjustments to the results obtained through a telephone survey can be made. In Table 7.2, characteristics of the household which determine these groups in this analysis and the estimated percentage of the sample falling in each group are given. The effects of the location variables city, state and area are excluded from the Table since they can be controlled by sampling techniques. The income level at which splits of home owners are made varies between the two surveys from $175 in 1974–75 to $200 in 1975–76, and the appropriate division has been used in estimating the percentage of the sample in each group.

Since the household expenditure surveys were carried out in 1974–76 there has been some increase in the percentage of private households with a telephone service, which is now estimated to be about 80 per cent nationally. Without access to more recent, large-scale data, it is not possible to say whether this is due to areas with low access catching up, to increasing access among particular subgroups or to a fairly uniform increase in telephone access. It is therefore possible

Table 7.2   Characteristics of head of household by level of household telephone access

	% of sample 1974–75	1975–76
Extremely Low		
Manual employee or not employed, aged under 30, living in rented accommodation		
or Aged 30 and over, renting a furnished flat	9.1	8.6
Very low		
Manual employee, aged 30 and over, renting a house or unfurnished flat		
or Professional, managerial or white-collar worker, aged under 30, living in rented accommodation	11.6	10.3
Low		
Not employed, aged 30 and over, renting a house or unfurnished flat		
White-collar worker, aged 30 and over, living in rented accommodation		
or Manual employee, aged under 45, income less than $175 ($200) per week, home owner (or living rent-free)	15.6	14.0
Average		
Professional or managerial worker, aged 30 and over, living in rented accommodation		
or Self-employed manual worker living in rented accommodation		
or Manual employee, aged 45 and over, income less than $175 ($200) per week, home owner (or living rent-free)	13.4	11.6
High		
Home owner (or living rent-free) and manual employee, income $175 ($200) per week or more		
or Not employed, income less than $50 per week		
or Professional, managerial or white-collar worker, aged under 35, income less than $175 ($200) per week	20.0	22.9
Very High		
Home owner (or living rent-free) and not employed, income $50 per week or more		
or Professional, managerial or white-collar worker, aged 35 and over, income less than $175 ($200) per week		
or Self-employed manual worker	16.1	19.5
Extremely High		
Professional, managerial or white collar worker, income $175 ($200) per week or more, living in own home	14.1	13.0

that the internal homogeneity of the subgroups defined in Table 7.2 has altered and the extent of the differences between subgroups has changed. I believe however, that the basic relationships and subgroups determined by the AID analysis will remain reasonably stable. Data from interview surveys which include a question on telephone access can be used to determine current estimates of the level of access within these basic subgroups and hence to modify, if necessary, the combinations of these subgroups suggested here.

IMPLICATIONS FOR TELEPHONE SURVEYS

The purpose of this analysis has been to identify subgroups of the population with distinctly different levels of telephone access but which are internally relatively homogeneous, with the aim of improving population estimates made from telephone surveys. Within each of the subgroups presented in Table 7.2, the predictors used in this analysis have little effect on a household's decision to have a telephone, so that weighting the results of a household telephone survey to take account of the different level of telephone access within each subgroup would at least provide fairly precise estimates of the distribution of households over these predictors. It should also have the effect of improving estimates for other variables, since the controls applied through the predictors should reduce differences between households with and without telephone access. The principle being applied is that of 'post-stratification' or 'stratification after selection', a procedure which is commonly used in analysing survey data to ensure that the distribution of selected characteristics obtained through the sample matches the known distribution of the population.

Suppose for example that one wants to estimate the proportion of intended ALP voters using a telephone survey. If a simple random sample of private telephone numbers is taken, then clearly the low-access subgroups in the population will be underrepresented, and this may bias the result significantly. If information is also obtained which allows respondents to be allocated to the appropriate subgroups and the numbers (N_i) in the subgroup in the population are known, weights can be applied to the responses to take account of the differences in telephone access. If p_i is the estimated percentage of ALP voters in the i'th subgroup in the sample, the estimate for the population is:

$$p = \frac{\Sigma N_i p_i}{N}, \text{ where } N = \Sigma N_i \text{ is the total size of the population.}$$

Alternatively, if the proportion (t_i) of households with a telephone service in each subgroup is known and n_i is the number of sample households in the i'th subgroup, the estimate is:

$$p = \sum \frac{n_i p_i}{t_i} \Big/ \sum \frac{n_i}{t_i}$$

since n_i/t_i is proportional to N_i. In either case, the sample must be large enough to provide a sufficient number of cases for each subgroup, and in particular to ensure adequate representation of households in the 'extremely low' and 'very low' access categories. This can only be achieved either by increasing the sample size and hence the cost of the survey, or by designing the sample so as to increase the probability of selection of households in these subgroups.

Consider for example the design of a telephone survey of residents of one of the state capital cities. Particular telephone number codes are allocated to particular areas and by matching these areas to the Census Collector's Districts (CCDs) or Local Government Areas (LGAs), the latest Census data could be used to provide details of household characteristics within telephone code areas. The sample could then be designed to give a greater probability of selection to telephone code areas with a greater proportion of households in the low-telephone-access categories, with appropriate weights being applied, to form population estimates.

It should be noted that the AID analysis showed differences between capital cities, between states and between metropolitan, urban and rural areas within the subgroups specified in Table 7.2 so that some stratification by area would also be required in a statewide or national sample. Sydney and Melbourne households have a relatively high level of telephone access across all subgroups, with Adelaide households also relatively high among 'high access' households. Households in Queensland in particular have low access levels. Within states, households in the capital cities and in rural areas are generally more likely to have a telephone service than those in 'other urban' areas.

The post-stratification procedure suggested above ensures that selected characteristics estimated from the sample match those of the population, but further research is required to validate the usefulness of this approach in estimating other characteristics. Many face-to-face interview surveys include a question on telephone access, and these data provide a valuable source of information on the differences in attitudes, behaviour and other facets of residents of telephone and non-telephone households. By comparing estimates made from the responses of these two groups, the variables in which significant differences are found can be isolated, and suggested procedures for adjusting for the differences can be tested. In this way we would gain knowledge of those characteristics which could be estimated using a telephone survey rather than through the more costly face-to-face interview.

What this comparison ignores of course are the differences in response that might arise through the method of data collection itself, and there is certainly a requirement for extensive evaluation on that topic. In fact once levels of telephone access become sufficiently high, this is the only major problem facing the user of telephone surveys. Nevertheless, if there are significant differences between estimates obtained from telephone users and non-users which cannot be adequately reconciled when there is no difference in survey method, what hope is there of achieving comparable results when different methods are used?

8

T. A. CUTLER AND K.F. SHARP

Telephone interviewing in Australia: some aspects of using the telephone network

Telephone interviewing has emerged as a cost-effective survey method largely because of developments which facilitate the interfacing of telephone networks and computer facilities, and the provision of economical trunk services such as Wide Area Telephone Service (WATS) which facilitate centralised interviewing and the application of sophisticated computer-assisted techniques.

The potential of these developments for survey practice is illustrated in experimentation with the use of interactive cable systems, and videotext services such as Prestel, for the remote administration of computer-based questionnaires in respondents' homes. More immediately, technical developments have facilitated the growing use of computers both for call generation and 'on-line' coding of interview responses.

In the United States the availability of WATS has contributed greatly to the economic attractions of telephone surveys. WATS simply involves providing outward access to an extended area for a fixed charge, thus enabling centralised interviewing at a reasonable cost. At present Telecom Australia has not announced any plans to introduce a WATS service. (WATS or OUTWATS is a completely different service from the INWATS service that has been introduced.) Changing attitudes to WATS in the US have a definite bearing on the prospects for such a service in Australia.

In America there is evidence of moves either to severely restrict the WATS service or to eliminate it altogether. It would appear that telephone companies there are under increasing pressure from the Federal Communications Commission (FCC) to reduce the tariff differential between WATS lines and trunk rates. This is in line with the general FCC policy that pricing differentials for services are only justifiable if they can be related to cost differentials. Given that WATS is, in reality, only a bulk discount on calls, it is now being viewed as discriminatory tariff that contravenes trade-practice moves to restructure regulations. Any move to restructure the tariffs would, of course, undercut the advantages of the service to users, including survey researchers.

PRIVACY AND CONTROLLING THE USE OF THE NETWORK

The growing use of the telephone network for unsolicited 'commercial' calls, whether they represent market research surveys or direct selling campaigns, has promoted widespread discussion about whether such calls represent an invasion of privacy. Telecom itself receives many complaints about such 'nuisance' calls, particularly when the person called has a silent line. Most of the problems raised tend to relate to the issue of privacy within its wider social context and the general concern about the misuse of personal information in computer databases. Special difficulties with telephone calls relate to such questions as the often inconvenient timing of calls and the intrusiveness of calls which represent an invasion of people's lifespace. Problems also arise in establishing the legitimacy of a call and the credentials of the caller.

Various groups have argued that the use of the telephone for some types of unsolicited calls should be restricted. One solution advanced by the NSW Privacy Committee was for Telecom to print an asterisk alongside the directory listing of subscribers who wish to give notice that unsolicited calls are unwelcome. Besides being somewhat impractical from Telecom's point of view, such a solution would not help in the case of the growing use of random digit dialling to generate calls.

Telecom itself, as a public utility charged with providing a public network service, is not competent to impose far-reaching restrictions on the use of the network. From a business point of view, the increased traffic generated by commercial calls for market research is attractive to any telephone company. This is, however, counterbalanced to the extent that, over time, such calls disrupt and dislocate established patterns of telephone usage.

Given the difficulty of establishing practical mechanisms to regulate unsolicited commercial calls, it is likely that many telephone subscribers will begin to take corrective action themselves. Not only are public concerns about privacy likely to be reflected in response rates to surveys, but there is likely to be a growing and wider interest in the type of call-interception and screening facilities already widely used in the business sector. Recent surveys by Telecom have found considerable consumer interest in such possible services as: the visual identification of the caller; calling-party number identification; centralised call-intercept and message store-and-forward systems; and centralised call-filtering services where only nominated calling numbers are accepted.

The interest in such services reflects some people's active concern to control the manipulation of the telephone by other people. The widespread adoption of mechanisms for screening incoming calls would have a direct and obvious effect on telephone surveys and the accessibility of particular groups in the community.

TECHNICAL CONSTRAINTS OF THE ACCESSIBILITY OF SURVEY POPULATIONS BY TELEPHONE

Telephone penetration and the incidence of telephone ownership has been widely discussed as a source of survey bias. In addition, the question of the *accessibility* of survey populations by means of the telephone raises difficult technical problems affecting the actual achievement of a desired sample through more or less 'random' diallings.

Table 8.1 contains the latest available estimates (1979–80) of telephone ownership by household. As other chapters present more detailed discussions of telephone ownership, only a few general points need be made here. These survey estimates of telephone ownership show that 75.8 per cent of Australian households have a telephone. These cross-tabulations show significant variations in the geographical distribution of ownership, particularly between town and country.

In terms of sampling bias, it is particularly important to characterise non-owners. From various studies we know that important categories of non-owners include migrant groups, low-income families, and the mobile, migratory groups who are presently denied 'ownership' by limitations of the technology. In sociological terms, many of the non-owner groups represent the 'information poor' who, irrespective of ownership, are unable to use telephone services effectively. This relatively large group contrasts with the small elite of the 'information rich' who account for the bulk of telephone usage.

In considering such figures it is essential to bear in mind that telephone surveys sample telephones, not people. The sampling problem is one of the accessibility of a relevant population by means of the telephone, and is not necessarily a simple question of household telephone ownership. What matters is whom you can contact by means of a telephone. To labour this point slightly, the accessibility of people to researchers is very different from the accessibility of the telephone to

Table 8.1   Household telephone ownership by areas of Australia

Area	Household has phone		No phone in household	
	No. ('000)	%	No. ('000)	%
New South Wales				
Sydney	822	79.7	210	20.3
Newcastle/Wollongong	108	73.0	40	27.0
Rest of NSW	276	65.8	143	34.2
Victoria				
Melbourne	743	83.7	144	16.3
Geelong	28	74.0	10	26.0
Rest of Vic	217	72.0	85	28.0
Queensland				
Brisbane	246	76.3	76	23.7
Rest of Qld	214	62.1	130	37.9
South Australia				
Adelaide	263	79.5	68	20.5
Rest of SA	96	66.8	48	33.2
Western Australia				
Perth	172	79.1	46	20.9
Rest of WA	95	69.9	41	30.1
Tasmania				
Hobart	41	73.4	15	26.6
Launceston	15	55.2	12	44.8
Rest of Tas	35	67.9	16	32.1
ACT				
Canberra–Queanbeyan	75	81.6	17	18.4
Total Australia	3447	75.8	1101	24.2

Source: Telecom Australia and Roy Morgan Research Centre (1981)

people and users. This is evident from the use by non-owners of Redphones in flats and shops, public telephones, party lines, mobile services, and so on. For the researcher, the initial telephone contact will always be just one step in the screening of respondents.

The question of telephone penetration and ownership is only part of a larger problem for telephone surveys: the fact that the population of telephones cannot be directly related to any population that is relevant to a particular survey. This is simply a function of the way the telephone network is technically organised. This is well-illustrated by two examples which are very relevant to the conduct of telephone surveys: the allocation of number ranges, and the categorisation of working services by telephone exchange.

In the first stage, the available number ranges within any one exchange area are determined by a complex set of technical factors. The allocation of numbers from these working ranges to any particular terminating point results in the random distribution of numbers in a radial pattern from the exchange which bears no relationship to the 'identity' of a subscriber. There are exceptions where groups of numbers (rotary groups) are reserved for specific purposes, although these allocations are not likely to be consolidated within any one numbering module. The discontinuous allocation of numbers across a number range creates particular problems for random digit dialling, as will be discussed below.

Second, it is useful to look at the way working telephone services are categorised because this highlights the problems in differentiating a subgroup of telephone numbers related to the population requirements of a survey sample. Not all exchange working services are subscriber services. In addition to subscriber services there is a proportion of working services and number allocations. These include a fixed 5 per cent of capacity retained as working reserve (this allocation might be increased in cases where traffic volume exceeds switching capacity); Telecom test lines; number blocks reserved for special connections; effective reserve capacity available to meet anticipated new demand; and cancelled numbers held for a fixed period before reallocation. The effective number occupancy of telephone exchanges will vary significantly over time as new number blocks are installed as part of the forward provisioning program.

Working subscriber services can be divided into the three categories of business, non-business, and Telecom lines (including coin telephones). The estimated proportion of services in each category for the Melbourne and Sydney metropolitan areas is shown in Table 8.2.

Table 8.2   Categories of telephone services

	Melbourne (1980) %	Sydney (1980) %
Business	27.8	24.4
Non-business	70.9	74.1
Telecom	1.3	1.5

The technical organisation of the telephone network therefore makes it difficult to identify any one specific population within the whole population of telephone numbers and working services. Survey researchers have attempted to solve this problem in two ways. Telephone directories can be used to differentiate subscriber populations for sampling, or alternatively, some form of random digit dialling can be used to derive a relevant population sample from the overall telephone population. It is interesting to look at each of these techniques in terms of the probability of achieving an effective interview.

TELEPHONE DIRECTORIES

Both Yellow Pages and White Page Alphabetical directories are used. Yellow Pages directories can be used to separate business populations and special-interest groups. The directory listings of business telephone services, however, tend to underrepresent large businesses. Small businesses often have more than one number allocated to them, whereas large businesses often have a single number servicing a large and complex switchboard. The White Pages' alphabetical listings can be used to separate 'non-business' and, in more complex sampling using exchange area prefixes, regional subgroups of 'non-business' subscribers.

Some of the sampling problems of these directories centre on the fact that the White Pages does not clearly distinguish between business and private 'residential' services. Also, there are special problems associated with two-line households, two-household 'families', silent lines and unlisted numbers.

It is estimated that at present about 0.5 per cent of residential services represent a second service in a household. The forecast potential demand for a second line (not extensions) will lead to sampling bias through the overrepresentation of these households. It is also estimated that about 1.5 per cent of residential services represent multiple residence connections. Once again this leads to the overrepresentation of those households. An estimated 2.5 per cent of services are silent lines which do not appear in directory listings. (For the Sydney metropolitan area, 2.2 per cent in 1980 against 1.4 per cent in 1975.) It is difficult to estimate any recent growth in the number of silent lines because of inadequate statistics and the unknown effect of a recent surcharge of $10.00 per annum applied by Telecom.

Any directory becomes increasingly inaccurate during its currency as new services are connected and existing services are cancelled. Amendments to directory entries do not represent a problem because the telephone number will still be listed. In the case of cancelled service, however, some proportion of listed numbers will cease to be working services because the number will not be reallocated until the next directory issue. In the worst case, and using calculations based on the 1980 Sydney White Pages as an example, some 25.5 per cent of services might not be accessible from the directory sample, either because a service exists not without a listing or because there is a listing but no service.

In general the overall 'churn' in directory entries does not present a sampling problem as long as a listed number continues to be a working service. What does affect sampling is the probability of achieving an effective population sample since a directory sample may give access to as little as 69.5 per cent of the population of telephones.

RANDOM DIGIT DIALLING

The use of various forms of random digit dialling involves even more problems for deriving a survey sample. One of the main problems is to minimise the number of calls made to non-working numbers and to non-subscriber working services. Some simple calculations will show the probabilities of achieving an effective interview.

If one were to assume 80 per cent number occupancy in a metropolitan area, and given the ratio of business to non-business services, the probability of an effective call would be 0.81. The probability of getting a domestic working service would be 0.56; and the probability of getting a business service would be 0.24.

The usefulness of digit-added dialling in reducing the probability of ineffective calls is limited by several factors. Numbers are often allocated individually. Numbers, when allocated in blocks, are allocated in different-sized blocks, and numbers are often allocated from all parts of available number ranges.

CONCLUSION

It is difficult to estimate the overall probability of effective calls within the Australian telephone network because of the variations in both occupancy levels and the ratio of business to non-business services. This difficulty is well illustrated in Table 8.3 which shows the distribu-

Table 8.3 Exchange service population distribution (service type by exchange area, 1980)

Exchange district	Business services %	Non-business services %	Telecom services %	Total %
A	15.9	83.2	0.9	100
B	87.8	4.0	8.1	100
C	86.8	6.6	6.6	100
D	29.2	69.2	1.6	100
Total for region	54.7	40.9	4.4	100
Total for metropolitan area	24.4	74.0	1.6	100

tion of the population of exchange services across four exchange districts within a region of the Sydney metropolitan area. This table clearly shows that, exchange by exchange, the problem of sample design is acute. For example, in area B the probability of getting a residential service is 0.04. If a researcher had designed a study on the average probability within the metropolitan area as a whole, up to 18.5 times more calls would be needed to achieve a required sample than would have been budgeted for at the design stage. Of course, the distribution across service categories also highlights the problems of sampling validation: how does one interpret non-answering as either non-response or a number outside the population of interest?

9

T. A. CUTLER AND K.F. SHARP

Telephone interviewing: the meaning of the medium

Interviewing is a special form of communication. All the classic texts on interviewing include discussions on how 'dysfunctional' communication habits might be controlled for within the situation of a structured interview. In order to be able to control the communication that takes place within the context of an interview, however, the processes of communication need to be well understood. But virtually all reviews of methodological developments in survey research begin by noting that many basic questions remain unanswered:

> Before major advances can be made, it is necessary to learn more about what happens in the interview situation and to develop some theories about the cause and effect sequences that occur. (Cannell, Marquis and Laurent, 1977)

In this chapter it is argued that in the case of telephone interviewing, the medium of the telephone has significant effects on the interview situation. This has important implications for the conduct of survey research by telephone.

One of the questions raised in this chapter is how survey researchers can reconcile the evidence from communications research about the significance of media effects with research into techniques. A comparative review of the literature on telephone interviewing and the literature on mediated communications shows that there is considerable divergence between the issues being investigated. In many cases the research findings tend to be contradictory.

Within the field of survey research most of the comparative studies of telephone and other data collection methods concentrate on the comparability of survey results arrived at by the different methods. The starting point with research into mediated communications is the investigation of the internal dynamics of communication processed within the various contexts of human interaction. An examination of the communication process, particularly where that process is mediated by artefacts of technology, is necessarily concerned with the question of construct validity. Some theories of communication would suggest that 'communication' *is* construct validation. Evaluation of interviewing-as-communication would therefore involve establishing the necessary conditions for question validation. At the stage that telephone interviewing is applied to survey research, however, it seems difficult on logical grounds to test for construct validity and to establish a legitimate 'range of convenience' for telephone interviews as a survey device. In comparative field studies of data collection methods the question of validity seems to have been translated into one of survey reliability.

Anyone working in the area of telecommunications has a particular interest in trying to reconcile the different thinking that distinguishes research work in the area of telephone interviewing from that being carried on in the area of communications research. This apparent divergence poses some real difficulties. The research techniques used within Telecom Australia, for example, are at the same time the subject matter of its research studies. This situation does, however, provide a useful perspective from which to ask reflexive questions about the nature and meaning of the telephone as a medium for interviewing. We present here the results of some studies of the telephone as a communications medium and suggest some hypotheses about the dynamics of a telephone interview. If the medium does matter, and if there are systematic differences in the way people use the telephone in communicating, then it becomes quite important for researchers to consider the implications for data collection by telephone.

RESEARCH INTO TELEPHONE INTERVIEWING

In reviewing the literature on telephone interviewing it quickly becomes evident that one of the greatest obstacles to coming to grips with the subject is the initial problem of information overload. Contributions come from a diverse range of interests and cover applications varying from psychoanalysis and welfare counselling to commercial market research studies and public opinion polls.

Table 9.1 provides us with a cross-section of available literature on telephone interviews. The incidence of publications on a given topic is ordered by date of publication to highlight any shifts in the focus of discussion over time. Despite the volume of the material, the range of issues discussed is somewhat restricted. Few publications cannot be fitted into one or other of the eleven categories used. Half the published literature is accounted for by the three categories of sampling, interviewing techniques, and the comparison of survey methods. These studies express considerable consensus on the issues of telephone sampling, special telephone sampling techniques, and comparisons

Table 9.1   Categorisation of reviewed literature relating to telephone interviewing by topic and date of publication

	undated	1940	1950	1960	1970–74	1975–79	1980–	total	%
Application to surveys	—	2	1	7	8	17	2	37	9.4
Telephone ownership	5	1	—	4	2	7	—	14	3.6
Sampling methods	—	—	—	6	11	34	5	61	15.6
Response rates	—	—	1	4	4	24	5	38	9.7
Privacy	—	—	—	—	—	2	1	3	0.8
Usage and behaviour	2	—	1	5	2	8	4	22	5.6
Increasing techniques and effectiveness	1	3	3	8	8	35	4	62	15.8
Assisted techniques	2	—	—	—	3	8	—	13	3.3
Survey comparisons	5	—	6	18	10	33	3	75	19.1
Telephone counselling	—	—	—	1	—	14	12	27	6.9
Telephone selling	—	—	—	—	7	3	—	10	2.6
Other	30	—	—	—	—	—	—	30	7.6
Total	15	6	12	53	55	185	36	392	—
%	3.8	1.5	3.1	13.5	14.0	47.2	9.2	—	100.0

with other interviewing techniques. Indeed, given the considerable effort that has been devoted to investigating these issues, it is rather surprising that there has been so little debate and disagreement. One possible explanation of this might be the restricted capability of these studies to examine rigorously the relation of media variables to survey results. Perhaps more effort should have gone into looking at the distinctive characteristics of different interviewing media within the context of the function of sample survey research. In other words, the literature suggests that telephone interviewing has mainly been assessed within, rather than tested against, the prevailing notions of validity widely accepted in survey practice.

An equally noteworthy feature of Table 9.1 is the finding that 56 per cent of the literature has been produced since 1975. There can be little doubt that this is related to the rapid emergence of telephone interviewing as a widely used survey method. This probably accounts for the dominance of issues such as sampling and comparability as part of a process of legitimising telephone interviewing as against the more traditional methods of interviewing and data collection. Over the time series there appears to be a shift in emphasis from general discussions of the application of telephone interviewing to the detailed examination of techniques and augmented computer-assisted systems.

The survey of the literature relating to telephone interviewing leads to several conclusions. There is extensive discussion of a limited amount of issues; there is considerable consensus about these issues; and critical reference to theoretical models of survey research is absent, or at least lacking.

MEDIATED COMMUNICATIONS

As in the case of telephone interviewing, even the most superficial scanning of the literature on communications shows a disarming array of books and articles. To some extent this reflects the broadness of a subject with no natural boundaries. Even when such a review is limited to the literature concerning the role of the medium in interpersonal communications (thus excluding 'broadcast' media) and excluding all the literature on technical aspects of the media, there is still a great volume of publications representing a wide range of perspectives. Titles range from *Understanding Media* (McLuhan, 1964) with its intriguing chapter on the telephone, to *Electronic Meetings* (Johansen et al., 1979), from *The Social Psychology of Telecommunications* (Short et al., 1976) to the *Social Impact of the Telephone* (Sola Pool, 1977).

The range of issues canvassed is equally diverse. This is well illustrated in the critical review of recent research on electronic meetings conducted by Johansen and others (1979). For the purposes of this review electronic meetings were defined as 'alternatives to face-to-face meetings involving small group communication through an electronic medium': 127 research studies were analysed, all but eleven of which were conducted in the last decade. Table 9.2 shows the diversity of that research effort:

Table 9.2 Interviewing research

Type of study	Frequency
Theoretical reviews and discussion	9
Literature reviews	28
Laboratory experiments	48
Field trials	23
Surveys	20
Descriptive analyses (by participants/observers)	16

Almost all this work concentrates on the role of the medium in telecommunications: discussion of the research results takes a variety of forms and the terms of the debate diverge. Some researchers concentrate on differences in conversation protocols and discussion procedures in order to discern and explain differences between media. Others study the appropriateness of different media for different activities or tasks. Laboratory experiments have been carried out comparing different media in terms of individual task completion, and surveys have been conducted to assess the substitution of telecommunications for travel. While some researchers generalise their results to various societal impacts of different media use, others restrict their analyses to individual attitudes to the ease of use, and perceived outcome of using, different media under certain circumstances.

Throughout this research there is significant disagreement based on contradictory evidence. As one researcher (Sola Pool, 1977) observes, the telephone has puzzling and evasive impacts contradicting the many hypotheses which have been put forward to explain its effects on society.

Two areas of research can be used to illustrate the dimensions of this disagreement. In the debate on travel/communications substitution, one end of the dichotomy is represented by the 'telecommunications as a travel substitute' position. It examines the occasions and conditions under which this substitution effect is apparent. Those maintaining this position argue that for certain communication events telecommunications is totally adequate and, therefore, able to be substituted for travel. At the other extreme, those arguing the complementarity of telecommunications and travel marshal evidence for the way the two apparently complement each other within any communication environment. The second example concerns the conflicting evidence on the appropriateness of the telephone for particular tasks. The telephone is in turn judged to be either satisfactory or unsatisfactory for 'forming opinions of others' (Young, 1974; Stapley, 1973), 'persuading others' (Stapley, 1973; Short, 1973), 'generating ideas' (Williams, 1975; Craig and Jull, 1974) and a variety of other tasks. It is arguable that reference to a well-developed theory of communications may resolve many of these areas of apparent conflict, and this leads to a further feature of the telecommunications literature.

Much attention has been focused on theories of communication. An attempt in 1957 to integrate the theoretical literature (Cherry, 1966) only served to highlight the complexity of the subject and the diverse range of issues pursued by researchers from a variety of disciplines. The extensive and continuing discussion of theories of communication involves explicit recognition of the inadequacy of models being used and of the fact that the development of a recognised, comprehensive body of knowledge is still at a formative stage.

All the research, however, suggests that the outcome of all mediated communication can be significantly affected by the medium of communication. This is recognised by applied researchers and theoreticians alike. Thus, the literature is primarily concerned with the direction and amount of influence exerted by the medium. It can be hypothesised, therefore, that the medium is never 'transparent' to communicators but is always open to both conscious and unconscious manipulation. Further research conducted by Telecom Australia supports this hypothesis.

In summary, several consistent themes emerge from the literature on the role of the medium in communications. The discussion of the topic is diverse and there is often disagreement on the relevance of issues; research produces much contradictory evidence on media effects; significant effort is devoted to formulating theories of communication; there is general agreement that the medium affects interpersonal communications. Above all, little has been done to weld the growing bodies of knowledge in interviewing theory and of the role of the medium in communications into a cohesive whole.

THE TELECOM EXPERIENCE: THE MEDIUM MATTERS

The preceding review of the literature on both telephone interviewing and mediated communication highlights some interesting differences between the two areas. The literature on mediated communications starts by examining the proposition that the medium affects communication processes and proceeds to investigate the nature of these effects. The literature on telephone interviewing suggests that survey researchers assume media effects have been accounted for and the major variables are somehow controllable in survey practice. The continuing debates among communication researchers suggest that it might be very necessary to look again, and perhaps in different ways, at the media effects on interviewing and their implications for survey techniques.

The nature of the questions addressed in Telecom's market research program has provided a useful perspective on the problems of reconciling these different viewpoints. The distinctive feature of research into telecommunications is that the subject matter and the methodologies converge. All the research into Telecom's markets has indicated that the medium is important. The discussion that follows presents the results of studies that not only point to the importance of media effects but also suggest some of the kinds of problems that might constrain the effective use of the telephone in survey research. Such an assertion is not unequivocal. Much work remains to be done before the power of these suggestions can be understood.

Telecom's Line Quality Study

Telecom's Line Quality Study was initiated in response to a need recognised within the organisation to assess the technical standards of line quality against the customers' opinions of what constituted 'good'- and 'bad'-quality telephone lines. The quality of any local telephone connection is affected by two factors—the drop in the speech volume level from one end to the other, and the amount of spurious noise introduced to the connection from a variety of sources. By carefully controlling and manipulating a number of key technical conditions, various combinations of these two detrimental factors were tested, thus simulating the full range of 'quality' as it is experienced within the local telephone system. Customers were asked to respond in a variety of ways: to the 'volume', 'noisiness', and general 'quality' of each interview telephone call. As it was believed that the interviewers would also contribute to the assessment, they too were asked to respond to the same questions. After rigorous training of interviewers and testing of the questionnaire the study proceeded with a survey of some 3000 customers.

All respondents answered the questionnaire in an apparently meaningful way. The conditions referred to (noise, volume levels and general quality) were concepts which were clearly recognised by respondents—Telecom's complaints area is further evidence of this. At no stage was the medium totally 'transparent', at least at the quality level offered by local telephone call conditions in the Australian network.

Significantly, interviewers rated the telephone connections as inferior when compared with the rating given by customers. Figure 9.1 shows a comparison between the two response sets on the 'volume' dimension. Even at 'optimum' conditions interviewers gave a higher frequency of adverse ratings ('too loud' or 'too quite') to particular connections (see Table 9.3). The same result was obtained for the 'noisiness' dimension and the general 'quality' dimension (see Table 9.4) It was hypothesised that this result might be explained by the interviewers' wider experience in telephone usage and, consequently, their familiarity with how good a 'good call' could be. An analysis was therefore undertaken of customers' opinions by categories of telephone usage (see Figure 9.2). Although a general trend towards high users being more critical is

Figure 9.1 Adverse opinion (too loud/too quiet) of loudness by measured loudness of line

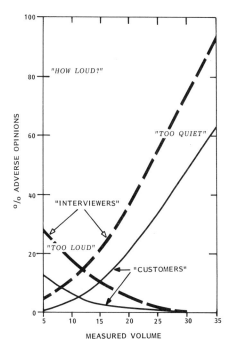

Table 9.3 **Adverse opinion (too loud/too quiet) of loudness of three 'optimum' volume levels**

	% Adverse opinions	
Volume level	Customers	Interviewers
1	13	59
2	13	32
3	19	38.5

Table 9.4 **Negative opinion of line quality for four categories of line quality (line quality a composite of volume level and spurious line noise)**

	% Negative opinion	
Line quality	Customers	Interviewers
1	4	6
2	8.5	14
3	12	29
4	28	50

Figure 9.2 **'Intolerable' rating of line quality by telephone usage**

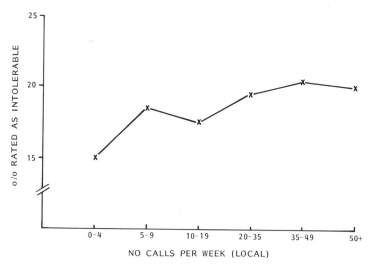

apparent, it is not statistically significant and does not appear to explain the difference in interviewers' opinions. From the results of this study it can be hypothesised that the distinction lies in the different *tasks* involved. Furthermore, it appears the task involved had an asymmetrical effect on the rating of line quality.

A field trial of new telephonist headsets

Evidence about the effects of line quality and the 'intrusiveness' of the telephone as a medium emerged from an extensive field trial designed to establish users' requirements of a new model of telephonist headset. The trial, which was conducted over a period of nine months (1978–79), involved a sample of 270 participants at five locations representative of the range of situations in which headsets are used. This study looked at telecommunications-usage behaviour in work contexts not at all dissimilar to Computer-Assisted Telephone Interviewing. In each area telephonist functions were associated with VDU operation at varying levels of complexity, such as airline bookings and reservations, newspaper classified advertisements and Telecom Directory Assistance.

The surprising result was the overwhelming importance of factors associated with the telephone medium itself in comparison to the specific aspects of the terminal equipment which was being evaluated. Line quality, volume control, and the integrity of message transfer emerged as critical variables, but the quality of voice reception or line quality was consistently rated as the most important factor in the evaluation of headsets. Ratings of the quality of voice reception became progressively more negative during the trial, and as many as 51.5 per cent of respondents described themselves as being 'slightly hard of hearing' or 'rather hard of hearing' *within* their work context. Only 12 per cent of these associated this problem with a physiological condition.

Tolerance for inadequate line quality was inversely correlated within the complexity of the information transaction and the level of precision required in the transcriptions of data. It was found that the different impedance characteristics within the range of transmission levels effect distortions in the relative clarity of speech elements. Where the total accuracy of transcribed information was essential, awareness of and problems with line quality were highest.

The study showed that these media effects significantly increased the level of difficulty experienced with cultural mismatches of speech habits and accents between an operator and the other party, the impact of background noise, and fatigue and information-processing errors with extended calls.

Telecommunications control studies

It became apparent from a number of other Telecom studies that a wide cross-section of telephone users were either consciously or unconsciously using the telephone to create a 'communications environment'. This manipulation was achieved by the way in which they used the telephone or in their expressed preference for particular features in a telephone system, and was discernible in both business and domestic situations. Two specific studies provide evidence of this manipulative use of telecommunications media. These involved research into business facilities and the Brisbane Telelink Trial.

In research aimed at determining the facilities required of a business telephone system a high level of demand was associated with features such as 'calling party identification', secretarial interception, call-transfer facilities and selected intercom facilities. While these features were initially justified (and could probably be paid for) on the basis of savings in telephone costs or time, the reasons were supported by others related to communications control.

In this respect some facilities were reported as being needed to provide a controlled communications environment where calls could be screened and only those 'permitted' would be allowed to enter that environment and be connected. This phenomenon is similar to situations described in Toffler's *Future Shock* as a response to information overload—in this case communication overload. Other facilities were apparently required to reinforce the perceived role of the user within the organisation by making an individual accessible to a greater or lesser number of other individuals. This acts as a status barrier created through the manipulation of communication channels. Finally, some facilities were reported as necessary to create an objectively perceived organisation and management structure through control of communications. While McLuhan in *Understanding Media* suggests that the telephone breaks down organisational barriers, the selective manipulation of the telephone can, and often does operate in the opposite direction.

This 'telelink' trial, conducted by the Brisbane City Council in 1974–75 with support from Telecom, involved the participation of socially isolated, housebound people in regular 'group conversations' by means of telephone conference facilities. After 'meeting' in this way for six months, the participants decided to organise a face-to-face gathering. This turned out to be a complete failure. Some interesting reasons were advanced to explain this. The telephone link was preferred because it did not necessitate 'dressing up' to appear respectable to others. Apparently respectability could more easily be conveyed over the telephone. Also, because of age or illness some participants know themselves to be physically unattractive but found that such features became irrelevant in the case of telephone contacts. Some participants were indeed surprised and dismayed to find that the others did not match their 'images' of them.

The telelink groups, it was found, had been able to manipulate the telephone to create adaptive social support systems; the purported limitations of the telephone as an audio-only medium served to increase its effectiveness in this context. 'Getting to know someone' by means of this telephone link meant developing a construct of the person from verbal and vocal cues alone; each participant was able to manipulate an 'image' depending on his or her trust and confidence in other group members.

These findings about the manipulation of affect were confirmed in subsequent field trials, and agree with findings from the growing body of research in the area of telephone counselling. Hence the difficulty of controlling for affect poses problems for the maintenance of proper client–counsellor role relationships. The fact that the telephone interaction is unverifiable, ambiguous and deniable is undoubtedly the reason why such services attract many of their clients. On the other hand, professional counsellors complain that too many telephone sessions 'degenerate into conversation' (Lester, 1977).

At the very least, Telecom's research into 'Telelink' and the studies of user requirements for business communication facilities show how people do actively manipulate telecommunications to gain organisational, operational, and emotional control over their communication and social environments. In all these cases the medium is not only visible, but it is also manipulated to secure specific behavioural outcomes.

Telephone usage behaviour—a usage-segmentation study

A study was commissioned by Telecom in 1977 to segment the market for telephones and calls. Because the research started with the question of what phone usage does or does not do for people in the actual act of phoning, many of the results are of particular relevance to a discussion of telephone interviewing.

This work confirmed the findings of previous studies about the importance of the telephone as a medium. Importantly, the telephone is shown *not* to be a 'phoney' substitute for face-to-face communication. Convincing evidence is marshalled to suggest that the telephone, together with its essential ambiguity as a communication channel, has to be seen as a unique medium in its own right.

The significance of this study lies in the attempt to bridge the gap between a purely scientific understanding of the telephone as a medium and an understanding of this medium within the context of its use. The results demonstrate convincingly that people use the telephone for different purposes, and that different people converse differently over the phone even when it is used for the 'same' purpose.

In this study the telephone market was segmented in terms of three distinct types of telephone usage. Two of these types are relevant to the present discussion. They are business callers making work-related calls, and social callers making personal calls.

Work-related usage is where the telephone is used very pragmatically as a tool for getting information and controlling people's activities. Such usage, which may be regarded as networking, involves the coordination of actions and decisions with other people. It is all about 'playing the system' and is outcome-oriented with little concern for the personal experience or satisfactions of the communication. This type of usage is associated with busy people—managers and administrators, energetic middle-class women, aggressive skilled working-class males—who have mentally demanding jobs, crowded schedules, or who are anxious to influence what goes on about them.

The style of telephone call is best characterised as a 'talking telegram'—brisk, short, straight to the point. It is obviously just for this type of user that Parkinson promulgated his Telephone Law:

> The effectiveness of a telephone conversation is in inverse proportion to the time spent on it.

Lapses into a 'conversational mode' are not encouraged, and usage behaviour is not sensitive to affect.

The *command*, or demand, is the typical communication associated with work-related calls. The command, and the response to the imperative of that command, is the purposeful message exchange that is characteristic of bureaucratic communications. This type of communication is asymmetrical because the initiator and recipient cannot interact on equal terms. The outcome required by a command is a response, not a reply. While the context of work pressures dictate that most people will use the telephone in this manner in specific situations, the study characterised some 17 per cent of the survey sample as being predisposed *only* to use the telephone in this way.

Within the segment of social callers a telephone call is not so much a means to an end as an experiential end in itself. These users are primarily interested in the telephone *conversation* in so far as it satisfies personal needs through the affirmation of social relationships. The phone is not seen as a tool, but as a 'friend': the medium of a telephone conversation acquires a 'social presence' as 'sensitive', 'warm', and 'personal'. The conversational mode of personal/social usage is ideally suited to 'keeping up with what's going on in the world', to the reassurance of self-image. Calls tend to be long, rambling, and indeterminate.

The *question* forms the basis of the interaction that constitutes a *conversation* in this style of usage. It is a sort of independent reciprocal behaviour carried on by two or more parties. In personal/social telephone calls the conversation is characterised by its *complementarity*: the conversation is an interaction that is negotiated by the parties as it proceeds.

While this type of usage is widespread—with a considerable overlap with work-related usage—the study identified some 10 per cent to 12 per cent of the population as being exclusively predisposed to it.

The results of this study show clear links between call type, message type or style and the characteristic communication behaviours of different groups within the population. Figure 9.3 summarises the finding that while most people were associated with mixed-type telephone behaviours, as many as 25 per cent of the population could be characterised as having a personal predisposition to an 'extreme' type of usage behaviour.

Such findings pose some intriguing questions about the use of telephone interviewing. What is the effect on interviews of the different attributes of the telephone as a friend or as a tool? What of the difference between an outcome orientation and an experience orientation on the part of respondents? What is in store for survey interviewers calling samples of business people during the day and the same or other people at home during nights or weekends?

Since different people appear to be predisposed to use or respond to a telephone call in different ways, what effect might this have on the interview process and the validity of responses? What sort of people should telephone interviewers be? In considering the questions raised in this review of some of our research, it is helpful to refer to a simple

Figure 9.3 Types of usage behaviour

BUSINESS CALLERS	MIXED TYPE	SOCIAL CALLERS
(est. 10 -12% population)	(est. 75 - 80% population)	(est. 10 - 12% population)

• Telephone usage is OUTCOME oriented	• Telephone usage is EXPERIENCE oriented
• Usage as "Commands + Demands"	• Usage as "Conversations"
• Telephone viewed as "tool"	• Telephone viewed as "friend"
• Communication is Asymmetrical -	• Communication is reciprocal -
"the talking telegram"	"the social chat"

149

model of the process of mediated communication as a way of developing further insights into the impact of the medium on telephone interviews.

A MODEL OF COMMUNICATION

Any model of the communication process should perhaps begin by accounting for the interaction between two people. Many widely used models do not start from this point; such pervasive cybernetic models as Shannon's theory of communication imply that people can only function as 'noisy' impediments to effective information transfer. Nevertheless, those models which have proved useful in social science begin with man as a communicator and then look at the extent to which media technologies introduce 'noise' into human discourse. One such model which has proved its usefulness in many fields is Newcomb's A-B-X model depicted in Figure 9.4 (Emery and Emery, 1975).

Figure 9.4 A model of the communication process

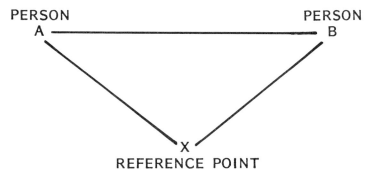

In this diagrammatic representation of the communication process X is the 'objective' reference point for the interaction between two people. This model presupposes that people can only interact or communicate with respect to something. This point, in fact, is seen to constitute an essential precondition for successful communication. Successful communication can only take place if two people can reach agreement that some object or thing is the common reference point for their interaction. Otherwise two people literally do not know what they are talking about.

Within this model the following relations are important: the extent to which X is an unambiguous referent for both A and B, and the extent to which A can develop a perception of B and BX and to which B can develop a perception of A and AX. For successful communication to take place between A and B there must be congruence between XA and XB. In the absence of this agreement, 'noise' and 'communication breakdown' results.

TELEPHONE INTERVIEWING AS COMMUNICATING

This model of communication is equally useful in elaborating the interview situation. In this instance the communication is asymmetrical as the communicants, the interviewer and respondent, take particular parts in the communicative act. Figure 9.5 represents this situation:

Here the interviewer has a topic X which he is representing through the telephone to a respondent for some sort of response. The respondent reacts to his perception of what the interviewer is presenting: X'. The congruence between the two, X, X', is a measure of the com-

Figure 9.5   Interviewer and respondent communication

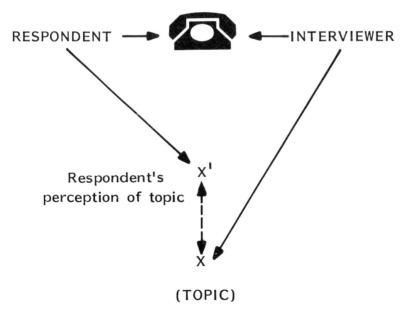

RESPONDENT ⟶ ⟵ INTERVIEWER

Respondent's
perception of topic   X'

X

(TOPIC)

munication achieved and of the *validity* of the interaction between subject and interviewer. It is the measure of the 'interview' achieved.

In the interest of objective research it is the interviewer's topic X which represents the 'reality' or the objective topic of the communication. All communication is based on adjusting the respondent's perception of this reality X' so that it matches the subject of the interview, thus giving the interview its validity. It is in this way that the communicative act is asymmetrical.

As with the previous communication model, congruence is achieved by positioning the topic in conceptual space through the use of referents common to both interviewer and respondent. Again this specifies the asymmetrical nature of the communication. The interviewer is not free to negotiate his topic (at least in questionnaire surveys) and so it is left to the respondent to do so. Where the topic X has obvious referents available to the respondent he will be able to achieve this congruence (i.e. $X'=X$); where a respondent has no useful outside referents the communication will be incomplete, $X' \neq X$, and no 'interview' will have been achieved. In this latter case, a response to a question may well have been elicited, but with little or no validity. This represents the standard problem of the validity of research questions.

So far this discussion simply describes interviewing as communication. However, where this communication is mediated by the telephone—a highly visible and manipulable medium—the interaction takes on a further dimension.

THE IMPACT OF MEDIUM USAGE IN TELEPHONE INTERVIEWING

While it is generally agreed that the medium affects the outcome of any mediated communication, the Telecom research shows that it affects individuals differently, but systematically, in their actual behaviour. In the interview situation these effects result in a response to the task involved in quite different terms, and involve the defining of the interviewing task in distinct ways. At one extreme the interview is dealt with as a 'business call', while at the other it is seen as a 'social conversation'. These task definitions have implications for both the way the interview is conducted and for the meaning the respondent places on the response he gives.

It is stressed that this phenomenon is the result of the medium itself, as a visible and objective intervening entity which provides the opportunity for individual responses of this kind. The medium becomes an object which can be manipulated so that it is either the tool or the friend of the respondent in his or her personal adaptation to the communication event. This is not to suggest that the extreme types described are wilfully manipulating the situation or being dishonest. But it does suggest that this 'telephone style' is an integral part of their definition of what happens during an interview. Nor can this process be controlled by a researcher through manipulation of interview techniques or devices; if a respondent cannot operate in a way which is adaptive to him, he or she will refuse to participate at all.

Using the previous model of the communication/interview process it is possible to describe the behavioural outcome of an interview with both the extreme types of telephone users, 'business callers' and 'social callers'.

The 'business caller' respondent will react to the telephone call as a means of accomplishing some end or outcome. He will define the interview as the business of handling this call, rather than attempting to establish an interview. He will therefore react to his initial understanding of any question and will tend to ignore any other referents being used to establish the validity of the subject matter of a question as simply noise. To him, all questions are precoded (albeit by himself) and he will assume that the interviewer has the right coding frame. To use the earlier analogy, he will 'read this telegram'.

Using the labelling of the model, X is irrelevant. It is the respondent's X' which is the subject matter of the interviews. Referents to X are therefore irrelevant (noise) and the link $X - X'$ is nonexistent in any case where the referents to X' do not automatically coincide with those of X.

The 'social caller' respondent will react to the caller—the interviewer—in a sociable manner as a means of making the whole interview a social event. The conversation itself takes precedence and again no attempt is made to establish an interview. The subject matter of any question is irrelevant except as a vehicle for affirming the social relationship of the conversation. He or she responds to the interviewer in any way which will make the experience of the call more pleasant and sociable. He or she will be preoccupied with the conversation and not the interview. Both X and X' are irrelevant. Referents to X will be based on the $A - B$ interaction and X will not be located in conceptual space but in emotional space.

In both these cases the outcome of the communication is affected by the medium in a way which has serious implications for researchers. In neither case is question validity relevant or capable of being established. The meaning placed on the event is internal to the respondent and is only at best coincidentally related to any objectivity associated with the interview. The medium, and the way in which these types respond to it, defines the message of the event.

In summary, the following characteristics are likely to be associated with each of these extreme types of telephone styles:

Business caller	Social caller
1 Resents calls and avoids answering	Welcomes calls and attempts to answer first
2 Establishes quickly and intuitively what the call is about	Seeks to establish who is calling through conversation
3 Completes the business in hand narrowly and quickly	Keeps the conversation going and tries to extend it
4 Call takes on format of 'talking telegram'	Call format amounts to a social experience
5 Ignores elaboration of questions and offers no comments	Seeks elaboration of questions by seeking comment from interviewer
6 Views call suspiciously and suspects manipulation	Welcomes call as another opportunity to respond socially
7 Ignores 'probes', silences, etc	Elaborates on 'probes' rather than answer and fills silences with 'warm chit-chat'
8 Views telephone as 'cool' medium	Views telephone as 'warm' medium
9 Makes short calls only when necessary to achieve an end, although this will happen frequently	Makes long calls whenever the opportunity for conversation occurs
10 Uses the telephone frequently as a tool	Sees the telephone as a friend

SOME GENERAL CONCLUSIONS

'Interviewing is communication' has been taken as the starting point for so many discourses on interviewing methods that it has become a truism. Certainly most models of the communication process are applicable to discussions of interviewing, yet even here the literature is almost totally devoid of attempts to make explicit any models of interviewing as communication and to develop a set of appropriate theoretical constructs.

This chapter attempts to take seriously this initial proposition and to investigate its implications. While the terms of debate in the fields of survey research and communication research are often incompatible, the research conducted by Telecom and by others points out serious anomalies which would seem to have significant implications for telephone interviewing. Telephone-communication behaviour is very much a matter of personal style for a large part of the population and as such is beyond the power of the researcher to control. Yet this style of telephone usage is intimately related to the outcome of any communication event in a way which raises questions related to the validity of many areas of investigation by means of the telephone. Furthermore, current research into the question of the validity of telephone interviewing has centred on comparisons between media and has proven to be inconclusive—to have found differences between media would have been conclusive, but having found none simply leads back into the area of validity and is not enough to be definitive.

On the other hand, communication research quite definitely claims that media differences are real and systematic. Furthermore, since communication is about validity, this research throws doubt on the use of telephone interviewing techniques and their application across the full range of research interests.

The general conclusion of this discussion, therefore, must be that there are many basic issues to be investigated and reconciled before telephone interviewing can claim the legitimacy it so desperately seeks. It is perhaps pertinent to ask why researchers are apparently willing to overlook these anomalies in their haste to adopt this economically attractive technique.

It is not suggested that the baby be thrown out with the bath water. Communications theory suggests that telephone interviewing has its perfectly legitimate areas of application. These are the areas where little or no construct validation, or 'rich' communication, is required within the interview situation. Yet even in these situations the use of standard research strategies, such as interviewer training, interview protocols, the use of 'probes' or 'comments' sections, interview length and the interpretation of response rates, require serious reassessment.

In summary, the main points of this chapter can be listed almost as a dichotomy of issues under the headings of 'Communications Research' and 'Techniques Research':

Communications research	*Techniques research*
1 The medium affects the outcome of mediated communication.	The medium has no effect on the results of interviews.

Communications research	*Techniques research*
2 The medium affects behaviour in a way which raises problems of construct validity.	No comment.
3 The medium affects different tasks in different ways.	It is assumed that media have universal application and validity.
4 Communication protocols are important in controlling the outcome of interaction.	Agree (but little empirical research has been undertaken).
5 For a part of the population, the outcome of a communications event is based on media 'usage style' and is thus highly personal. Researchers are therefore unable to predict or control outcome validity.	The ability to predict outcome validity has been assessed in ways which prove to be inconclusive.

FURTHER RESEARCH

From the points made in this discussion it is apparent that further research is required into telephone interviewing techniques at two levels. First, at the theoretical level more work is required in developing an understanding of telephone interviewing as a communications process. This work should consolidate the results of research in the areas of communications and interviewing and develop appropriate models, thus facilitating the identification of areas for further fieldwork. This work would also involve the development of appropriate strategies for testing hypotheses which would emerge from such a synthesis.

Second, further empirical work is required in a number of areas to test hypotheses which emerge from discrepancies in existing research. This includes: telephone interview applications and the 'range of convenience' of the techniques as a survey method; subject validity; interviewer training; interviewer methods and protocols; questionnaire design and length; response rates and response styles.

Within the communication area much more work needs to be undertaken to elaborate the concept of 'usage style' and to attempt to generate population descriptors for the various 'usage-style segments'. Finally, it is worth noting that most of the research on telephone interviewing has been conducted within the US. There is much evidence to suggest that cultural differences exist in communications behaviour as reflected by the significant difference in ownership and usage patterns between the major communicating nations (USA, Canada, England, France and Australia). This would suggest that similar cultural differences may affect the use of telephone interviewing, and this may prove to be a fruitful area of research.

10

P.J. KORBEL AND I.R. BELL

Fieldwork methodology: a survey of research buyers' concerns and doubts

In the business of market research one of the most costly areas, both in time and money, is fieldwork. How often do we sit down and really analyse the problems we are going to create by the use of one technique to collect the data we need, as opposed to another? If anything, we do the opposite—the agency or the client recommends that the study should be carried out by door-to-door interviews, or group discussions, or whatever, and then justifies the selection by listing various benefits of the selected technique and why it is therefore the most *suitable* way to conduct the fieldwork. Rarely, if ever, do we go through the more valuable process of eliminating techniques as being *unsuitable* because of the concerns or doubts we have about their ability to provide us with the data we need.

It was with this in mind that we approached the New South Wales Division of the Market Research Society to conduct a survey of research buyers to understand better the doubts and concerns they have about the validity and reliability of data collection techniques. The study was conducted under the auspices of the Society and questionnaires were mailed out for self-completion by research buyers who were members of the Society's NSW division. Eighty-seven completed questionnaires were returned and it is the results of these questionnaires that are presented here.

A profile of respondents revealed that up to 90 per cent had either supplied or commissioned group discussions, and that over two-thirds had experience of the other primary methods of data collection: face-to-face and telephone interviewing and mail surveys. The modal group of respondents had had more than ten years' experience in market research and two-fifths controlled market research budgets exceeding $100 000 annually (some 30 per cent did not know, or refused to specify the value of the research budget).

CONCERNS ABOUT VALIDITY AND RELIABILITY

Respondents were first asked to give their own concerns and doubts about the validity and reliability of various standard data collection techniques.

Group discussions

Concerns about group discussions were in three main areas: response accuracy and representativeness; moderator skills; and respondent selection.

As to the actual responses and opinions gained during a group discussion, a third of research buyers were concerned about the influence of a dominant personality within the group and how peer-group pressure will affect the individual respondent's expression of his or her own thoughts and beliefs, while the representativeness of opinions due to the group situation and the homogeneity (or lack of it) of the respondents was questioned by a quarter of research buyers.

It appears that this area of concern is related to the notion of the whole being greater than the sum of its parts, but in this instance there is a concern that the whole (the group response) bears any relation at all to its parts (the individual respondent's own opinions).

A third issue stimulates a concern about the reliability and validity of research buyers! We find it astounding that 20 per cent of our sample were concerned that they could not quantify the data from group discussions and extrapolate to a total population. It is heartening to know that they realised that they could not quantify; but it is staggering to know that they should even want to, and want to to such an extent that they should label this as a concern about the validity of group discussions as a technique. We feel this shows a complete lack of understanding of the role of group discussions and the uses to which they should be put. What compounds the problem is that this response did not come from those who had never had any experience of group discussions. In fact, it was quite the reverse: the response came exclusively from those who claimed some experience.

Almost one in three buyers (30 per cent) had misgivings about the experience and skill of group moderators, while one in four were concerned that the results of a group discussion-based study depended too heavily upon the interpretation put upon the discussions by the moderator. We see this as a fundamental area. We believe the value of a group discussion is closely linked to the skill of the moderator in eliciting information and with his or her ability to interpret information beyond merely reporting what was said to provide conclusions and recommendations—however extreme they may appear. Furthermore, these conclusions and recommendations should be seen as the starting point and not as the end of the research process.

The third major area of concern expressed by buyers was related to respondent selection and recruitment. Given the relatively small samples involved in group discussions, 25 per cent of buyers reported misgivings about how respondents are actually selected and recruited, while one in six (16 per cent) raised the uncomfortable spectre of the 'professional respondent'. Again, this is a fundamental problem. The validity of a discussion depends heavily upon the correct recruitment of respondents. Incorrect or shoddy recruitment can lead us to make totally invalid hypotheses and can ultimately lead the client to question the real value of group discussions.

There are perhaps many ways in which these concerns and doubts can be allayed, ranging from the decision to conduct group discussions in the first place through to how the brief should be prepared and how the results are to be presented.

Two suggestions are relevant to the main fears uncovered in this study. First, in the area of response accuracy and moderator skill, it is up to both the client and the agency to build up a close working relationship so that each realises and respects the skill of the other. The 'moderator' will continue to be simply what the word itself means—a mediator between the consumer and the client. But interpretative ability and willingness to make recommendations based on sound marketing knowledge is something more. The client has to be prepared

Table 10.1 Concerns about group discussions

	Total (N=87) %
Bias from peer group pressure/dominant personality	33
Skill/experience of group moderator	30
Representativeness of data/participants	26
Interpretation depends on moderator	25
Sample selection/recruitment	25
Extrapolation of data/can't quantify	20
Professional respondents	16
Misuse of technique/used for wrong things	7
Artificiality of group environment	5
Affinity groups	5
Lack of accurate reporting	3
Others (less than 3 per cent each)	13
Don't know/no experience	6
None	2

to accept and pay for that skill in hiring a skilled qualitative researcher and this is probably what is expected of the agency.

Second, on the issue of group recruitment, it should be standard practice among agencies to use a fully detailed recruitment questionnaire to establish respondent qualifications. The completed questionnaires should be made available to the client well before the group begins.

The full list of concerns about group discussions can be seen in Table 10.1. It is worth noting that only 2 per cent of buyers said they had no concerns or doubts about group discussions as a research technique.

Individual in-depth interviews

The major fears expressed about in-depth interviewing were related to the skills and qualifications of the interviewer (Table 10.2). More than one in four (28 per cent) of the total sample, and more than one in three (39 per cent) of those who had actually commissioned this technique, were concerned about substandard, underskilled and underqualified interviewers.

One in five (22 per cent) of all buyers and one in four of those who had commissioned in-depth interviews, doubted the objectivity and lack of bias on the part of the interviewer. Fourteen per cent of the

Table 10.2 Concerns about individual in-depth interviews

	Total (N=87) %
Unskilled/underqualified/bad interviewers	28
Interviewer objectivity/bias	22
Inability to quantify	17
Fictitious responses (to impress)	14
Interpretation depends on interviewer	10
Poor/biased sampling	9
Questionnaire design/poorly structured	9
Artificiality of interview situation	8
Misuse of technique by data extrapolation	8
Poor recruitment/respondents not meeting specifications	6
Standard of interpretation/generalisations drawn	6
Expensive technique if done correctly	3
Inexperienced researchers and companies	3
Don't get range of opinions/points go unmentioned	3
Others (less than 3 per cent)	28
Don't know/no experience	8
None	8

sample were concerned about fictitious responses (and presumably the lack of ability on the part of the interviewer to perceive them), while 10 per cent felt that the results of in-depth interviews relied too heavily on the interviewer's interpretation. The warning signs here are very clear: the research agency must train and provide, and the client must insist upon and be prepared to pay for, specialised interviewers who are experienced in the special skills of in-depth interviewing.

Again, the 'let's quantify the unquantifiable' brigade came through: 17 per cent complained about the inability of in-depth interviews to be quantified. This was countered somewhat by the 8 per cent who complained that the technique was misused because the results they received were quantified!

Door-to-door interviewing

The major concerns about validity and reliability of door-to-door interviewing were interviewer quality, sample and response bias, and fieldwork control. The strongest single concern expressed by buyers was related to the use of poorly trained, inexperienced interviewers— mentioned by over a third (38 per cent) of the total sample and by a half (47 per cent) of those who have commissioned a door-to-door survey (Table 10.3).

This is clearly a serious problem, and the research industry as a whole is aware of it. The Market Research Society has produced an

Table 10.3 Concerns about door-to-door interviewing

	Total (N=97) %
Poorly trained/inexperienced interviewers	38
Non-response/refusal rate	32
Gaining a representation/non-biased sample	24
Control and supervision of callbacks	22
Fictitious/boastful responses	15
Biased sample due to non-working/non-busy respondents	13
Badly planned/designed/over-long/complex questionnaires	9
Control of sample selection	8
Only good for short/superficial response	8
Respondents' lack of privacy	5
Cost of obtaining valid sample	5
Others (less than 3 per cent each)	20
Don't know/no experience	3
None	1

excellent Fieldwork Handbook and last September started an Interviewer Training Scheme at the NSW Institute of Technology in Sydney. However, the MRS will be limited in what it achieves unless the research agencies are more active in training fieldforces. Wherever possible, the client should become more involved by attending a formal briefing session.

The issue of sample and response bias emerged in several ways, the most frequent of which was the concern about low response rates—mentioned by a third (32 per cent) of buyers. This subject is a crucial area which will have obvious effects on the progress of market research worldwide. Also, a quarter of our sample (24 per cent) were concerned about the inability or difficulty in obtaining a representative sample by door-to-door fieldwork, while 13 per cent were concerned by the likely oversampling of 'at-homes' such as housewives and pensioners, particularly since most door-to-door interviewing is carried out during daylight hours.

Other concerns in this area were about how the sample is chosen (mentioned by 8 per cent) and the fear of fictitious responses (mentioned by 15 per cent). In the related area of fieldwork control, one in five (22 per cent) of buyers doubted the existence or effectiveness of controlling and supervising callbacks.

Perhaps there is no easy solution to these concerns. In a broader sense, the onus is on both the client and the agency to discuss all areas of sampling and how problems like respondent selection and response rates will be dealt with for each specific study, *before* going into the field. Too many clients leave it entirely to the agency and complain when something goes wrong—if indeed they are fortunate or intelligent enough to be aware that something has gone wrong. Clients should demand to see call record sheets, and completed questionnaires. They have every right to do so. If nothing else, they will at least have their eyes opened to the problems that the agency has in achieving what is often considered to be the straightforward and simple task of speaking to a 'good cross-section of the population', whatever that means.

Street interviewing

The main concern about street interviewing (Table 10.4) was the inability or difficulty of obtaining a representative sample, mentioned by one in four (26 per cent) of buyers. Specific concern was expressed about the bias resulting from the location, the day, and the time of interviewing (mentioned by a further 14 per cent). If a strict quota sample is set and the locations and times of interviewing are varied, the required sample should be achieved. There is no law that says street

Table 10.4 Concerns about street interviewing

	Total (N=87) %
Gaining a representative/non-biased sample	26
Short time factor leads to scanty response	23
Non-response/refusal rate	18
Fictitious/boastful responses	16
Poorly trained/bad interviewers	15
Biased sample due to location/day/time	14
Bias in respondent selection by interviewer	9
Only suitable for short topics	9
Depends on research topic/objectives	3
Others (less than 3 per cent each)	26
Don't know/no experience	14
None	3

interviewing, with adequate controls, will not achieve as good a sample as any other means of face-to-face interviewing.

A strong concern was mentioned by a third of our sample (32 per cent) that street interviewing is only suitable for a short interview. Perhaps with this technique it is a matter of selecting the fieldwork most appropriate to the study being conducted.

One in five (18 per cent) were concerned about non-response and refusal rates, whilst 16 per cent had misgivings about the possibility of fictitious responses. Fifteen per cent were concerned about poorly trained interviewers and the possibility of cheating by interviewers.

Telephone interviewing

Almost one in three (30 per cent) had misgivings about a biased sample due to non-telephone households (Table 10.5). In hindsight it would have been interesting for us to have obtained estimates of telephone ownership rates. Perhaps most would have found themselves to be sadly wrong. This is an area where our own company has undertaken some intensive investigations. Others like Roger Jones of the ANU Survey Research Centre, Telecom, STC, and the Roy Morgan Research Centre have also conducted detailed investigations.

Speaking on our own behalf we are in a position to give the best possible estimate of private-dwelling telephone ownership in Australia. We put this at around 85 per cent overall and around 92 per cent in metropolitan Sydney and Melbourne. Perhaps these figures destroy much of the myth about the so-called 'high' percentage of non-

Table 10.5 Concerns about telephone interviewing

	Total (N=87) %
Biased sample due to non-telephone population	25
Lacks face-to-face contact/no visual cues	22
Non-response rate	18
Short interviews limit scope/depth	16
Fictitious/'expected' responses	15
Skill/calibre/training of interviewers	14
Refusal rates	13
Lack of control over respondent selection	12
Can't show products or prompt cards	9
Poorly structured/designed/over-long questionnaires	7
Biased sample (non-specific)	5
Others (less than 3 per cent each)	26
Don't know/no experience	6
None	6

telephone households. There is little doubt that a bias operates in terms of socioeconomic status, where the so-called 'lower' groups are certainly underrepresented. However, anyone who conducts telephone surveys should be aware of this fact and cater for it by post-weighting of results if the demands of the target sample warrant it.

A less predictable concern emerged as the second most frequently cited and was mentioned by 22 per cent of the sample. This was the lack of face-to-face contact and the belief that the quality of the interview would be reduced by the inability of the interviewer to note and record any visual cues given by the respondent. Our response is one of surprise that there appears to be a sizeable number of research buyers who believe that in a face-to-face interview the interviewer takes notice of visual cues and that if she does, she actually records them in the questionnaire.

Another concern shown in Table 10.5 was non-response rates (mentioned by 18 per cent) and refusal rates (mentioned by 13 per cent). Our comment here is that our experience over the last two or three years has shown a response rate for telephone interviewing of 60 per cent on first calls compared to less than 30 per cent for face-to-face interviewing.

A further concern, mentioned by 16 per cent of buyers, was that telephone interviews must be short in length and limited in depth. Again, our experience shows we have successfully conducted telephone interviews of up to 30 minutes in duration and have covered the most sensitive of topics, including attitudinal and image questions.

Central location interviews

As might be expected, the most significant concern to emerge in relation to central location interviewing was that of gaining a valid random sample. Forty-three per cent of buyers questioned the representativeness of the sample, while a further 16 per cent felt the sample would be biased by the overrepresentation of non-working, non-busy respondents (Table 10.6).

Table 10.6   Concerns about central location interviewing

	Total (N=87) %
Non-random/biased sample	43
Rushed atmosphere affects response	17
Sample bias due to non-working/non-busy respondents	16
Poorly trained/non-supervised interviewers/cheating	12
Non-response/refusal rate	10
Depends on purpose of research/product tested	10
Artificial/noisy environment	9
Fictitious response	7
Lack of privacy for interview	3
Others (less than 3 per cent each)	12
Don't know/no experience	14
None	8

Perhaps we would all agree with that concern and that there is no effective way of totally overcoming the problem. Interviewing on Thursday evenings and Saturday mornings helps, as does interviewing over weekly lunchtimes. However, we must balance the benefits of being able to show a product display, conduct a taste test or research a television commercial with the drawbacks of the difficulty in gaining a representative sample. In many instances, of course, the sample specifications will be very suitable for central location testing.

The only other major concern (mentioned by 17 per cent) was that limited time led to the interview being conducted in a rushed atmosphere and therefore affected the depth of response. Again, this is something we must accept, and the design and length of the questionnaire should reflect this.

Mail questionnaires

The uppermost concern about the use of mail-out questionnaires is obviously the low response rate. Table 10.7 shows that this concern was

Table 10.7 Concerns about mail questionnaires

	Total (N=87) %
Low response/return rate	59
Biased response towards those interested in subject	24
Non-representative sample	14
Respondents' willingness to be accurate	13
No control of/don't know who completes questionnaire	12
Validity relies on respondent comprehension	12
Poorly designed/structured questionnaires	10
No way of assessing respondents/selection criteria	9
Administration of questionnaire can't be controlled	3
Increasing costs/expensive technique	3
Lack of visual/physical contact	3
Others (less than 3 per cent each)	14
None	2

expressed by 59 per cent of the sample. Even with the use of incentives, it is unlikely that the response rate will be greater than 30–40 per cent (as shown by this study itself in which some 227 questionnaires were mailed out and only 87 were returned—a response rate of 38 per cent).

A further problem mentioned by one in four (24 per cent) of buyers was that the sample was likely to be biased by the fact that those who are most interested in the topic are most likely to return the question-naires. The 'silent majority' are unlikely to put pen to paper.

Other concerns were that the accuracy of response and questionnaire completion would be affected by the respondent's willingness to cooperate in the survey (mentioned by 13 per cent), the fact that we do not know who actually fills out the questionnaire (12 per cent) and the validity of data which relies heavily on the respondent's own under-standing of the questions (12 per cent).

Again, this is an area where we must accept the limitations of the technique and balance them against the benefits to be gained by using that technique. The important thing is to be aware that these limitations exist and make every effort to allow for them in the way the survey is set up, administered and interpreted.

TRENDS IN THE USE OF RESEARCH TECHNIQUES OVER THE NEXT TWO YEARS

Respondents were asked to rate each of the data-gathering techniques on a 5-point scale in terms of how they felt the use of that technique would progress over the next two years. The results are shown in Table 10.8.

Perhaps the most significant result was the vast difference in trends over the next two years in the use of telephone versus door-to-door interviewing. Two-thirds (68 per cent) of research buyers believe that telephone interviewing will gain in popularity. It is perceived to be the one technique which will show the greatest increase in use over the next two years. In comparison, 40 per cent of buyers believe that door-to-door interviewing—for so long the major quantitative approach—will drop in popularity: it is perceived to be the one technique which will show a real decrease in use over the next two years.

The future of street interviewing, again one of the classical styles of fieldwork, would also appear to be somewhat in the balance, with research buyers evenly split about its progress over the next two years. Central location interviewing would appear to be set to show an increase in use, while the group discussion—ever-popular in Australia—would also appear to have a rosy future.

PERCEIVED COST-EFFECTIVENESS OF RESEARCH TECHNIQUES

Respondents were asked to rate each technique in terms of 'cost-effectiveness' or 'value for money', using a 5-point scale. Table 10.9 suggests there is the very high correlation between the relative positions of the various techniques in the cost-effectiveness ranking and the previous ranking of trends in the use of each technique. Telephone interviewing again emerges with the top rating, while door-to-door is again rated the least cost-effective.

Although it is clear that the cost of each technique has had a considerable influence on research buyers' perceptions of how the use of these techniques will progress, we sincerely hope that other issues such as the quality and the suitability of an approach to a particular need have also entered into the research buyer's mind. No one will benefit if the decision about what technique to use for a particular study is based solely on cost.

We hope that the results of this review of research buyers' opinions towards fieldwork methodology will be regarded as important. If nothing else, it highlights the obvious need for buyer and supplier to discuss the benefits and drawbacks associated with each fieldwork approach and to work together to arrive at the most suitable methodology for a particular study.

Table 10.8 Progress in data-gathering techniques

	Telephone %	Groups %	Central Location %	In-Depth %	Mail %	Street %	Door-to-Door %
A great increase	32	9	3	16	13	2	2
A slight increase	36	43	33	23	31	18	17
Stay the same as now	12	30	37	25	24	43	33
A slight decrease	8	8	8	18	15	18	32
A great decrease	2	2	—	2	8	5	8
Don't know	9	8	18	15	9	14	7
Mean score	+0.96	+0.53	+0.39	+0.38	+0.28	−0.05	−0.28

Note. The mean scores have been calculated on a +2 to −2 scale, with 'don't know' responses being omitted from the base for each calculation.

Table 10.9 Relative cost-effectiveness of different techniques

	Telephone %	Groups %	Central Location %	In-Depth %	Mail %	Street %	Door-to-Door %
Very good	20	20	9	20	2	10	6
Good	40	32	25	21	21	22	16
Average	16	28	35	22	36	25	37
Poor	10	12	8	16	20	18	26
Very poor	5	2	3	7	5	15	6
Don't know	9	7	20	15	17	9	9
	+0.66	+0.59	+0.36	+0.35	−0.04	−0.06	−0.11

CONCLUSIONS

Several conclusions can be made about what research buyers think about fieldwork procedures at present and in the future. Regardless of fieldwork methodology, there are two major concerns in the minds of those who pay for the research which suppliers provide. There is a genuine concern for the validity and reliability of our samples, and concern about the skill, qualifications and expertise of the interviewer is almost as strong. Although both concerns are of obvious importance, it is perhaps the latter which is more crucial to the progress of market research practice. In relation to sample validity we can justify the use of various statistical weighting procedures to arrive at the representation we require. In relation to interviewer quality, there are no such handy formulae which can overcome the weakness of a poor interviewer. It may be that it is the quality of the fieldforce—whether it be the part-time door-to-door interviewer or the omniscient group discussion leader—that will be the fulcrum upon which the rise or fall of market research in Australia balances.

E.K. FOREMAN

Appendix A: Workshop opening address

Melbourne, 18 November 1981

First let me say it is a great pleasure to be here to welcome all of you who are participating in this SSC/CASSR Advanced Workshop on Survey Methods. I must say at the outset that meetings on survey work of any kind are all too infrequent in this country. Perhaps there really aren't enough to us with a professional interest for them to be more frequent. Meetings on the subject of measurement, if I might use the general term, are even rarer—yet this is probably the most perplexing, and potentially the most rewarding, of all the studies in survey research methods.

I must first welcome on your behalf our principal guest, Professor Charles Cannell from the University of Michigan's Institute for Social Research. I might mention that I first visited the Institute in 1953 when it was pioneering some very difficult surveys in agriculture and consumer attitudes—they were very brave and novel surveys. I was pleased to be able to go there again ten years later and that was when I first met Charlie Cannell. I remember vividly one of the things that he made a point of showing me. It was their advanced work with computers, and in particular, developmental work on high-level languages, as applied to statistical surveys. This was of great interest because our Bureau at that stage was yet to get its first computer. In retrospect, you will realise that twenty years ago this was very advanced work. It is characteristic of the Institute that it has pioneered advanced work in all areas related to our craft and this meeting represents advanced facets of survey research which the Centre has continually shared with the research community.

Professor Cannell was one of the founders of the Institute, which today is certainly one of the oldest and most respected in the world. He is visiting Australia as a Fulbright Senior Scholar. The University of Sydney and Flinders University have conferred the honour of Visiting

Professor in recognition of his eminence. His visit was made possible through the support of the Australian–American Educational Foundation and we must owe that body a debt of gratitude for making this very useful meeting possible.

I must also welcome the workshop support staff. You will all have before you the list of distinguished people who have come here to assist in running this meeting. The careful work of that body of very skilful people is an essential for the organisation and success of the meeting. And finally I must welcome you all.

It is of interest to note that the balance among our 45 participants is fairly equal—people from industry, from the academic world and from government. I am also pleased too that some of my own colleagues from the Australian Bureau of Statistics have been able to attend this meeting.

You might like to know of the interest that our Bureau has in this meeting. Official statistical offices are thought of as being interested only in factual information. Perhaps to academic and business people this is understandable. They use it as background to many of their studies. You may think of this more factual information as the more straightforward part of survey work. But one particular problem has drawn us at the Bureau beyond factual or 'hard' information: what some people misguidedly call 'hard' information. Because of this problem, official statistical offices cannot avoid measuring some things that are not matters of fact. Matters of opinion, of expectation, satisfaction and approval are becoming increasingly important for survey research among official statistical offices. Ill-advised, ill-tested measurement methods could get us into a lot of trouble. Our Bureau is asked not infrequently to obtain statistics bearing on the likely use of some actual or proposed facility or service. If you think of an example, like the use of childminding centres—a big subject ten years ago—there are two kinds of questions to be asked. The first is, how many people are there who would qualify to use those services—that is, parents of children of the appropriate age? The second set of questions would elicit how many of them wish or are willing to use those services. That is not a 'hard' factual statistic: it is a matter of attitude and opinion. I suppose most of you have been in the position of having to ascertain answers to questions like, 'Would you use this service?' As you will know, asking that question is a good way of getting very misleading answers. A more skilful approach is necessary to obtain reliable answers to questions of that kind.

There is also another reason for our being interested in advanced measurement techniques. It is the need to appraise the answers we get to factual questions. When we appraise them skilfully, it can be horrifying to discover that asking what appears to be a straightforward factual question can produce answers that are by no means reliable. Appraising the questions we ask is another reason for our taking a very serious interest in survey measurement techniques. Of course, we are quickly drawn into other difficult questions. For example, the planning of household expenditure surveys, which incidentally were pioneered by the University of Michigan, requires not only a great deal of skill in devising suitable questions, but in developing techniques for appraising their validity as well.

A principal concern of this workshop which is perhaps not explicit in the preliminary list of topics is the validity and reliability of survey measures. It is one thing to talk about techniques; it is another thing to talk about their reliability. This is an underlying theme for many of the workshop papers and one of the principal concerns of the people organising this meeting, as it is to practitioners generally.

A highlight of the workshop program is the controversial subject of survey interviewing by telephone. I note that among the workshop supporting staff are officers of Telecom Australia. Their presence is very much appreciated. As an aside I should mention, as some of you perhaps know, that official statistical offices have been rather reluctant to use telephone interviewing. I should explain a particular reason for this. I do not mean to impune in any way the usefulness of the method, but merely to explain one of its possible limitations. In undertaking survey research—and most of you will be well-aware of this—the key statistics for which surveys are looked to provide are proportions of people, and proportions of households in the population that have particular characteristics. This means getting statistics from a representative sample of people, one representing the entire population. Consequently, official statisticians have to be very careful of their surveys' coverage and of the benchmarks they use for survey estimation, to make sure the statistics they obtain represent, and can be related to, the whole population. The most difficult aspect of telephone interviewing, as we understand it, is to be sure that the coverage of people about whom answers are obtained is actually in accordance with the coverage rules to which we must adhere in all of our survey work. Because of this, we are at present reluctant to use telephone methods. We want to see our informants to ask the coverage questions on the spot because it is often a matter of probing to find out who are the people occupying the dwelling and who should be included in our survey under the survey coverage rules. I trust that this is one matter to which you might direct some attention in this workshop. I have no doubt the problems will eventually be overcome. We are pursuing what we think is an obvious way of overcoming it; that is to visit each sample household once to establish the coverage to be accepted in successive surveys. But it is a difficult problem, one that is very important to official statistical offices—perhaps relatively more to them than to commercial survey firms or academic researchers.

In meeting here with you and reflecting on my own work, I cannot help thinking of the prophetic words of one of my teachers, William Edwards Deming, whom I had the pleasure of seeing not very long ago when he visited the Philippines for the International Statistical Institute meeting. Many years ago he was explaining to me the relationship between standard errors and biases, including measurement errors. He explained it in terms of a right-angled triangle—which he proceeded to draw. He pointed to the bias and the sampling error, reminding me that the square of the bias plus the variance of course adds up to the mean square error. He said then that we now know a lot about the calculation of sample errors. We don't know very much at all about the measurement of bias. He added that he didn't know how it could be done. Deming is a very big man and has a very deep voice. In his deep voice he concluded by saying, 'The last word on sampling has not yet been said.' Ladies and gentlemen, you will appreciate that this is still true 30 years later.

I must finally commend Terry Beed and Bob Stimson on their initiative in arranging this meeting and again thank Professor Cannell for being here to make this meeting, I am sure, an outstanding one. Ladies and gentlemen, I have very much pleasure in declaring this meeting open.

Appendix B:
Workshop conclusion

One of the fundamental problems affecting Australian survey research is the lack of a distinctive program of education in survey methods at the tertiary level. Very few institutions offer comprehensive courses in this area of growing importance. We are acutely aware of the difficulties the universities and colleges face in developing new teaching programs, but by holding workshops built around distinguished researchers we hope to provide a forum for change in both the classroom and the applied settings. The people who have participated in this first workshop represent a diversity of academic and applied interests and we hope they will pass on experiences gained here to their teaching and research colleagues.

Charles Cannell has given us a very intensive exposé of the state of the art in interviewing theory and techniques and his is unquestionably a view straight from the research frontier. The great strength of the Survey Research Center in Michigan is its ability to conduct applied survey research while at the same time advancing our theoretical understandings of survey practice. We are indeed fortunate to have spent the last three days sharing in the accumulated wisdom of Professor Cannell and his colleagues, all of whom have been pursuing the elusive goal of minimising total survey error for several decades.

In planning these workshops we felt everyone's interests would be well served by focusing on telephone interviewing in survey research. This proved to be a most appropriate decision, and to learn of the advances in this area at Michigan has been breathtaking. Professor Cannell's review of fundamental research into telephone interviewing will certainly have considerable impact among those who are now offering this service in their agencies, as well as among those who are contemplating its use or considering further theoretical research. Professor Cannell was very ably supported by Terry Cutler, Kevin Sharp and Roger Jones with their papers on aspects of telephone interviewing in Australia. All of these contributors have done much to sensitise us to the substantial problems of local application in this country. Yet this is no doubt that this technique of data collection will assume increasing importance in Australian survey practice. As Professor Cannell has observed, this is about the only area of real technical innovation in the survey business. We are fortunate that the workshops have presented much in the way of local experimental work, particularly at Telecom Australia. The lively contributions from the floor have teased out many details of these experiments which so often languish behind the closed doors of a government, commercial or academic agency. It is to be hoped that this spirit of experimentation and sharing of results continues.

As a workshop on interviewing theory and techniques we also felt it would be worthwhile exploring other areas of application outside telephone interviewing. Again, Professor Cannell set the framework for this with his coverage of response bias and validity, and of the role of the interviewer as well as the respondent. The papers by Ken Brewer and Bill Faulkner extended the range of these concerns by looking at some older and newer techniques of data gathering and verification. One of the very interesting things about Brewer's paper was his thorough documentation of an elaborate experiment. The fact that the hypotheses he set out to test were rejected is salutary. There needs to be more of the sort of communication about where things fail as well as about where they succeed. Faulkner's work on data-gathering procedures at the Bureau of Transport Economics again demonstrates the value of having run a workshop where progress with intriguing techniques can be aired in stimulating company.

Tony Cleland's 'grassroots' account of the role of panel or group discussions as a means of data gathering and problem circumscription makes many necessary points which we feel should be made over and over again. There is, after all, a real danger that many of the buyers of market research in Australia see group discussions as a complete substitute for surveys, complete with powers of estimation. In this regard Paul Korbel and Ian Bell gave a fascinating (and entertaining) insight into the current state of play in the consumption of market research services among buyers.

The fact that nearly 100 people have attended these workshops speaks of the interest such a program can generate. Unwittingly to us, the program has taken on a national flavour, with participants drawn from all over Australia. And this was no passive audience. They provided a stimulating setting for us as organisers, our workshop staff and their fellow participants.

By holding this and future workshops we hope that we can create a forum for people who are experienced in surveys as well as those who are not, and to bring together practitioners from the universities and colleges, the government and the private sectors. In this way these gatherings can operate more or less as a retooling and re-education process to redress something which is quite sadly lacking in Australia at the moment. Before we invite our distinguished guest to bring the proceedings of the last three days to a close, may we express our deep gratitude to our support staff for their contribution to what we regard has been a highly successful experiment in educational outreach.

WORKSHOP CLOSURE: C.F. CANNELL

I had the opportunity on Wednesday to announce the 'Invocation' and now I have to pronounce the 'Benediction'. I think that what we have been looking at during the last three days is a kind of basic problem that started when people first began to make up a few questions and send out a couple of graduate students to do interviews. Then they would suddenly announce great findings. In other words, survey research method is a deceptively simple technique—why can't anybody just sit down and dream up a few questions, send out a couple of graduate students or somebody's wife or something of this sort, take a few interviews, analyse the results, publish it up on nice stationery and call it a survey?

Something ranging from that type of endeavour to what we like to think of as a scientific survey are worlds apart. We would not attempt to do the kinds of measurement we presently do in other branches of science, because we would recognise the frailty of the method. If we conducted experiments in physics in which somebody sat down and designed a piece of equipment, used it a couple of times and then came up with a great theory, everyone would laugh him out of existence and say, 'That isn't science, that isn't anything.' We have some of these same problems of doing studies that really in many cases I suspect should not have been done.

I was interested in the last paper. I was interested in it because it seemed to me what the buyers of research were saying is, we are worried about the quality of our surveys. If I had been one of those 35 per cent who entertained this fear I think I would have responded the same way. I would have been worried about sampling; I would have been worried about response bias; I would have been worried about interviewer training. All of the things that those people were worried about, I would have been worried about. I am probably more worried about it than they are because I know the problems involved in it. I think they have spelled out the kinds of issues and the kinds of problems that survey research makes. It seems to me the solution is not to convince them that they are wrong to worry—because they are not wrong, they are right. The proper procedure here is to try to refine and develop the methods to the point where we don't have to worry about such things as response bias and non-response levels of 50 per cent or things of that kind. I was saying earlier that one could do haphazard surveys using a couple of graduate students, or gimmicky surveys could be done to put something in the newspaper just to amuse the public about whether gentlemen prefer blondes. For these surveys it just didn't make a lot of difference how good the methodology was—it wasn't important.

But more and more survey research is now being used for important government, business and academic decisions. Theories are being based on it in academia. Policy planners are using it in government. Important business decisions are being made on the basis of survey findings—hopefully not on surveys alone, but they have a heavy impact on the level and the type of decisions that are made. This seems to me to provide a really ethical and moral challenge to survey researchers to feel sure that when they give somebody data, they can stand in back of these data and say it is valid. In some cases it may mean that you have to say to the person who wants to purchase the research: 'I am sorry but the questions you are asking are either unanswerable or they are only answerable if we have money enough and time enough to investigate the methodology to be sure we can get good measures.' I feel very strongly about this. I think that this is the challenge of survey research. What do we do about it? It is clear that we are not going to stop doing surveys; we would all be out of business, or a lot of us would. Yet it is also clear that we are not going to get a million dollars to suddenly improve our methods. Furthermore, it is clear that even if we had a million dollars we could not solve all the problems at present facing us. Nonetheless, the responsibility rests on us to contribute to an improvement of methods.

My proposition is that we ought to commit ourselves to the idea that in each survey we conduct we will try to build in some small piece of methodological investigation. It does not even have to be something that is suitable for publication in the annals of science or anything of this sort. And incidentally, negative findings here are quite as useful as positive findings. Look at Ken Brewer's work—that was very useful. We all tend to think if things are negative they are not worth anything. They are worth something. We learn something from negative findings. I am surprised at how many ideas I have picked up today, and indeed over the last three days, by just talking with people. Somebody says, 'I did this at one time', and I say, 'Gee that is a great idea—I had not thought about this'. Now it is in these sorts of episodes that I believe the methodology of survey research is going to be improved.

Our first priority should be to insist on standards, to do surveys only when we can be reasonably sure we can come up with good data. Each of us should commit ourselves to doing small investigations and circulating them, sending them for example to one of the organisations sponsoring the workshops or in some way getting the information around to the rest of us. We will all benefit from that and this is the thought I would like to leave with you. It has been a pleasure to meet with you.

Appendix C: Workshop staff

CONVENORS

Dr T.W. Beed, Director, SSC, University of Sydney
Dr R.J. Stimson, Director, CASSR, Flinders University

WORKSHOP LEADER

Professor C.F. Cannell, Research Scientist and Program Director, Survey Research Center, Institute for Social Research, University of Michigan, Ann Arbor

WORKSHOP SUPPORT STAFF

Mr K.R.W. Brewer, Principal Research Scientist, Department of Mathematical Statistics, CSIRO, and Project Director, Schools Resources Study, Schools Commission
Mr E.A. Cleland, Senior Lecturer in Psychology and Research Associate, CASSR, Flinders University
Dr T.A. Cutler, Manager, Commercial Planning, Commercial Services Department, Telecom Australia
Dr H.W. Faulkner, Principal Research Officer, Special Studies Branch, Bureau of Transport Economics, Canberra
Mr R.G. Jones, Acting Head, Social Science Data Archives, Australian National University, Canberra
Mr P.J. Korbel, Director, Spectrum Research (NSW) Pty Ltd, Sydney
Mr I.R. Sharp, Manager, Market Research, Telecom Australia

GUEST SPEAKERS

Professor M.G. Taylor, Deputy Vice-Chancellor, University of Sydney
Mr E.K. Foreman, AM, First Assistant Statistician, Australian Bureau
of Statistics, Canberra

WORKSHOP RESEARCH ASSISTANTS

Ms L.D. Hayes, SSC, University of Sydney
Ms L.B. Gibbons, SSC, University of Sydney
Mr A.J. Goldsworthy, CASSR, Flinders University
Ms A.M. McKnight, Bureau of Transport Economics, Canberra

ADMINISTRATION

Ms P.F. Keane, Secretary, SSC, University of Sydney
Mrs B. Flynn, Secretary, CASSR, Flinders University

Workshop participants

Ms Elizabeth Ampt	State Transport Study Group, Sydney
Mr Gerry Bardsley	Australian Bureau of Statistics, NSW Office, Sydney
Ms Celia Berry	Hoare Wheeler & Lenehan, North Sydney
Ms Annie Burfitt	BIS Shrapnel Pty Ltd, Chatswood, NSW
Miss Lorna Chatterton	WD & HO Wills (Aust) Ltd, Sydney
Ms Rosemary Connell	Reark Research, North Sydney
Dr Brian Crabbe	Department of Psychology, University of Sydney
Ms Susan Edwards	Kuring-gai College of Advanced Education, Lindfield, NSW
Mr Murray Goot	Department of History, Philosophy and Politics, Macquarie University
Mr John Goodhew	Department of Economic Statistics, University of Sydney
Mr Allen Grant	Australian Bureau of Statistics, Canberra
Mr Geoff Hall	Telecom Australia, Queensland
Mr Peter Harrington	Illawarra Regional Information Service, Wollongong
Mr Chee Mun Hong	Telecom Australia, Sydney
Ms Margaret Kruse	Reark Research, North Sydney
Ms Julie Le Fevre	NSW Hospitals Planning Advisory Centre (HOSPLAN), Sydney
Mr Terry Lewis	Australian Bureau of Statistics, Perth
Mr Dennis List	ABC Audience Research, Sydney
Mr Kay Loong	Bureau of Transport Economics, Canberra
Ms Noeleen Lott	Australian Bureau of Statistics, NSW Office, Sydney
Mrs Pamela Manley	Sample Survey Centre, University of Sydney

Mr Rupert MacLean	Centre for Education, University of Tasmania
Dr Terry Purcell	Architectural Psychology Unit, University of Sydney
Ms Elisabeth Quinlan	Australian Bureau of Statistics, Sydney
Mr Barry Reardon	Australian Bureau of Statistics, Brisbane
Mr Neil Richardson	Agrimark Consultants, Sydney
Ms Concetta Rizzo	Law Foundation of New South Wales, Sydney
Ms Glen Rose	Australian Veterans' Herbicide Study, Sydney
Ms Jane Rothman	Traffic Accident Research Unit, Traffic Accident Authority, Sydney
Mrs Robin Rowe	Cottees General Foods, Gordon, NSW
Mr Michael Scott	The Treasury, State Statistical Coordination Unit, Sydney
Mr Graeme Sheather	Department of Administration, Social and Political Studies, Kuring-gai College of Advanced Education, Lindfield, NSW
Ms Elaine Simmonds	Market Research Centre, Brookvale, NSW
Ms Colleen Strotton	Traffic Accident Research Unit, Traffic Authority, Sydney
Assoc. Professor Wendy Walker	Department of Behavioural Sciences in Medicine, University of Sydney
Mr Brian Wallace	Retail Banking, Westpac Bank, Sydney
Mr David Watson	Research and Statistics Section, Department of Veterans' Affairs, Canberra
Mr Robert Whelan	Overseas Telecommunication Commission, Sydney
Dr Margaret Wilson	Education Commission of New South Wales, Sydney
Dr Robert Zehner	School of Town Planning, University of New South Wales

MELBOURNE WORKSHOP 18–20 NOVEMBER 1981

Mr J.K. Austin	School of Business, Prahran College of Advanced Education, Melbourne

Mrs Mary Baxter	Royal Melbourne Institute of Technology, Melbourne
Dr Floyd H. Bolitho	Department of Social Work, La Trobe University
Miss Carol Bottomley	Directories (Aust) Pty Ltd, Melbourne
Ms Jacinta Burke	Australian Broadcasting Tribunal, Melbourne
Mr Dennis Challinger	Department of Criminology, University of Melbourne
Mr Michael Christie	Preston Institute of Technology, Victoria
Mr David Collins	Australian Bureau of Statistics, Canberra
Mr P. Collins	Australian Bureau of Statistics, Adelaide
Dr Peter Dowling	Graduate School of Business, University of Melbourne
Mrs Barbara Evans	Department of Administration and Law, Swinburne Institute of Technology, Melbourne
Ms Eve Fesl	Aboriginal Research Centre, Monash University
Dr Cecily Gribbin	Division of Building Research, CSIRO, Victoria
Mr Rodney Hall	National Mutual Life, Melbourne
Dr Bruce Headey	Department of Political Science, University of Melbourne
Mr David Hill	Anti-Cancer Council of Victoria
Dr B. Kabanoff	Flinders University
Ms Geraldine Lazarus	Caulfield Institute of Technology, Victoria
Mr Steve Lettkowitz	Agricultural Extension Department, University of Melbourne
Mr John Miller	Bureau of Transport Economics, Canberra
Ms Debbie Neuhaus	Australian Bureau of Statistics, Canberra
Mrs Kym O'Neill	Hospitals Benefits Association Ltd, Melbourne
Mr Raivo Rahni	Department of Architecture and Building, University of Melbourne
Mr Jim Reark	Reark Research, Melbourne
Mr Lawrence Robertson	Department of Administration and Law, Swinburne Institute of Technology, Melbourne

Mr Chris Robinson	Swinburne Institute of Technology, Melbourne
Dr Hilary Schofield	Centre for the Study of Higher Education, University of Melbourne
Ms J. Schornikow	Australian Bureau of Statistics, Melbourne

Appendix D: Notes on the workshop discussions: Sydney

Small discussion groups were held on a variety of topics, including experimental design, self-administered and mail surveys, response rates, and survey ethics. The main points arising from these discussions are outlined below.

A EXPERIMENTAL DESIGN

Two workshops were held on the topic of experimental design. Similar issues emerged in both:

1 Attachment of methodological modules to a survey designed mainly for substantive purposes
   a Ken Brewer noted that this is typically achieved by dividing the main sample into random subsamples and applying one variant of the proposed methodology to each such subsample. Charles Cannell pointed out that this is rather easily achieved in the context of the telephone survey. In face-to-face interview surveys it is an advantage if each interviewer has parts of each subsample in his or her workload.
   b Two differing interpretations of the term 'experimental design' were raised. These were the use of surveys within experiments, and the use of alternative experimental techniques. Reservations were expressed about the experiment described by Cannell on commitment, feedback, and pace. These reservations related to differential effects depending on which item was considered, and the creation of a contrived interview situation by the techniques. In the light of these reservations, two suggestions were made. The first was the use of another group of interviewers not trained in the technique. The second suggestion involved

having a pre-test and post-test design, where the interviewers use both and do not use the new techniques. It was suggested that it would be necessary to alternate the order in which the interviewers used the techniques. This would lead to a large number of experimental groups. Ken Brewer discussed a survey on the role of women in CSIRO, in which three samples were used: females, and matched and unmatched samples of men. The three samples were used in order to overcome the confounding effects of age, seniority, and type of work.

2 Examples of models that could be used in methodological modules
  a Response level is equal to mean plus effect due to the length of the questionnaire. Null hypothesis: the length-of-questionnaire effects are all zero.

3 Control groups
  a It was noted that the term 'control group' was sometimes used incorrectly by clients to refer to a replication of the same survey techniques on another sample. (If both samples give the same answer, the client is reassured.) In other cases it can refer to another comparison group in the total population.
  b In methodological studies, the procedures used for control groups tend to be unrealistic in that feedbacks, for example, which come naturally to an interviewer are prohibited, and 'control' really means 'no feedback'. That is, the 'control' group is a 'neutral' procedure with which others are compared. However, a methodological study was being planned in which these 'natural' responses would be simulated by writing indiscriminate positive feedback into the control group questionnaire. Particular attention was given to the appropriateness of a control group for a survey of risk perception in the Botany Bay area.

4 Validity of assumptions used in the analysis, e.g. independence of observations
  a The assumption that the model used is realistic is subject to the usual reservations and the data may, and often does, conflict with it.
  b However, the randomisation of the sample into subsamples goes a long way towards validating the assumption of independence.

5 Questions and questionnaire design experiments
  a The problem of how to design questions for surveys of children was raised. Suggestions were that there should be discussions with children, speaking with primary school teachers, consulting education departments and higher education research centres.
  b The use of different rating scales to assess attitudes was raised.

Experience was cited in use of a 7-point scale. Respondents answered in the range 5–7, despite expressing dissatisfaction during the interview. It was suggested that the investigators experiment with reversing the direction of the scale. A more common result reported with 7- or 9-point scales is that people will not use the extremes.

c The question was asked whether there is any accepted conventional wisdom in the type of scale to use for particular areas of research. Reference was made to Oppenheim and ICPSR books on existing attitude scales in the workshop library.

6 Measuring quantitative data

a This issue was raised in the context of problems in industrial research, of recall and fear of a breach of confidentiality (market share being discovered by one's competitors). Suggestions were:

i the use of diaries (for which there is a cost increase and possible increase in non-response);

ii putting sensitive questions in the middle of the questionnaire;

iii use of randomised response techniques (but possibly not appropriate for a small sample size).

b It was suggested that the questionnaire could be split into qualitative and quantitative sectors to reduce the length of the questionnaire. This could be appropriate if the question sets are completely self-contained.

7 Dangers in using experimental designs

a The need to follow slavishly instructions in experimental designs can produce inappropriate interviewer responses.

b Use of incentives may modify behaviour.

c Withholding information from or lying to respondents may introduce the ethical problems of manipulating the person and causing anguish. Instances of this in psychology experiments were discussed. The possible conflict between the standards of the NSW Privacy Committee and Market Research Society Code of Professional Behaviour on the respondent's right to know a survey's sponsor was mentioned.

8 How to tell whether the techniques are getting at the 'truth'

a It was noted that there was a real danger that elimination of interviewer variability might lead us to assume that all interviewers were getting the 'right' answers. It was suggested the only way to check on this was to use external records on what was 'right' or 'true' as in health records kept by hospitals or doctors. Even this has dangers. For example, hospital records might indicate a particular respondent had been diagnosed as having a particular disease, but if no one had ever told the

respondent, then the name of that disease would be the 'right' answer, and the respondent would not legitimately know.
b In the case of trying to estimate the incidence of de facto relationships, it would already be known that the natural tendency of the respondent was to fail to report such a relationship. Consequently, any technique which revealed more relationships than another could be regarded as a better technique.

SELF-ADMINISTERED AND MAIL SURVEYS

1 The use of the optical-scan technique
  a CASSR experience suggested that the optical-scan technique was not cost-efficient. Problems experienced included the inadvertent destruction of questionnaires, and the precision of marking required that the coders have to go through each form before machine processing.
  b Terry Beed suggested the technique was suitable for extremely large surveys with samples in the tens of thousands. One issue however, is the high professional cost of preparation for design and printing of the questionnaire, particularly when the print run is small. Liz Ampt suggested response rates may be lowered if the questionnaire looks like a computer-read form.
2 Multiple mailings
  a Both SSC and CASSR use approximately a two-week gap and two follow-ups to non-respondents and remail the entire survey package, not just a reminder letter. The usual pattern of response is 50 per cent of non-respondents at each mailing. The need for the collection of current data on response rates in Australia was pointed out. There is a problem of people working with textbook information from the UK or USA, which is 10–12 years out of date and which takes no account of modern, computer-controlled mailings.
  b The SSC Survey Management System for monitoring response and mail-backs during a self-administered survey and for producing status reports was discussed. The SSC also has available a rich body of data on response rates monitored through multiple-wave mail surveys.
3 The need to study non-response
  a A study by Liz Ampt and Bob Stimson was discussed, in which statistically significant differences were found for those non-respondents who were sampled. Differences were also found in

the characteristics of respondents to first and second mailings. The problem of not being able to compare behavioural variables with census data, as is possible for demographic variables, was also noted.

b Bob Stimson suggested that where the response rate is less than 60 per cent, results are not worthwhile. Concern was expressed by various people that commercial mail surveys often get response rates around 20 per cent. In response to this concern, the following points were made:

i It is not cheap to get reliable information.

ii Attempts should be made to sample non-respondents. Terry Lewis suggested a phone survey follow-up in which the respondent completes the questionnaire over the phone. In doing the phone follow-up, records could be kept on why people have not responded. It was noted however, that the phone survey misses a proportion of the population.

iii Alternative ways of collecting information should be considered when a low response rate is expected, for example, quota sampling; sampling a few small areas that can be compared with census data; and the use of quasi-experimental designs for hypothesis testing.

iv The drop-off and pick-up method was considered to be a cost-effective compromise.

c It was also noted that response rates are dependent on levels of vested interests in the target population, e.g. the high response rate (over 80 per cent) on the Williams Committee educational surveys. Non-response varies across issues and time.

4 Frames/mailing lists

a The need for up-to-date frames and mailing lists was discussed. The Electoral Office publishes lists of electoral roll updates, and the coverage of these varies significantly across geographical areas. Many people are delinquent in registering to vote.

b There is also a need to gauge the extent to which the mailing reaches the target audience. It was noted that there is a need in diary surveys to judge whether the diary is being kept up to date. This can be achieved by 'surprise' visits to respondents in whose households diaries have been placed.

C ETHICS

a Tony Cleland raised the issue of whether the researcher has the right to go into people's homes and ask questions. This generally involves telling the respondent that he/she will benefit from the research, which may in fact not be true. Cleland suggested that the researcher could be considered under an obligation to take the results back to the respondent.

b The issue was also raised of whether the researcher has the right to 'frighten' people by asking questions. The example was given of a survey sent through the mail with social security cheques.

c The question of control over information was discussed, both in relation to aspects of privacy and in relation to the use of surveys by other groups without the researcher's knowledge or approval. Various forms of control, including regulating bodies, were discussed. Reference was made to the Survey Guidelines published recently by the NSW Privacy Committee and the Code of Professional Conduct of the Market Research Society of Australia (which is binding only on its members).

Appendix E: Summary of the workshop discussions: Melbourne

The group that examined experimental design issues discussed methodologies for obtaining control groups to compare with experimental groups and focused on a rather large survey that was being done in Queensland by Sue Payne on evaluation of driver-education programs. The study was used to highlight the processes of obtaining comparable groups by matching on a selected group of variables. It was suggested that selected variables be chosen by using the AID procedure. There were advantages in terms of having a trade-off between improving the comparability of the two groups by weighting and increasing the variance of the weighted mean.

A very large workshop meeting was held on the question of interviewer training. It focused on motivation of the interviewer. Discussion ranged over the various motivation procedures that could be used and was an outcome of the background material Professor Cannell had given on the first day. Some of the questions raised by members of that group were in terms of how much and how intense interviewer training should be. Also discussed were the problems of cost and whether the use of costly experienced interviewers or relatively inexperienced interviewers at lower cost was more desirable. From information given by people from the ABS and discussion based on Professor Cannell's experience in America, there seems to be some evidence that more experienced interviewers are getting higher response rates but that the reliability of the data tends to go down somewhat. This perhaps could be related back to interviewer motivation. There were many complex issues arising in these discussions and obviously within the Australian context there is a need for a lot of experimental work to be done on the question of interviewer motivation and response rates. More particularly, data reliability using interviewers with different levels of pre-survey training and with different levels of actual interview experience needs to be explored.

A number of other issues emerged, such as, can one develop more effectively the notion of broadly based manuals for interviewer training and can these be used very much as a replacement for the specific training usually given for each survey? It appears that there is considerably less time spent on interviewer training in Australian survey research than in the US. Professor Cannell had made the point that there were very good reasons for having five-day training periods for interviewers for most academic surveys.

Among the other points to emerge was an important one which related to the need to have high standards of quality control and monitoring of interviewer performance. This is very important to ensure that interviews have in fact been carried out, and to ensure that interviewers do not become obtrusive in matters which are not directly related to the questionnaire itself. There is a danger of the interviewer getting on too familiar terms with the respondent, as this invites bias. It is significant that all agreed that much more research needs to be done in this area.

There was a small workshop on interviewing in multicultural societies. The emphasis was on the problem of different ethnic groups and particularly on Aborigines in Australia. To raise briefly the points that were discussed: difficulties arise through the necessity of interviewing migrant families, and non-English-speaking families; and difficulties are imposed by the use of the child or other family member as an intermediary or proxy for others in the non-English-speaking household. The problems of translating questionnaires from English into the native tongue of migrant groups were discussed. It is apparent that direct translations can often result in different meanings being assumed by the person responding to a given question. With respect to surveys of specific minorities, ethnic or non-English-speaking groups, there are both advantages and disadvantages in having ethnic community organisations involved by supplying translators who do not have experience or training as interviewers. Perhaps this was a bigger problem some years ago. Considerable attention was given to the problems experienced in conducting survey research with Aboriginal communities, particularly the influence on the type and reliability of data collected where white interviewers as distinct from black interviewers are used. The conflict of cultural values was canvassed in this meeting. A further problem discussed was the difficulty of drawing probability samples when the target population is a specific ethnic group. This presents serious sampling problems and costs if one is going to make inferences to a specific ethnic population.

A rather large gathering at the workshop on self-completion questionnaires went on into the evening and into the second session. We defined a number of different situations in which self-completion techniques were being used. These included the drop-off and pick-up type, supervised self-completion in classrooms to the hybrid design of combined face-to-face interviews and self-completion forms; and the classic all-mail type of self-completion survey. Areas of application were widespread, ranging through the medical and farming areas, surveys of electors, students and even disqualified drivers, focusing on the problems with those types of groups. The major issues which emerged were non-response and what you do about handling it. We talked about strategies for looking at non-response and its possible influence. This included follow-up interviews of non-respondents to mail surveys and the possibility of telephone interviews with non-respondents, and we broached some of the problems of the types of universe and sample lists which one might work with in the self-completion setting. One of the biggest contrasts in sampling methodology in Australia is between working with electoral rolls to represent the general population and the use of specific lists—such as lists of students in universities, colleges and schools.

Non-response received most of the attention. Ironically, there is a great lack of hard data on it in this country. Yet it would be very simple to start assembling some high-quality data. One mechanism is through organisations such as the newly formed Social Science Data Archive at the ANU which has an interesting collection of substantive survey material. But if we can somehow encourage depositors of data to hand over performance information on the running of their surveys, this would be of great assistance not only in self-completion surveys but in face-to-face interview surveys. A unified approach to the non-response problem in general is very much overdue in this country.

Appendix F: Some questions put to Professor Cannell at the workshops

INCREASING SURVEY RESPONSE BY COMMITMENT AND FEEDBACK TECHNIQUES

I am interested in the commitment side. We in the Bureau of Statistics often get people to sign a form at the very end. Now you are suggesting a signature at the beginning. Going through my mind is the fact that Billy Graham demands a commitment which tends to be at the end rather than at the beginning but then at Alcoholics Anonymous, a man stands up and says, 'I am a compulsive drinker', and then he gives his testimony. Also in a court of law, a man stands up and gives his commitment on the Bible. I am just interested to know if there are more ways of killing the cat than just signing the top of the form. What other ways of plunging into commitment have you experimented with?

That is about as much as we have experimented with. When we were talking about this in some other sessions, other people had done a lot of things that they hadn't really called commitment at that time. But they were committing themselves. We did a couple of other things. Incidentally on the commitment procedures we do something like Billy Graham does by telling them, 'Here's what it takes to do a good job but before you agree to it, let us ask you a few questions so you understand what this interview is like and the kinds of things we are asking about.' We don't ask them to commit themselves in the dark. We ask a few questions and then say, 'All right, now here are the kinds of questions...now do you commit yourself?' I think the answer to those questions themselves are committing. We tried the introduction by attempting to get them to ask questions the right way: 'This is the Survey Research Center calling, we want to ask you about your health: what is the state of your health?' Now by simply getting this interview underway we may be committing the respondent to a better performance. It turned out that this approach didn't work at all. That is about the extent of it, but I am sure that most of you have done some sort of commitment procedures that you may not have called commitments, and I think a number of these sorts of things have been widely used.

Did you find there was any resistance by respondents to putting up their signatures, considering the fact that we as interviewers are taking their time or asking them to commit themselves to an unknown 'pig in the poke'? I have often gone for verbal commitment, where you say, 'Would you mind answering the question?' This is basically their commitment but I would hesitate to ask any of my students to get a signature from a person—the doors would slam in their faces I think.

Ninety-six per cent of them didn't. I guess it all depends on how you do it. You would not walk in and say, 'Sign here!' Two things, first of all. We said, let us tell you a little about what the interview is like and then we would let you ask a few questions first. So they got warmed up to it. Second is that we left the commitment form with the respondent. We told them at the beginning these were confidential interviews. The interviewer actually signed at the bottom of it and then said I agree to keep all this information confidential. So it was a 'mutual pact'. Incidentally, it is being used a lot these days in psychotherapy where the therapist and the patient sign a contract, the patient signs an agreement to talk about things that are important and not waste a lot of time and to be on time at these sessions. Likewise, the psychiatrist or the psychologist signs a statement that they will do their best and spend all their effort to try to help out. I think there are a lot of commitments of this kind. We are happy with an initial, they don't have to sign their whole name to it, but we give them the reason we want the signature so they understand what we are asking. Respondents don't react negatively to it.

You mean American respondents?

I venture to say all respondents.

Did you ever try any experimental or organised way where the interviewer signs his commitment before the respondent?

No. We told the respondent, however, that the interviewer would sign it. The interviewer said, . . . 'And I will sign down here.' I am not sure, I am interested in the cultural difference notion because there are clear cultural differences—I hope someone will try this here.

I would suggest that one of the differences in Australia is the notion of actually signing something—the idea of you just signing something is often considered very dangerous by many people.

That is why we accept initials. We got some resistance to signing a whole name. Two things—we accepted an initial and we said, 'You keep the form'. So the respondent was going to keep the form and he knew that. I think it was nowhere near as threatening. I hate to say this ladies, but among the 4 per cent who did not sign it, almost the universal answer was, 'My husband told me never to sign anything.' So much for chauvinism for the moment.

96 per cent of what? 96 per cent of response rate?

No, 96 per cent of respondents who were asked to, did so.

What happened to the 4 per cent who didn't sign the commitment?

We didn't conduct the interview.

Are they 4 per cent who you would normally give an interview?

A number of them said, 'Well, I would be glad to give you an interview but I just don't want to sign a form.'

So there is a 4 per cent loss as compared with other procedures?

Yes, I want to be very clear that you understand. This is experimental so we didn't care what we lost. If we had lost 50 per cent, we would have cared a lot but we didn't care about that 4 per cent because we were not trying to make population estimates. If we had lost a lot we would have been concerned about it. But in that case we told the respondent if he didn't want to sign, we didn't want to proceed with it, and we did not proceed.

Would that upset the randomness of the sample in the sense that they were excluded? I tend to think that in this country it would.

That would be very interesting to test here. I guess we need to compare notes area to area. In most things there does not seem to be great cultural differences but this might be one where there is. I think there is another one which we will talk about later on—the use of the telephone—where I think cultural differences may be great. But this is a sufficiently powerful technique which someone ought to try here and find out how it works.

Could you describe it again—the form, the whole questionnaire was kept by the respondent?

We have already distributed a copy of the form to everyone. This afternoon we will look at some of the things which lead up to this but that is the actual form we use. It is all nicely set up on good quality paper, and so forth.

Now it is this form you actually left overnight, not the actual survey instrument?

This is the form that was left with the respondent. They could frame it or do anything with it. We told them at the beginning, this is for you to keep, so there was no malice or forethought in thinking this was a sneaky way of getting their name. If there was any question at all, we told them we only need to get your name or even your initials—we just want to be sure that you have read and understood the form.

It seems to me that the commitment of the interviewee is in some way going to be associated with commitment of the interviewer. Perhaps many interviewers do not expect people to be willing to sign. In this case your chances of getting them to sign are very slight. I wonder whether this would be much stronger than anything which may be cultural—that this may be the cultural thing you are talking about, that the Australian interviewers may not expect to get what they want. They may not even think what they are trying to collect is important enough to get what they want.

You are absolutely right. Our interviewers in the South always think the South is so different from the North: what works in the North won't work in the South and they will all tell you, 'That may work up there in your country but down here this does not work at all.' Well, we say try it, and they come back and say, surprisingly it did work. You are absolutely right, what controls a very great deal of this is the attitude of the interviewers. For example, if you look at the response rate in surveys by interviewer, and the number of interviewers who have trouble getting income from people—it varies tremendously and it varies tremendously because of the attitude of the interviewer. You can reproduce this over and over again but the attitude of the interviewer is all-important, not the perception of the respondent.

The best example of this was a recent one I know of, a study done before the last US Census—there was a big argument between the Census and the Congress and the National Center of Archives as to how long the information would be kept confidential. The statement that the interviewers were giving to the respondents was that this information is private, and that nobody will ever see it. It turned out the National Archivists said, 'Now wait a minute, 75 years from now we are going to let all this data out' and the Census said, 'You can't do that, we have told people. . .' The Archivist said, 'It is my data at this point.'

So the question is, what difference does it make what you tell people about confidentiality? An experiment was done, a survey conducted of attitudes, information and so forth and there were five statements of confidentiality. One was, 'and these data are going to be kept completely confidential forever.' Second, they were going to be kept confidential for 75 years. A third, they will be kept confidential for 25 years. The fourth made no statement of confidentiality, and the fifth said, any agency which wants this data can have it. These were given to random samples of respondents. Really the only difference in response rates occurred before the statement of confidentiality was made at all.

That is, the interviewers had the feeling that if you gave them those last two options, they weren't going to get an interview and the response rate dropped down about six percentage points. When the respondents were actually given the information, the response rate differences were virtually zero, maybe one percentage point. What determined the difference was the attitude of the interviewer. They thought, 'People are not going to give this to me', therefore they were sure that the respondent was going to refuse and the respondent refused before any statement of confidentiality was made. It is a beautiful example of that power of the interviewer.

It is just possible that the interviewers were right and that they triggered the refusal of the very people who would have refused once that statement had been made.

They may just have been very good predictors of that. The only thing that applies in the face of that is they varied by interviewer. There are some interviewers who get many more respondents; well, they may have been cleverer. You are right, it may be possible. I would not bet much on it.

Would you expect these techniques to be as useful in a sort of survey where people had no commitment to the issue—advertising research, market research, that sort of thing?

There have been about four studies done; two were on the use of media, and a couple of other topics were covered too and they seemed to work as well. I will give you the one on media as that is an interesting one [Miller, 1979]. It was a small study that was done using these three techniques and the results are as follows; the reporting of the use of television increased using these techniques, especially how many hours of programs they watch; the reading of editorials in newspapers dropped in the use of these techniques; the watching of X-rated movies went up, the reading of books went down. In other words, it was pretty clear evidence that you were not just getting 'yea-saying', that you were getting really more honest reporting of it. The second study of media showed a substantial increase in the amount of television watching that had occurred during the course of a week. It seems to work. The place in which it is not yet very clear how well it works is in attitude surveys. They seem to yield a fuller response—well, we know they are fuller responses; we know that they tend to report more embarrassing things; we tend to think they are getting less acquiescence. But the feedback for attitudes is still not clear—just how in the world do we do that? That is what we need to work on now. That is where I say again these techniques are experimental. Yet, their potential is great and there is a long way to go.

Surely if someone who has been a good respondent and a nice person by being a good respondent, particularly in the area of attitudes, wouldn't that lead to a greater socially desirable respondent and create a new set of operational problems?

I certainly hope not. If however, they interpret a nice person as being a good respondent I will accept that, because that is what I want. I think if it is done properly, operational problems do not occur. Hopefully what the respondent would say after the interview, if you said to him, 'What was this interview about and what was your role?' would be, 'I worked hard and I did the best I could for that person because what they wanted was really very accurate information and I tried to do it.' That was what one would hope he would be saying. But if they also did say, by the way, it was an enjoyable experience, there would be no negative problem attached to it. I would like again to see somebody do some studies—why don't you try it—to find out what the respondent did take away with him, what did he understand had gone on. That is pretty critical to this whole approach.

In the question of feedback, you tended to put a lot of emphasis on verbal feedback. What about the question of a raised eyebrow, a smile or whatever it might be—the 'body language' of feedback?

We haven't looked at the effect of it, but we have tried to control it. We have tried to say on these control groups there is a lot of feedback which is of the non-verbal feedback. We say you are to sit there: well, don't sit there and look unpleasant, look pleasant but don't nod, don't use posture changes, don't do other things which might give those cues. I don't know how successful that was but we certainly are very much aware of that kind of feedback—that is one of the advantages of doing it by telephone. You reduce that kind of feedback and the results seem to be pretty much the same.

I am interested in the degrees of commitment—especially where it involves a monetary reward. Have you done any experiments where commitment was raised progressively in this fashion?

I don't know any good evidence for that and I worry about it. I have a feeling that it is all a matter of motivation, that it may be a good motivation or it may be a very bad motivation and it depends much on how it is used and how it is structured. We use it for example on panels—we have had a panel going now for about fifteen or sixteen years where we have interviewed those people every year. In that case we have said to them, 'We want to make a lot of demands of your time and we will at least partially reimburse you for some of this time.' Again it is like some other kinds of feedback—we are trying to make very clear what is being paid and what is not because the evidence suggests that they may interpret money as buying their opinions. I guess my feeling is that if a commitment is to a one-time survey, I would not pay them because I think it raises all these potential dangers. But if some real commitment of time is to be made I would approve it only on that basis. It is a field that I am very surprised has not seen more systematic research. There are a couple of studies but they weren't really very well designed and they tend to show one thing or another fairly inconclusively. The answer is I don't think anyone really knows what happens. But due to sufficient inherent danger there, there ought to be more research.

What about the effect of a different type of feedback, which also can be interpreted, I suppose, as an incentive? If an interviewer comes and knocks on a door and says, 'I am carrying out a particular survey', I have found that perhaps making a promise of an outcome for the respondent—even a general summary of the results seems to act as an incentive—helps you get the foot in the door. I was just wondering if you have done anything to look at the effects of that sort of feedback in terms of increasing the response?

No, we have not. We usually tell them we will send copies of the report if they are interested in it and we do it as a kind of polite gesture, but we have never used it as an experimental variable and I don't know how effective it would be. We did explore the use of the letter prior to the interview. The interviewers always said that a letter prior to the interview was a good way to get responses so we used two kinds of letters—a short letter and a long letter, and no letter at all. They were all about the same in response rate. It didn't seem to make much difference to the quality of the response. But again that is not even experimental. It is just a series of simple ideas gathered from our experience at ISR.

I have a feeling that some participants in social surveys may well feel ripped-off if they do not get feedback because quite a number of studies in my experience do not provide any feedback whatsoever.

That comes close to being an ethical issue. I think respondents ought to expect it—we automatically tell them that they will be getting it, if they want. Most of our studies are anonymous, so we say, 'If you want this, here's a card you can fill out and I will make sure you get a copy of the report.' The respondent's name doesn't get associated with the interview and our procedure is to print up about a three- to four-page summary of the main findings. A small number do write in. I think that is very desirable and really something that ought to be done for them.

If a Japanese bows to another Japanese, the other fellow feels a social contract to bow back again. If a member of a church comes to a front door, he offers a fairly cheap gift from a commercial point of view, he offers to bless the house, and this creates a social obligation, a social contract and gets things going. Have you done any experimentation with, not cash payment for commodity, but establishing a social contract of that type? At Christmas time, exchange gifts, that type of thing? No we have not. It is a different form of getting a commitment. I just have the feeling there are lots of these kinds of commitments that we have not tried, that are legitimate and would help—we haven't tried that. We will try to tell our interviewers to bless the house if that will help!

These techniques interest me very much. I was wondering what would happen if I requested the market research company that does most of my surveys to use them? I think one thing you might say in regard to the commitment would be a piece of folklore in market research—never ask people to agree to do anything—just proceed and let them stop you if they can. The question is, do you have evidence as to whether asking for the commitment reduces your response rate and may I ask the same question about feedback?

To answer the last issue first—is it necessary to tell the respondent they are doing a good job to get an interview completed? My answer would be no. I don't think it is necessary. You may want to give a little thought to making the question itself somewhat more respondent-oriented. It seems to me that most good interviews and most good questionnaires are a combination of statement of the variable you want to measure with some attention to the respondent. Explain to the respondent why you want it or what is to be done so that the respondent does feel that he or she is not just sitting there and answering a cold questionnaire. Actually, by the time you put these instructions in, the questionnaire itself has taken on a more conversational sound. It says, 'The next thing we want to ask is about this...' and your people have a hard time remembering it. You will need to work hard at this but it helps to break up that cold clammy part of the questionnaire.

You say that using these techniques doesn't increase the drop-out rate in the course of the interview.

In our experience it has not increased it at all. If you look at those five groups, the response rate for each was almost identical. There is no evidence there that the same interviewers get different results with different techniques.

Could there possibly be a different goal between your getting a response rate because you are working for a federal department instead of a market research agency which did not perhaps inspire the same kind of cooperation and commitment?

I am absolutely sure of it. The Census Bureau gets a response rate on the health surveys of about 97 or 80 per cent. I guess 96 or 97 per cent.

When the Survey Research Center at the University of Michigan does the same thing it gets a response rate of 80 per cent. I am sure that is the case and it does mean that there are problems, but those response rates occur not as a result of variations in technique but are due to the 'legitimacy' of the organisation and the approach of the interviewer. Again it is the interviewer attitude: she says to herself, this is the Federal Government, this is the Census Bureau, I am going to get an interview. Our people often tend to approach it by saying, 'You wouldn't want to give an interview would you?' to themselves and the Census Bureau tried it in that experiment I was telling you about—a split half experiment—because we were interested in the difference between ourselves and the Census. They got 85 per cent response rate, we got 80 per cent response rate.

In the preliminary question, before you require the signature of commitment, do you give any indication of the time that the interview is going to take and how accurate is that indication?

I think we do not. If the respondent asks we say to them, 'Well, it will take a half-hour or sometimes longer or shorter depending on how much we have to talk about.' I don't think we make a point of it. I am a little vague on that.

You said the response rates are going down generally, you mean generally over all kinds of interviews?

Yes. We have not been in the telephone business long enough to know what is happening to rates there. But the face-to-face interview rates had been going down generally in the US over the past ten years.

Any reason—is there a sort of saturation point?

I think it is due to the kind of things we were talking about earlier—some are concerned about letting people into the house—more concerned about violence. I think also the people have got an easy out—they can say this is an invasion of privacy. It isn't really a very serious issue but it gives them a good rationale for refusing if they want to. It may very well be that some people are concerned about surveys but it doesn't seem to be a major national issue.

I was wondering if we would have to face it one day. For instance, the place where I come from—Wollongong—is a sort of strip on the coast which has a very finite population and we are always worried about 'wearing it out' with surveys. I think if it is possible to do anything, you can do it. In a place like the US, how quickly can you reach a saturation point at which people just won't listen to surveys any more?

I don't really think that is the issue. I think there is an issue of the conflicting use of the phone for different purposes, such as selling and the volume of these other uses far exceeds the volume of survey interviewing. Saturation is therefore more likely to be general, rather than entirely specific to surveys.

TELEPHONE INTERVIEWING

When fowls are running around and browsing in the paddocks we think that is fairly healthy, but when we see fowls laying eggs in batteries we get a bit upset, it seems unnatural. Now, interviewers have a pretty boring job but at least they have to read a map and travel from house to house. A vision of 40 girls cooped up day after day puzzles me a little bit and I just wondered if fatigue sets in with ordinary interviewers? How many days does it take for a girl to go off her brain in this sort of environment?

We only hire ones who are off their brain to begin with! This is a problem, we use about five- to six-hour shifts and we live in an academic environment so nobody is standing over them with a whip to see that they are working all the time. But I understand people are doing this in the commercial field all the time and they run longer shifts. There is a large turnover of staff and it is to some extent due to exactly what you are saying, 'No I can't stand that any more.' That does disturb them because the proportion of time they spend interviewing is a lot greater than in a face-to-face interview. We run two shifts of interviewers because we follow the clock across the country. We run from about 2.00 in the afternoon to midnight and there are two shifts coming in at various times (overlapping shifts) and it does wring those interviewers out—there is no question about it. They are cooped up in that sense—they are in cubicles. We do all kinds of things to make it easier for them but there is a heavy turnover. We tend to use wives of graduate students who need money and will work there until they find something better. Some of them seem to thrive on it and have been with us for years. I asked somebody just before I left what the turnover rate was and they didn't know but they said it was very high, probably something like 50 per cent.

Earlier you said the response rates were falling. Did you say that the phone interviews tend to be better? What is the overall rate you are talking about? You said something between 60 and 90 per cent for an interview.

Let us talk about the face-to-face interviews then we can subtract them. It is hard to come up with a general rate because while the Census Bureau is still getting 97 per cent this is not the case for the rest of us. The rate for a face-to-face interview with a probability sample would be somewhere around 75 per cent and it would range from 72 to 80 per cent. It used to be 80 to 85 per cent. So it is a significant drop. The telephone rate is slightly lower, although on that health study, we got 80 per cent, but that is unusual: it is usually 70 to 75 per cent—these are very rough figures. The other thing is that the cost is just about one half for telephone interviews compared to face-to-face. It is far more cost-effective.

One of the factors that you mentioned earlier was related to the question of cost. I recall some figures quoted in 1979 about the ISR operation that the face-to-face interview had a cost of around about $150 and the telephone interview had a cost of around about $55 to $60. Would that still be roughly the difference in these?

The cost differential is about two to one when comparing personal and phone interviews. It depends on what you put into the cost factors. Our usual figure when we are making estimates for the interviewing, if you figure all the interviewing and sampling procedures—not the analysis and not the coding—is that they run between $60 and $75 per interview for face-to-face and about half that for telephone. That figure you are giving is either a special survey or it is the total cost of the survey, including all the analysis.

Can you expand on interviewer turnover and the problems it causes?

The main reason for concern is the tremendous difference in turnover amongst our face-to-face interviewers, which is very low, at under 20 per cent per year, and our telephone interviewers. The biggest reason for turnover is that they either get pregnant or move. Aside from that they stay with us for a long time. The job is just different and it attracts a different kind of person but the telephone interviewers do turn over more quickly. Part of it is pay—we pay slave labour rates—and they get better jobs elsewhere and go on to better jobs. But that is not entirely the answer and I really don't know what the answer is.

Can I just change the subject? What sort of weighting do you apply to your telephone interview surveys?

We try to look at the distribution of the population and usually if the phone ownership fits well there is no problem. We are more concerned about response rates because unfortunately the non-response tends to look like the non-ownership; that is, they tend to be the lower educated and with lower income. There are all kinds of studies going on now to perfect post-survey adjustments. I say none of them are very satisfactory but by the same token we do weight for non-response when we know what the response characteristics are. Usually we try to use the income, education, age and sex variables.

Do you make adjustments for people having more than one phone?

Yes, we do. That happens very rarely—not a lot of people have more than one phone. When they do, it tends to be a child's or a teenager's. If the phone is listed you get the child's phone number and you eliminate it. The trend to child's phones will increase as phones are relatively inexpensive—and you can give the children a Christmas present by giving them their own phone!

Can you please explain more about CATI—is it a particular piece of software?
No, it is a whole suite of programs to support CATI. It is called by various things, CATI is the generic name for the computer-based interviewing. The hardware we are using is a PDP 1170. Let me say before going on that the real problem with all of this is the relatively high cost of development.

Is the data that are being generated as a consequence of that particular interview filed in a data file and then called upon—what software do you use, OSIRIS or what?
The output is taped. It is a rectangular data set—you can take the tape off our machine, put it on an IBM machine, use OSIRIS or do whatever you want.

Are the variables coded in at the time the questionnaire screen program is being generated so there is no need to reorganise the data set?
It is reorganised a little but it is done instantaneously—as soon as you get through with that interview those data are stored. When you get through the last interview it is all stored and it is available for using in aggregate form except for the open-ended questions. These have to go through a coding process, the same as any other open-ended data would. It is not quite clear to us yet what is the most effective way of coding open-ended data. At present we do all our coding on-line using the same PDP 1170 equipment. For the open-enders we get hard copy of the responses and give it to a coder who codes it into the main system. We want to bypass this manual step but the computer methodology hasn't been worked out yet.

How much down time do you have with that system?
Zero, so far. We have had two serious crashes due to voltage change since we have had it but aside from that, there is no down time.

When is the machine maintained?
They do that during the night. We run coding shifts from 8.00 in the morning until 5.00 pm and we run the interviewing from about 2.00 in the afternoon until 12 midnight, bearing in mind the US time zones. So there is a free shift from 12 midnight to 8.00 am and the programmers do whatever they need to do for maintenance and development.

Is the interview data processed on the same machine so as to produce tabulations?

No. The data are taken off that machine and put onto a big machine. The interesting thing I find about this system is its real potential for future development. We are using a mini-computer. There are now micro-computers available that are much smaller yet much faster. At least two major organisations in the US are using these micro-computers.

Could you put a price tag on the Michigan CATI in US dollars—including development costs, hardware and software?

You sound like my boss. I used to keep hiding the figures as well as we could. I don't really know what it is. We have a contract with the market research group to produce software for us. We have three people in our own organisation—three programmers—who have been working for at least six months full-time to develop the system internally. I just don't know what the total of all this is but the machine itself is about \$200 000. Then the consoles are about \$1000 a piece and we have about 50 of them. So you are already up into sizeable money. The original programming alone represented seven or eight years of development work—some of that are quite a highly sophisticated program level and some of it at a lower level.

Are you going to market CATI as a package?

We hadn't thought of it. I suppose one could, but I think our people feel to market it just gets them into problems and that they don't want to get involved. There are some on the market now I think. If you were content to have a simple machine that just flashed questions up and coded information, they are rather readily available. It is all those added sophistications we have talked about which add very appreciably to the cost. The way our organisation works, they wouldn't buy anything but a Cadillac and the Cadillacs are obviously very expensive. Now we can justify at least part of it on the basis of better control and better ability to handle different kinds of data. The market research people from whom we acquired our basic system had this operating for two years. When we contracted with them it took them another year at least to carry out the development we needed for our work. Their surveys were much simpler and shorter and they could handle what they needed to but they couldn't come anywhere near touching us, particularly in the area of sampling. Our sampling is very difficult: they were using much cruder samples.

We have a cassette tape that shows something about the system. It doesn't have high quality to it but it is enough to give you an idea of how the system operates and what it looks like. The person who presents CATI on the cassette, Mary Dawson, is now a programmer—

shortly she will be the person who is in charge of the CATI system. Five years ago we hired Mary as an interviewer—she had no computer experience at all and she turned out to be an absolutely superb interviewer. About six months later we made her a supervisor and she was a field telephone interviewing supervisor for a couple of years. When we were looking forward to CATI she took a couple of courses in programming and she is excellent. She does all the minor program changing that we need to have done from day to day. She knows the system 'up one end and down the other' as you will hear when she talks about it.

Would you be prepared to say that a long-term trend resulting from this type of interviewing might be that small-scale market research firms might be swallowed up by larger-scale ones?

As in most of these developments I think what will happen is that small market research firms will either go right along doing pencil-and-paper questionnaires and will do them about as inexpensively and with the competitive advantage that the companies originally had. Saying they had a computer system will not be crucial to them. I also think these CATI-type systems will be marketed at competitive prices so that literally anybody could buy them. This is occurring now and there are numerous coding packages you can buy off the shelf now. They are not expensive, $3000 or $4000 or so. I don't think it has any implications for larger firms swallowing the smaller ones. I think it is like most things, it is going to get simpler.

Yesterday you mentioned retaining information on industrial phones and perhaps second phones, today you are mentioning retaining information on when it is best to ring back. This means there will be increasing retention of names and addresses. Do you think this might worry people?

It worries me. Those data are of course all lost as soon as the interview and the survey is ended. The interview data is entered with no reference to phone number or anything of that sort in it. One could maintain the names and addresses of respondents in face-to-face interviews, if one so wanted. When we want to recontact people, I guess we do keep their phone numbers but even I am not quite sure in what form they are kept for the duration of the survey.

What do you do when that data is lost after the interview is completed? What prevents the same number being used again?

We don't do anything. It is purely a chance phenomenon that it might occur. We take probably 1500 interviews per month—purely by generating all these random numbers. You can have some control over it by drawing different telephone office area codes, but I guess at the moment they don't worry about it very much. Incidentally, our Census

Bureau is also heavily involved in CATI system development at the moment. They are doing a lot of experimentation on it because they see some real advantages to it and I think within another year they will probably be using this system very widely. They have already done two experimental studies and, like all the Census work, they insist on developing their own system.

Are telephone numbers generated in the same software?

No. At the present time they are generated in another computer and then transferred to the 1170 but the next routine that will be developed at Michigan is the generation of random numbers on the 1170. After that we will introduce an automatic dialling device so in this case the interviewer won't even know what the telephone number is—the telephone number will be rung automatically. The ringing machine costs about $25 000. In terms of the time it takes to get through punching all those numbers in, it will probably pay us to buy a dialling machine. Everything will be automatically handled up to the point where somebody answers the phone.

Has anybody tried sending a reward to somebody in the hope of getting them to ring up rather than their being rung up by the University?

No, because we don't know how to get in touch with them. The only thing we know—and this is one of the disadvantages of random digit dialling—is the telephone number. We have some idea, because we know the location of the telephone office code but we don't within that have any respondent's address: it is really a blind ring. One of the advantages of starting with lists is that we would be able to send them something ahead of time. The problem with telephone directory lists or any other lists we know of is that they are so far out of date. The best estimate our samplers can come up with is that if you started with the telephone numbers published in the directory, then between the private numbers, the unlisted numbers, and the out of date, you would only cover 50 per cent of the population. So the most effective way to implement probability samples on the telephone is on the basis of random digit dialling. But there is still the disadvantage of not being able to contact people ahead of time. While on this subject, we are about to do a study at Michigan of an organisation which has a list of all its subscribers and their telephone numbers and addresses. This is being funded by an insurance company. We have drawn a sample of subscribers and we are going to send a letter to them ahead of time telling them we will be calling on them—that is the nice way of doing it. I expect it will reduce the refusal rate.

What about administering 5- and 7-point scales over the telephone? Have you done any experimental work on this yet?

The problem is that the data from our experiments in this area have not been fully analysed. In one of our studies the analysis is now proceeding on a 5- to 7-point scale. Our own guess is that by the time you get much over 3- or 4-point scales you have got troubles. You may have to use some unfolding technique by starting with a 3-point scale and divide the two end points. You could say, 'Are you for, opposed to it or not?', and then, 'How much are you opposed to it, very much, somewhat, or how much are you in favour of it...?' There is evidence that when you do that you get significantly different data than you do when you give them the 5-point scale. What this difference represents, one doesn't know. If you started with a 3-point scale and then extend it to a 5-point scale, you tend to have more in the middle category as respondents split themselves up in three equal parts. There is a new book by Howard Schuman and Stanley Presser on question design (Schuman and Presser, 1981). Howard works in the same program as I do at Michigan and they have been doing a great deal of work on question form, particularly the use of middle alternatives. If you ask the question without the 'don't know', or the mid-category you get a very different distribution for a lot of the items than if you put the mid-category in. Howard has done quite a bit of work to understand the meaning of this. That book should be on the market by now—it opens up a lot of these issues. My guess is that we will go a lot more to either the unfolding techniques or some other device for getting people to identify their position—it may be something like a semantic differential where you have 10 points.

I work for a market research company which uses telephone interviewing quite heavily. All we simply do is tell them at the outset of the interview they are going to require pencil and paper and we read out the 7-point scale and they jot it down.

Does everyone get a pencil and paper?

The majority—some of them say 'can't be bothered' and hang up.

That is a very reassuring thing to do. We have not tried that yet because we were trying to experiment so far to see how far we could go with delivery of scales and collection of responses entirely on the phone.

Even with the visual presentation scale—when they write down the 7-point scale—they may get a tiny piece of paper, the size of a postage stamp. There are still problems with that.

Yes, there are still problems—there are great problems in how you present by phone what you would normally put on a show card in a face-to-face interview.

Are you employing any blind telephonists at all? This is an occupation which blind people could perhaps handle very well.

No, but we did try to get handicapped people working for us. We used people with paralysis and similar handicaps and we thought this would be a great opportunity for them, but the transportation problem was so great especially on cold, stormy winter days in Ann Arbor, they were not able to get into the office and they dropped out rapidly. We have never tried using blind interviewers, but I still think if we could organise it better for handicapped people this would be a very good occupation for them, provided of course it isn't a speech defect.

How many people did you actually have in the room doing the interviewing at once?
About 30.

There were no interferences in the background?
We have sound-absorbent booths that are built in with sound insulation equipment all round. The interviewers are sitting there with earphones carrying on the communication. Occasionally when you get a faint line and it is hard to hear, an interviewer will start speaking loud and everyone will look around. Aside from that it is just a kind of constant buzz.

So the person being interviewed can't hear any other noise but the interviewer?
No. At least I think not. We were more concerned about the interviewers hearing each other and being disrupted—but that is not a problem. Perhaps it would be if you were in a non-airconditioned room.

SELF-ADMINISTERED QUESTIONNAIRES

There was one other question that was asked that we might come back to for a moment which is quite different. Somebody asked if there was information on how well people handled self-administered questionnaires and I just have one piece of evidence that has always intrigued me and I will pass it on to you.

On one of our earlier hospital studies there was a hypothesis that you could get people to do a better job of reporting their hospitalisations if you left the form and asked them to fill it in and mail it back. Supposedly they would consult other people and get more complete information and they would be more likely to report some of the embarrassing things because it could be more anonymous. In about one-third of the interviews the interviewer simply left the form with them at the completion of the interview and asked them to fill out the hospitalisation data. In that study, which was a study I reported earlier in the workshop, we knew that every family we interviewed had had a hospitalisation during the year. So we knew for each address, what the situation was. The Census Bureau interviewers used the form, they left the form, then if they didn't get it back in, they followed it up with another letter and asked them to send it in. If they didn't get one then, they made a telephone call to get it back in. If they didn't get it back in that way, they went out with an interviewer and almost beat the respondent over the head to get it. They got about 97 per cent of the forms back in. The data from the mailed-back forms showed no real improvement in validity when compared with the information collected in person.

The most interesting finding was that if you looked at the validity of the various ways, the self-administered questionnaires that came back in the first instance were of the highest validity. In the second wave of the collection the validity dropped significantly; in the third it dropped again, and in the fourth wave the validity went way down. In other words, it illustrated that people were conforming to behaviour, in this case, the behaviour being to fill the form out and send it back in—but this behaviour had nothing much to do with how good the data were. If one were to make an estimation of hospitalisation on the basis of the first returns, it would be beautiful—but the more you add the later returns, the worse the data look. Of course you can't always look at data that way but in fact the data from the fourth return were much much worse and of considerably lower validity than the rest.

This reinforces the message I was trying to convey earlier that the major criterion of a survey's success should not just be the response rate. Our people were very proud of the fact that we got over 90 per cent of the potential response, but they clearly did it at the expense of the quality of information. The real question therefore is getting accurate responses, not just getting a piece of paper back through the mail. I don't know how we can achieve this but you are going to lose something if you don't recognise this trend and try to do something about it. In this sample, the respondents were all underreporting their hospitalisations. But the later returns were underreported much more than the first ones. Now understand again, we could not tell exactly how much underreporting there was. We only had figures to show that the person was in the hospital on a specified date so we could only check on whether that event was reported, and not how long they were there.

Is underreporting more common? What about overreporting?

In general, situations for which we collect information can be positive or negative. If it is voting behaviour for example, or a probe about good things in one's experience, there is a tendency to overreport. There tends to be a consistent overreport of past voting intention favouring the winning party or candidate. If, however, it is a simple memory-recall task like, 'Did you do something or other?' it is more often underreported because it is harder work for the respondent to get it right. So you have to think in each case what kind of data am I dealing with? The advantage of these experimental techniques we were looking at appears to be that they reduce both the over- and underreporting, but there is much work to be done yet.

Let me close by saying that here we are some forty years into the survey business and we are still grappling for the answers to some of these basic and simple questions.

Appendix G: Household telephone connections, Australia, March 1983

The ABS conducted a survey throughout Australia in March 1983 to obtain information on whether households in private dwellings did or did not have a telephone connected. Households which did not have a telephone connected were asked the main reason for not having it connected. Information was also obtained on the composition of the household and on characteristics of household members.

The survey was conducted as part of the regular monthly population survey which is based on a multi-stage area sample of about 33 000 private dwellings. The information about telephone connections was obtained from a responsible adult member of the household in a personal interview by specially trained interviewers. Results from the survey are now published (ABS, 1984), from which the following summary is drawn.

The table below gives the percentage of households which have a telephone connected by area. The results indicate an overall increase in household telephone connections of 9.5 per cent over the last three years when compared to the 1979–80 results reported by Cutler and Sharp (p. 131). The increase appears to have been fairly uniform across states, although the differences in connection rates between metropolitan and non-metropolitan areas have narrowed slightly.

Percentage of households in private dwellings which have a telephone connected by area, March 1983

	NSW	Vic	Qld	SA	WA	Tas	NT	ACT	Total
Capital city	89.0	90.9	85.0	90.0	88.1	81.9	*	*	89.0[a]
Rest of state	79.0	82.5	76.5	81.2	71.3	76.5	*	*	79.1[b]
Total	85.4	88.5	80.5	87.6	83.5	78.5	76.1	91.1	85.3

Notes: a Excludes Darwin and Canberra
       b Includes Darwin and Canberra

Other tables published by the ABS give the number and percentage of persons aged fifteen years and over in private dwellings with or without telephone connections by sex, age, and employment-status groups, and the percentage of household types with telephone connections. The main features of these tables reported by the ABS are:

Of the 748 200 households not connected 382 500 (51 per cent) gave cost as the main reason for non-connection, and another 279 400 (37.3 per cent) said they had the use of a telephone elsewhere, did not need one, or were in rented/short term accommodation.

Households consisting of married couples with or without children were most likely to have the telephone connected, and persons living alone and one parent families with all children under fifteen years were least likely to have the telephone connected. Cost was the main reason for non-connection for the one parent households but was not as important a reason for persons living alone.

Employed persons were more likely to live in a household with the telephone connected than unemployed persons, 89.0 per cent compared with 72.0 per cent.

Of the 212 900 males and 447 500 females living alone, 86.2 per cent of the females had the telephone connected compared with 59.9 per cent of the males.

Of the 1 965 300 persons aged sixty years and over, 90.1 per cent were members of households with the telephone connected. However, of the 444 900 persons aged sixty years and over who were living alone only 63.2 per cent of males compared with 90.0 per cent of females had the telephone connected.

Unfortunately the survey contains very limited information on the variation in levels of telephone access over many other subgroups of interest. Tenure and occupation, the two most important background variables explaining variations in household telephone connections in the HES data, were not collected in the survey. Nevertheless, some additional tables have been produced by the ABS which relate characteristics of the head of household to household telephone connection and release of a unit record data file from the survey is promised. Researchers wishing to pursue more detailed, and more interesting, analyses with these data should therefore contact the ABS.

Bibliography

Abernathy, J.R., et al. (1970) 'Estimates of induced abortion in urban North Carolina' *Demography* 7, pp. 19–29

ABS (1977) *Household Expenditure Survey 1974–75 Bulletin 1, An Outline of Concepts, Methodology and Procedures* Catalogue No. 6507.0

ABS (1978) *Household Expenditure Survey 1975–76 Bulletin 1, Summary of Results* Catalogue No. 6516.0

ABS (1984) *Household Telephone Connections, Australia, March 1983* Catalogue No. 4110.0

Abul-Ela, A.A. et al. (1967) 'A multi-proportions randomized response model' *J. Amer. Stat. Assoc.* 62, pp. 990–1008

ATC (1975) *Telecom 2000* Telecom Australia Melbourne

Berkeley, E.P. (1968) 'The New Gamesmanship, A Report on Urban Games' *Architectural Forum* 129, pp. 58–63

Barton, A.H. (1958) 'Asking the embarrassing question' *Public Opinion Quarterly* 22, pp. 67–8

Bourgeois, D.A. (1969) 'Planning for the Model City in St Louis' in R.F. Campbell, L.A. Mart and R.O. Nystrands (eds) *Education and Urban Renaissance* pp. 113–20 New York: John Wiley

Brog, W., and Erl, E. (1980) 'Interactive Measurement Methods: Theoretical Uses and Practical Applications' *Transport Research Record* 765, pp. 1–6

Brog, W., Haberle, F., and Ribbech (1981) 'The Mobility of Persons Needing Nursing who live at home—pilot study on mobility research for the handicapped' *60th Annual Meeting of the Transportation Research Record* Washington, DC

BTE (1982) *Transport for the Disabled in Canberra.* Occasional Paper 54, Canberra: AGPS

Cannell, C.F., Fisher, G., and Bakker, T. (1965) 'Reporting of Hospitalization in the Health Interview Survey' *Vital and Health Statistics* Ser. 2, No. 6

Cannell, C.F., and Fowler, F.J. (1963) *A Study of the Reporting of Visits to Doctors in the National Health Survey* (Research Report) Ann Arbor: MI Survey Center, The University of Michigan

Cannell, C.F., Marquis, K.H., and Laurent, A. (1977) *A Summary of Studies of Interviewing Methodology* Rockville: National Center for Health Statistics. As cited in a review by S. Angrist, *J. of the Amer. Stat. Assoc.* 73, 362, 1978

Cannell, C.F., Miller, P.V., and Oksenberg, L. (1981) 'Research on interviewing techniques' in Leinhardt S. (ed.) *Sociological Methodology 1981* pp. 389–437, San Francisco: Jossey-Bass

Cantril, H. (1947) *Gauging Public Opinion* Princeton: Princeton University Press

Carter, D., and Thorne, R. (1972) 'Attitudes to Housing: A Cross Cultural Comparison' *Environment and Behaviour* 4, pp. 3–32

Chapin, F.S. Jr (1971) 'Free Time activities and the Quality of Urban Life' *Journal of the American Institute of Planners* 37, pp. 411–7

Chapin, F.S. Jr (1974) *Human Activity Patterns in the City: What People do in Time and Space* New York: John Wiley

Chapin, F.S. Jr., and Hightower, H.C. (1965) 'Household Activity Patterns and Land Use' *J. Amer. Inst. Planners* 31, pp. 222–31

Cherry, C. (1966) *On Human Communication* 2nd edn Cambridge, Massachusets

Craig, J.G., and Jull, G.W. (1974) *Teleconferencing Studies: Behavioural Research and Technological Implications* Ottawa: Communications Research Center, Department of Communications

Emery, F., and Emery, M. (1977) *A Choice of Futures* Canberra: Centre for Continuing Education

Faulkner, H.W. (1981) 'Journey Pattern Adjustments on Sydney's Metropolitan Fringe: An Exploratory Study' *Australian Geographer* 15, pp. 17–26

Faulkner, H.W., and Rimmer, P.J. (1982) 'An Approach for Identifying Transport Gaps: A Southwest Sydney Case Study' *7th Australian Transport Research Forum* pp. 529–45

Fielding, A. (1977) 'Binary Segmentation: The Automatic Interaction Detector and Related Techniques for Exploring Data Structure' in O'Muirhearteigh and Payne (eds) *The Analysis of Survey Data* vol. 1, New York: Wiley & Sons

Folsom, R.E. et al. (1973) 'The two alternative questions randomized response model for human surveys' *J. Amer. Stat. Assoc.* 68, pp. 525–30

Goode, T., and Heine, W. (1978) 'Surveying the extent of drug use' *Stat. Soc. of Aust. Newsletter* 5, pp. 1–3. Reprinted 1979 in *Survey Statistician* 1, pp. 10–2

Goodstadt, M.S., and Gruson, V. (1975) 'The randomized response technique: a test on drug use' *J. Amer. Stat. Assoc.* 70, pp. 814–8

Goodstadt, M.S., Cook, G., and Gruson, V. (1978) 'The validity of reported drug use: the randomized response technique' *Internat. J. Addictions* 13, 3, pp. 359–67

Greenberg, B.G. et al. (1969) 'The unrelated question randomized response model: theoretical framework' *J. Amer. Stat. Assoc.* 64, pp. 520–39

Greenberg, B.G. et al. (1977) 'Respondent hazards in the unrelated question randomized response model' *J. Stat. Planning and Inference* 1, pp. 53–60

Hoinville, G. (1971) 'Evaluating Community Preferenes' *Environment and Planning* A.3, pp. 33–50

Hoinville, G., and Berthoud, R. (1969) 'Value of Time, Development Project Stage 2 Report' *Social and Community Planning Research* London

Horvitz, D.G., Shah, B.V., and Simmons, W.R. (1967) 'The unrelated question randomized response model' *Proc. Social Stat. Section, Amer. Stat. Assoc.* pp. 65–72

Johansen, R., Vallee, J., and Spangler, K. (1979) *Electronic Meetings* Addison-Wesley

Jones, P.M. (1979) 'Hats: A Technique for Investigating Household Decisions' *Environment and Planning* A.11, pp. 59–70

Lansing, J., Withey, S., and Wolfe, A. (1971) *Working Papers on Survey Research in*

Poverty Areas (Chapter 12), Ann Arbor MI: Survey Research Center, The University of Michigan

Lester, D. 'The Use of the Telephone in Counseling and Crisis Intervention' in I. de Sola Pool (ed.) *The Social Impact of the Telephone*

Liu, P.T., and Chow, L.P. (1976) 'The efficiency of the multiple trial randomized response technique' *Biometrics* 32, pp. 607–18

Locander, W.F., Sudman, S., and Bradburn, N. (1976) 'An investigation of interviewer methods, threat and response distortion' *J. of the Amer. Stat. Association* 71, pp. 269–75

McLuhan, M. (1964) *Understanding Media* Abacus

Madow, W.G. (1967) 'Interview Data on Chronic Conditions Compared with Information Derived from Medical Records' *Vital and Health Statistics* Ser. 2, No. 23

Michelson, W. (1966) 'An Empirical Analysis of Urban Environmental Preferences' *J. Amer. Inst. Planners* 32, pp. 355–60

Miller, P.V. (1979) 'Applying health interview techniques to mass media research' *Health Survey Research Methods* NCHSR Research Proceedings Series (PHS) 81-3268, pp. 101–13

Miller, P.V. (1981) 'Alternative Questioning Procedures for Attitude Measurement in Telephone Surveys'. Paper presented at American Statistical Association, August

Rogers, T.F. (1976) 'Interviews by telephone and in person: Quality of responses and field performance' *Public Opinion Quarterly* 40, pp. 51–65

Rowley, G., and Tipple, G. (1974) 'Coloured Immigrants within the City. An Analysis of Housing and Travel Preferences' *Urban Studies* 11, pp. 81–9

Rowley, G., and Wilson, S. (1975) 'The Analysis of Housing and Travel Preferences. A Gaming Approach' *Environment and Planning* A.7, pp. 171–7

Schuman, H., and Converse, J.M. (1971) 'The effects of black and white interviewers on black responses in 1968' *Public Opinion Quarterly* 35, pp. 44–68

Schuman, H., and Presser, S. (1981) *Questions and Answers in Attitude Surveys: Experiments on Question Form, Wording and Context* New York: Academic Press

Sharp, L., and Frankel, F. (1981) 'Correlates of Self-Perceived Respondent Burden: Findings from an Experimental Study'. *Proceedings of the annual meeting of the American Statistical Association* Detroit

Short, J.A. (1973) *A Report on the Use of Audio-Conferencing Facility in the University of Quebec* London: Communication Studies Group

Short, J.A., Williams, E., and Christie, B. (1976) *The Social Psychology of Telecommunications* London: John Wiley

Sola Pool, I., de (1977) *The Social Impact of the Telephone* Cambridge, Massachusets

Stapley, B. (1973) *Collected Papers on Remote Meeting Table* London: Communications Studies Group

Sudman, S., et al. (1977) 'Modest expectations: The effects of interviewers' prior expectations on response' *Sociological Methods and Research* 7, pp. 177–82

Telecom Australia (1976–1977) The Brisbane Telelink Trial, unpublished working papers, Marketing Research Section, Telecom HQ Melbourne

—— (1978) *The P.A.B.X. Marketing Study* Marketing Research Section, Telecom HQ Melbourne

—— (1979a) *The Line Quality Study: Interim Report* Marketing Research Section, Telecom HQ Melbourne

—— (1979b) *The Marketing Trial of Lightweight Headsets* Marketing Research Section, Telecom HQ Melbourne

—— (1979c) *The STD/CCR Marketing Study* Marketing Research Section, Telecom HQ Melbourne

—— (1980a) *A Report of Studies on Telecom Billing* Marketing Research Section, Telecom HQ Melbourne

—— (1980b) *The Business Environment for Telecommunications* Marketing Research Section, Telecom HQ Melbourne

—— (1980c) *Domestic Market Segments for the Telephone and their Implications* Marketing Research Section, Telecom HQ Melbourne

—— (1980d) Telephone Ownership Data: Market Research 1964–78, unpublished report, Marketing Research Section, Telecom HQ Melbourne

Warner, S.L. (1965) 'Randomized response: a survey technique for eliminating evasive answer bias' *J. Amer. Stat. Assoc.* 60, pp. 63–9

Webb, E.J., Campbell, D.J., Schwarts, R.D., and Sechrest, L. (1966) *Unobtrusive Measures: Non-creative Research in the Social Sciences* Chicago: Rand McNally

Williams, E. (1975) 'Coalition Formation over Telecommunications Media' *European Journal of Social Psychology* 5, 4

Wilson, R.L. (1962) 'Liability of the City: Attitudes and Urban Development' in F.S. Chapin and S.F. Weiss (eds) *Urban Growth Dynamics* New York: John Wiley

Wiseman, F., Moriarty, M., and Shafer, M. (1975) 'Estimating public opinion with the randomized response model' *Public Opinion Quarterly* 39, pp. 507–13

Young, I. (1974) *Understanding the Other Person in Mediated Interaction* London: Communications Studies Group

Zdep, S.M., and Rhodes, I.N. (1976) 'Making the randomized response technique work' *Public Opinion Quarterly* 40, pp. 531–7

Index